Praise for *The Making of an Educator*

This is the story, both personal and professional, of a teacher and academic studying and reflecting throughout his educational career on key facets of professionalism and core purpose. Essentially this is about the essence of professionalism and the essential need to combine both practical classroom wisdom with theory.

Dame Alison Peacock, CEO, Chartered College of Teaching

As an educator who has relied on Dr Hargreaves' scholarship for almost 50 years, *The Making of an Educator* has given me a renewed sense of pride, optimism, and resolve to take our work to new heights.

Avis Glaze, International Education Advisor, former Ontario Education Commissioner

In this intriguing memoir, noted educator Andrew Hargreaves reflects on the experiences that led him to become a teacher, a scholar in education, and a leader of thoughtful educational innovation.

Howard Gardner, Hobbs Research Professor of Cognition and Education, Harvard University

In this very readable and accessible book, we discover some of the background to the events and experiences that shaped Andy's career and the evolution of his thinking on education.

Professor Steve Munby, CBE, former CEO of the National College for School Leadership, England

As an avid reader of Andy's books for the better part of two decades, I think this is the keystone upon which everything else should be placed.

David H. Edwards, General Secretary, Education International

Andy's book helps us understand how the personal and professional are deeply intertwined, mutually informing one another. Importantly, it generates critical insights into the rise of neo-liberalism in educational policy and practice and captures key insights for educational improvement in our current moment that speak to both the pursuit of educational quality and equity.

James Spillane, Spencer T. and Ann W. Olin Professor in Learning and Organizational Change, Northwestern University, Chicago

In *The Making an Educator* you see Andy in flesh, blood, and as he was up to the age of 37. You understand what makes him tick and be ticked off. You can't understand and get the full brunt of Andy's magnificent contribution to practice and theory without absorbing the making of the early man.

Professor Emeritus Michael Fullan, OC, OISE/University of Toronto

Andy is keen to say that this is not a memoir and, in the sense that it isn't merely an account of the past, he is right. However, it is an invaluable 'bringing together' of the journey that school policy has taken over almost half a century and offers wise and rooted advice for the next generation of education professionals. As such, it provides us with a shared foundation for navigating the future.

Rt. Hon. Baroness Estelle Morris, former Secretary of State for Education

The Making of an Educator is a delight from the first page to the last, with direct relevance for all of us today who are dedicated to improving teaching and learning, wherever we may be.

Dennis Shirley, author, *The New Imperatives of Educational Change*

The Making of an Educator

Living Through and Learning from the Great Education Shift

Andy Hargreaves

Crown House Publishing Limited
www.crownhouse.co.uk

First published by
Crown House Publishing Limited
Crown Buildings, Bancyfelin, Carmarthen, Wales, SA33 5ND, UK
www.crownhouse.co.uk
and
Crown House Publishing Company LLC
PO Box 2223, Williston, VT 05495, USA
www.crownhousepublishing.com

© Andy Hargreaves, 2025.

The right of Andy Hargreaves to be identified as the author of this work has been asserted by him in accordance with the Copyright, Designs and Patents Act 1988.

First published 2025.

All rights reserved. Except as permitted under current legislation no part of this work may be photocopied, stored in a retrieval system, published, performed in public, adapted, broadcast, transmitted, recorded or reproduced in any form or by any means, without the prior permission of the copyright owners. Enquiries should be addressed to Crown House Publishing.

Crown House Publishing has no responsibility for the persistence or accuracy of URLs for external or third-party websites referred to in this publication, and does not guarantee that any content on such websites is, or will remain, accurate or appropriate.

Cover image © James Thew – adobe.stock.com

EU GPSR Authorised Representative
Easy Access System Europe OÜ, 16879218
Address: Mustamäe tee 50, 10621, Tallinn, Estonia
Contact Details: gpsr.requests@easproject.com, +358 40 500 3575

British Library Cataloguing-in-Publication Data
A catalogue entry for this book is available from the British Library.

Print ISBN 978-178583752-4
Mobi ISBN 978-178583762-3
ePub ISBN 978-178583763-0
ePDF ISBN 978-178583764-7
LCCN 2025934435

Printed and bound in the UK by
CPi, Antony Rowe, Chippenham, Wiltshire

Foreword by Pasi Sahlberg

'The owl of Minerva spreads its wings only with the coming of the dusk.'* So wrote Georg Wilhelm Friedrich Hegel, a German philosopher and one of the most influential thinkers of the 19th century.[†] In Roman mythology, Minerva is the goddess of wisdom, and her pet owl symbolises knowledge, culture, and discernment. A common interpretation of Hegel's wisdom is that any given era of history can only be understood in retrospect – after it's over.

If you take what Hegel wrote to heart, it has several interesting corollaries for educational literature and research. First, in education, our power to foresee the future is limited – as we've seen over decades, and even centuries, of efforts to try to predict how education will renew itself. Formal education systems and how they operate have remained largely unchanged despite revolutions and shifts in our societies, technologies, and the world. Second, Hegel's notion of Minerva's owl suggests that our power to understand the

---

* https://www.oxfordreference.com/display/10.1093/oi/authority.20110803100258860.

† To be precise, in the original German, he wrote: 'Die Eule der Minerva beginnt erst mit der einbrechenden Dämmerung ihren Flug', in his book *Grundlinien der Philosophie des Rechts: Naturrecht und Staatswissenschaft im Grundrisse* (Nicolai'sche Buchhandlung, 1820) (known in English as *The Philosophy of Right*).

present and the shifts and underlying forces of any era is usually limited. To that end, Hegel's insight enables us to see that in education – as in other things – true understanding and wisdom about what we experience at any given moment often emerge only in hindsight, after a major shift has passed.

I've been a fan of Hegel and his idea about the owl of Minerva since high school. As a teenager living through the turmoil of the 1970s, I tried hard to understand the world around me – without much success at all. The nuclear arms race had pushed the world to the brink of another global war. The energy crisis and struggles for basic human rights made the world a complex and often confusing place. Hegel often came to my rescue. I would turn to history books and listen to philosophers to better understand the present. The more I read about the history of education and consulted the works of John Dewey, Kurt Lewin, Jerome Bruner, and Maria Montessori, the better I could make sense of what was happening around me.

The next time I encountered the owl of Minerva was in the early 1990s, when I was offered a job at the newly established National Board of Education in Helsinki. That was a period of great educational change in Finland. Waves of neo-liberalism were shaking public-sector management thinking around the world, including in the Nordic countries. Corporate management models and business jargon were appearing in education policy documents and reform narratives. Political leaders embraced the principles of the Third Way, seeking to combine the best of the past with the most promising aspects of new corporate management thinking. Sweden, and other Nordic countries, was more eager to follow this trend than Finland – perhaps because Finns have always tended to be followers rather than leaders when it comes to significant social or economic shifts. That later turned out to be a blessing for the Finnish education system.

Dr Vilho Hirvi was the first Director General of the National Board of Education and my boss during the time I worked for that agency.

Foreword by Pasi Sahlberg

He was a teacher and education scholar with a genuine passion for history and philosophy. I remember how many politicians, academics, and business leaders in Finland urged Dr Hirvi to jump aboard the moving train of modern ideas, which promised efficiency and quick improvements through corporate-driven education administration and policy. When Dr Hirvi spoke to his staff about the future of Finnish education in the early 1990s, he said that we would only make sense of the real significance of that time once it was over. We understood the wisdom of Minerva's owl and decided to focus on building a stronger sense of purpose in education through shared values, collective responsibility, and mutual trust. That work went on as planned. The rest is history.

I was a young educator when the Finnish educational reforms ran against the global tide of neo-liberalism and pursued a path that was more professional, more collectively responsible, and more focused on the public good. In many ways, these early experiences have shaped my own path as an educator and have subsequently influenced how I, as a policy specialist, have been able to take these values and accomplishments – of professional trust, shared responsibility, and public good – to the World Bank, the OECD, and national governments across the world, most recently, in my adopted home of Australia.

During this formative period in Finnish education, in the 1990s, I spent some weeks as a post-doctoral research fellow at the International Centre for Educational Change, which Andy Hargreaves had established in Toronto. There, I met Andy, just a few years on in his own professional formation, whose ideas had started to take shape when neo-liberalism came across his bows during the onset of Thatcherism in England, a decade before it was popularised in Finland. I soon realised that, like me, Andy had already chosen his own alternate path that rejected standardised testing and the deprofessionalisation of teaching in favour of alternative assessments and collaborative professionalism.

The Making of an Educator

What happened to both of us in the past, during the great shifts that we each experienced at different times when our respective world views were evolving, has stayed with us, and grown in strength, throughout our careers. Like two owls, we came together. With eye and claw, both of us have since swooped down upon the many enemies of equitable, inclusive, and humanistic purposes in education in our pursuit of wiser and more ethical answers to the never-ending challenges of educational change.

Andy Hargreaves' book reflects the spirit of the owl of Minerva. He surprises readers by revealing that this book is not a memoir. Rather, as he writes, 'It's not an intellectual biography either. It's between and beyond these things.' Anyone who reads this book will find that to be exactly so. It becomes clear, as you travel with Andy as a guide, from the early 1970s to the late 1980s, that the true meaning of the political and educational era that shaped him as an educator can only be understood in retrospect.

But it also works the other way around – awareness of key issues in the history of education can help us to make more sense of contemporary educational debates, as this book makes clear.

One such issue is the role of research and evidence in informing educational practice, especially teaching in schools. As part of post-COVID recovery, many education system leaders around the world now insist that teachers only use methods like explicit teaching and direct instruction, based on robust evidence. In some countries, like Finland, Singapore, and Canada, decisions about which teaching methods to use – and the evidence behind them – are left to schools and teachers. In other systems, though, education authorities select the evidence and determine which methods should be used. In Australia, some education ministers have gone even further by mandating which evidence-based teaching methods teachers are supposed to use in their classrooms and for how many minutes each day. These policy decisions are often made without looking to the past and considering what happened when such initiatives have been tried before.

Foreword by Pasi Sahlberg

What makes Andy's book different from other 'memoirs' is the way in which he reflects on contemporary issues and debates through the lens of history and his own experience. For example, when he writes about research and experience in education (especially in teaching), he explains how, in the dominant culture of teaching in the 1970s, the only thing that counted when teachers made judgements was their own experience in their schools and classrooms. It was rare for teachers to refer to educational theories, research, or conditions from other fields when designing their work. Andy reminds us that research on teaching and the teaching profession has significantly contributed to improved practice in schools, but the pendulum then swung too far – he shows – and now, the role of evidence is often misunderstood and overstated. Evidence-based practice, if not exercised thoughtfully, has led – and is leading again – to governing by numbers, top-down accountability, narrowing curricula, and chasing data and performance targets – all of which undermines the soul of teachers' professional autonomy and erodes societal trust in schools.

I've taught graduate students in education policy and teacher education at five universities over the past 25 years. It's surprising – and disappointing – how little students pursuing a master's degree in education are expected to read from the past. It's rare to find a recent graduate who has read John Dewey or classics like Willard Waller's *The Sociology of Teaching*,[*] Dan Lortie's *Schoolteacher*,[†] or Andy Hargreaves' *Changing Teachers, Changing Times*.[‡] The book you are reading now makes it clear that becoming an educator is a long process – not simply the result of earning a university degree. Sometimes, as Andy shows here, it takes an entire career.

---

[*] W. Waller, *The Sociology of Teaching* (Wiley, 1932).
[†] D. Lortie, *Schoolteacher: A Sociological Study* (University of Chicago Press, 1975).
[‡] A. Hargreaves, *Changing Teachers, Changing Times: Teachers' Work and Culture in the Postmodern Age* (Teachers College Press, 1994).

The Making of an Educator

How can today's education graduates make sense of the present if they have only a limited understanding of the past? And how can we imagine the future without knowing what has been tried before? In my mind, educating educators today should include at least a basic understanding of the most significant works, ideas, and thinkers of the past. If you read this book and ask yourself which writings have shaped Andy as an educator, you'll quickly see the wide range of books and articles that influenced his early career as a teacher and teacher educator, including those mentioned above. It's difficult, in my view, to be an educator without familiarity with some of the classics.

If you read memoirs, as I do, you know that it's all about storytelling. Every life is worth a story – if you know how to tell it. Without revealing too much about what will follow, I can say that the storytelling in this book is engaging, entertaining, and occasionally funny. And remember that this book is not a memoir; it's something between a biography and a memoir – and it's an incomplete one. There is still much more to come in the making of an educator.

In the end of a memoir or intellectual biography, one question remains: legacy? What is a legacy? In the Broadway musical *Hamilton*, Alexander Hamilton responds, 'It's planting seeds in a garden you never get to see.' I hope this quote serves as a bridge to Andy's story because it raises the essential questions that all serious educators will ask at some point in their lives.

The story here is the most important – the legacy will follow.

Preface

This is not a memoir. It is not an intellectual biography either. It is a book that describes my experiences as an emerging educator and academic in my 20s and 30s as a way of looking at a great historical shift in education and society half a century ago that is reverberating in another shift of seismic proportions today. The book shows how crystallising moments in early career at key moments in history can shape people generationally through the insights and agendas they carry with them as their careers evolve over time, and as they develop the capacity to exercise leadership and make an impact on an increasingly large scale.

Some readers may be aware of my work on teacher collaboration, educational change, and professional capital after I moved from England to North America in the late 1980s. It has yielded eight book awards and over 100,000 citations, so it is quite well known. This book is about my professional and, in some parts, personal life before that point, from 1973 to 1987. What I experienced and accomplished then is probably less familiar, but, like the early work of other professionals, it laid the foundations for much of what followed.

Like many immigrants, all the work I did and all the expertise I had developed before changing countries was, and still is, largely unheard of. It is as if my accomplishments were achieved afresh and due entirely to the country that apparently discovered and adopted me. Leaving England and moving to Canada, then the United States, was like beginning a new life and career as a man without a past – a man that never was.

In the 1980s, before the widespread use of email, the internet, and fax machines, taking a job on another continent was an act of professional disappearance, almost. My work in the 1990s on the teaching profession, school leadership, and educational reform may have reintroduced me and my research to the UK once telecommunications had advanced, but even that made no reference to anything I had done before I left. When novelists wanted to dispose of a British character, one common plot device was to say, 'And then (s)he went to Canada.' Nothing great or terrible happened to the character in question, but the explanation seemed sufficient for the reader never to have to think about them again.

This book explains how and why almost 15 years starting out as an educator and academic in England set up my contributions to research, writing, and policy advocacy on the teaching profession, and educational reform after that once my family and I moved to North America. More than that, it shows how these experiences took place at a remarkable moment in history – the mid-1970s to the late 1980s – when there was a Great Shift in education and society. This shift, through the eyes and experiences of my own life and work at the time, threw up issues about teaching, learning, and school reform that have had immense and lasting importance ever since. Half a century later, in the mid-2020s, we are witnessing another Great Shift of global politics and economics. How we understand it and deal with it can be informed by how we experienced the previous one.

Other than wanting to know about the life of a minor public figure in education, along with a series of events that all took place in the previous century, why might you want to read this book? Who is it for?

Preface

If you feel lost in a chaotic world that you don't fully understand, this book will draw on knowledge of the past, without dwelling on it or wallowing in it, to help you understand the world you are in now. Because it speaks of a Great Shift when the world order was changing, it will help you to not only improve your grasp of how the world order is changing again today, but also how to capitalise on that uncertainty by involving yourself in innovation, change, and leadership that can help shape the future for the young people you teach. It may help inspire you to make 'shift' happen in your own work and in the world around you.

If you are a teacher, this book, through the lens of my research on middle school teachers, should provide insights into why teachers teach the way they do – indeed, why we all do things the way we do, even when it doesn't make sense to other people, and even when it isn't really working any more. It should acknowledge and explain your frustrations when other people – in politics, business, your community, or the media – are quick to judge teachers and slow to understand them, their life issues, and their work conditions. And it should affirm just how important our colleagues are to us, whether we are teachers or academics, and why building communities where we collaborate with colleagues and where we give and receive great mentoring matter so much.

If you are a leader in schools, of schools, or of whole groups or systems of schools, this book should also help to persuade you that the most important factor when we are changing teaching and learning, or changing anything really, is not structures, plans, programmes, or accountability mechanisms. It is culture – what we believe and commit to, how well we push and support each other, and how functional or dysfunctional our teams are when we do things together. This applies just as much to universities and faculties of education as it does to schools.

If you use or are engaged in any kind of research or enquiry, then this book should help to deepen your understanding of what research truly is and involves. It should help you not to be intimidated by it on the one hand or mesmerised by it on the other. It will show you that school-based and university-based researchers and enquirers can and should be on a more equal footing where both are accorded dignity and respect, and that teachers should not just be recipients of external expertise from non-teachers but should be critical consumers of research and partners with researchers too.

Professional knowledge in education, or anywhere, combines three forms of valued knowledge and expertise:

1. On-the-ground, upfront expertise of professional judgement built up over many years of knowing people and circumstances in unique situations.
2. Knowledge about external research that does not falsely elevate some kinds of research – quantitative methods, experimental procedures, or blind-controlled studies – over others that use interviews and observations with people up close in the complex worlds of real schools and classrooms.
3. Knowledge of collaborative enquiry that teachers themselves conduct into problems and challenges in their own institutions.

There is good and bad research in all traditions – quantitative and qualitative alike. This book shows that qualitative research, when it is done well by you or anyone else, is scientifically rigorous and respectable and has a long history. It reveals things that quantitative research cannot. It shows what is happening on the ground now, what it means to the people involved, what is emerging in the experiences of teachers and young people before it comes to public or official attention, and how what teachers know can therefore be ahead of the game of what more traditional 'scientific' researchers claim. When schools and universities work as equal

Preface

partners and value multiple methodologies, as I have, research can advance knowledge and insight about teaching and learning, rather than teachers just being convinced or compelled to implement the findings that university researchers have come up with on their own.

If you are a starting-out researcher or graduate student, you will also learn from my own research experiences about the value of building your own theory. There is nothing more practical, we will see, than having a good theory. Theories are frameworks that we all develop or adopt to make sense of what is around us – why children behave badly, why attendance has fallen off, or why parents seem to complain more than they did, for example. Formal theories are constructed over many years by experts who are paid to have the time to read and think in depth. Sometimes, we latch on to a theory early because it makes sense to us, but then we can become overly subservient to it. This dependency on a singular set of sources can turn our minds into echo chambers of our own unshakeable beliefs. We can become overly enamoured of one single set of theories – growth mindsets, phonics, or critical race theory, for example – without examining their drawbacks or considering alternatives to them. We might attach ourselves too firmly to the ideas or beliefs of a single professor or group of professors who taught us or whom we have read, and then take no time to wander, with a sense of curiosity and intellectual adventure, outside their familiar paradigms into the unexplored theoretical terrains of others. This book will show what it takes to build your own theories with professional independence and integrity from multiple components, rather than from a standardised set of building blocks that are owned and produced by just one brand.

If you believe in free speech, intellectual balance, and academic integrity, this book will show you how to escape from your own echo chamber and treat your opponents' theories, research findings, and beliefs with curiosity, dignity, and respect, even when you continue to disagree with them. And it will show you how to develop that mentality of curiosity and independence among our young people in schools and universities, too, so that they do not become blinded by their own ideological lights.

If you are near the beginning or end of your career, you will look through a window into my own early adult life and career and, perhaps along the way, that window will become a kind of mirror for your own life and career, and the lives and careers of those around you. You might learn to develop greater generational generosity towards those younger and older than yourself, and towards their life struggles and accomplishments. Perhaps you will learn to judge less, empathise more, and not treat junior colleagues as flawed versions of your younger self or dismiss older peers and forbears as outdated and irrelevant people of privilege either.

If you are in early adulthood, near the start of your career, and sometimes get discouraged about a lack of progress, this book will share my own challenges in getting started, becoming recognised, trying to stand up for myself and stick by my principles, struggling with money, raising a young family, and having to keep moving from one job to another just to stay afloat. In doing so, it will also reveal how, when we feel like this, we are often making a lot more progress than we probably think. In chess terms, we are moving our pawns so that we can bring out our rooks and queens later. And we are making sacrifices that might well prove worthwhile in the end, perhaps spectacularly so.

Like a movie, the book zooms in and pans out from my own experiences of educational developments during early career to a larger landscape of key research and policy literature at the time, and back again. And like a multi-generational novel, it also loops back and forth between the present and the past to show how the themes that this literature exposes, along with my own and others' experiences, continue to preoccupy many educators and educational researchers now.

Preface

The language and vocabulary may from time to time feel unusual to readers in different countries. When I write about the UK, I will refer to pupils, head teachers, state education, and local authorities. When I fast forward to my career in Canada and the United States, these terms will be replaced with students, principals, public education, and school districts. I will talk about football and crisps in England and soccer and chips in Canada. Otherwise, the rest should be self-evident.

I have several people to thank for helping me assemble what is in this book with greater accuracy and coherence, and for preventing me from becoming captive to the distortions and vicissitudes of my own memory. Foremost among all these professional colleagues and friends is my namesake, David Hargreaves. David has known me from the very start of my university career in England until the moment my family and I left for Canada. We worked closely together for almost five years at Oxford University and connected in many other ways over those years.

My gratitude to David knows practically no bounds for the time he has spent in the middle of a long struggle with cancer to reply fully, freely, and frankly to ideas, drafts, and recollections as this book has evolved. We spent a delightful day at his home near Cambridge on a visit I made to England in the spring of 2024, and then, from his tablet in his hospital bed after yet another surgery, he engaged generously with an earlier draft of a chapter about the 1980s in Oxford. In return, I have been privileged to read, respond to, and endorse what he says is his last book on ethics and happiness.[1]

Martyn Hammersley, my friend, former neighbour, and first university colleague, gave detailed and direct responses, as he has throughout his career, to my recollections about the early seminars at St Hilda's College, Oxford, that we participated in, and on one occasion organised together, and about the two years I was employed by the Open University. Particularly helpful were his extensive

The Making of an Educator

published reflections on nationally controversial accusations about Marxist bias among some of the group of scholars I joined, and the implications of this event for intellectual balance and freedom today. Martyn also enabled me to access the university's archives and retrieve my first ever media broadcast, which was shown on the BBC, so that I can now verify that my course presentation as a 29-year-old was indeed as pedagogically wooden and sartorially challenged as I remembered it being.

Peter Woods, who figures large in several chapters, and who, in addition to hiring me at the Open University, worked with me as a co-author, showed nothing less than complete kindness, including times I didn't fully deserve it when I was in early career. He has shared his own memories about the university and the field in the late 1970s and early 1980s. In his 90s now, and as a mark of his unshakeable lifelong optimism and resilience, he told me that he has just bought a new dog!

Geoffrey Walford, Emeritus Professor of Education Policy at Oxford University, also responded to my recollections of the St Hilda's conferences and shared with me an important paper he has published about its history.

Eileen Baglin was a student of mine at Oxford. Already a Justice of the Peace as well as a middle leader in her local secondary school when we met, Eileen went on to have an impressive career as a senior local authority advisor. Although we were poles apart politically on some issues, she became a dear friend of our family and a co-author with me and her fellow students of a book on personal and social education. She too has reflected with warmth and honesty on draft chapters I sent to her, and she has helped me to edit down what was a heavy-going theoretical section in the middle of the book.

There are other readers who didn't know me, or who scarcely knew me at all during the years I was establishing myself professionally in England, and for that reason their feedback on how the manuscript might make better sense to readers of different gener-

Preface

ations today, as well as beyond the UK, has been especially valuable. Particular thanks go to my long-standing colleague and friend, Steve Munby (who also helped me to ditch some of the theoretical jargon); my co-author and close friend for the past 20 years, Dennis Shirley; the voraciously reading director of one of my local school districts in Ottawa, Tom D'Amico; another co-author, Dean Fink, now almost 90 years old, who provided me with my first research opportunity when I moved to Canada to study collaborative school cultures in his district; and, not least, Pasi Sahlberg, who I invited to write the foreword to this book. Pasi and I have known each other and collaborated in various ways for 30 years. However, this did not include the times I worked in England. He is, in this respect, especially well positioned to connect and communicate who he knows me to be now, and what he knows I have done since I moved to North America, to the years before that, as he views them from a greater distance of time and space.

This book is my second that has a life history flavour to it. Both books have the same purpose: to use my own experiences as a looking glass for compelling educational and social issues of the periods being explored, as well as their continuing relevance today. Alongside my educational background, they contain a lot of detail about family and community life.

The previous book of this nature – *Moving: A Memoir of Education and Social Mobility* – described my experience of growing up in a working-class family in the North of England and of being educated in local primary and secondary schools.[2] It cast light on the nature, importance, and obstacles as well as the opportunities that are created by social mobility. This second book goes on to describe what the first starting-out years of professionals are like when they move up from the working class with few resources other than their own qualifications and wits. As my publisher, David Bowman, commented when he read an earlier draft, my narrative has quite a bit of impecuniousness about it.

The Making of an Educator

People's careers cannot be understood apart from their lives and the world around them. Through the mirror of my own life and that of my growing family, this book relates the formative years of being a new professional to the life circumstances and struggles of getting a financial foothold in the middle class and to a generationally influential period when a Great Shift was occurring in education and society. My wife of 50-plus years, Pauline Hargreaves, and our adult children, Stuart and Lucy, have helped me to look back on this period and what it meant to us all, including the leaving of it all, for Canada.

Almost all the material in this book is entirely original in how it reports on my research and publications over the years. There are five instances of more extended extracts that are adapted more directly from previous publications, and I want to acknowledge the following sources for use of that material:

- A. Hargreaves, 'The Significance of Classroom Coping Strategies', in L. Barton and R. Meighan (eds), *Sociological Interpretations of Schooling and Classrooms: A Reappraisal* (Nafferton Books, 1978), pp. 73–100.
- A. Hargreaves, 'Experience Counts, Theory Doesn't: How Teachers Talk About Their Work', *Sociology of Education*, 57 (1984), 244–254.
- A. Hargreaves, 'Teacher Collaboration: 30 Years of Research on Its Nature, Forms, Limitations and Effects', *Teachers and Teaching*, 25(5) (2019), 603–621.
- A. Hargreaves, 'Tim Brighouse: Sustainability Maker', in D. Cameron, S. Munby, and M. Waters (eds), *Unfinished Business: The Life and Legacy of Tim Brighouse* (Crown House Publishing, 2024), pp. 39–42.
- A. Hargreaves, 'The Dark Side of Networks: and the Implications for School Leadership', *School Leadership & Management*, 45(1) (2025), 1–6. https://doi.org/10.1080/13632434.2025.2454157

Preface

Last, but not least, I am extremely grateful to David Bowman at Crown House Publishing for having faith in this book as a viable part of his impressive stable. Meeting David for the first time was an encounter and an experience that is becoming less and less common – a publisher who reads manuscripts inside out, not just to assess their worth as a market product but also out of intrinsic intellectual interest.

If you have got this far, you have obviously not given up yet. Hopefully, you will find the rest of the book just as engaging, if not more so. So, let's get started.

Contents

Foreword by Pasi Sahlberg   **iii**
Preface   **ix**

Introduction   **1**
   The Great Shift   **1**
   Divisions and Disputes   **5**
   Experience and Research   **8**
   Culture and Strategy   **14**
   Life and Career   **15**

1. A Shot at Teaching   **17**
   A Field, a Suit, a Gun, and a Teacher   **17**
   Primary Responsibilities   **19**
   Psychic Rewards   **21**
   The Disintegrated Day   **23**
   The Music and the Words   **28**
   The First and Last Time   **34**

2. The Paradox of Pupil Autonomy   39
    Open Season on Open Classrooms   39
    Progressivism and Pupil Autonomy   47
    Time and Freedom   51
    Three Ways Forward   57
    Progressivism with Pragmatism   59

3. Classroom Coping Strategies   61
    A Lucky Break   61
    A Few Firsts   63
    Evidence or Experience   67
    Coping Strategies   71
    Coping or Transforming   75
    Beyond Coping   80

4. How to Build a Theory   83
    The Loneliness of the Long-Distance Thinker   83
    Big Things and Small Things   87
    Round the Mulberry Bush   93
    A Cock-and-Bull Story   95
    New Tricks   97
    Thinking Together   100
    Six Secrets of Theory Building   101

5. Bias and Integrity   105
    Scholarship or Propaganda?   105
    Contortion or Complexity?   110
    Inconvenient Truths   110
    Distortion and Frustration   114
    Integration and Integrity   116
    Postscript   120

6. Cultures of Teaching   123
   From the Sewers to the Spires   123
   High Culture in Low Places   126
   Back to School   131
   Mentors and Tormentors   134
   Meeting in the Middle   138
   The Break in the Middle   143
   Culture and Change   144

7. The Great Education Shift   147
   Sent to Coventry   147
   Teaching Quality   149
   Alone Together   154
   Side Bets   155
   Assessment and Achievement   157
   Time and Tide   169

8. A Shot in the Dark   173
   Exeunt   173
   The Knowledge   177
   A Particular Set of Skills   179
   Better Coping Strategies   182
   Leaving Home   190

Endnotes   191
References   205

Introduction

The Great Shift

The book begins in England in the 1970s. This was, at first, a period of public investment, pursuit of equality, commitment to education for a common good, belief in autonomy and choice in learning for children and teachers, romantic attachments to the idea of educating the whole person, enthusiasm about engaging in innovation, and support for a strong and highly qualified teaching profession as an attractive and well-regarded career. Although the lustre of this golden age began to tarnish and fade in the second half of the decade, it was still a time of public confidence in the value of state education, of education as a path to upward social mobility, of schools as places that could help to change society, and of teaching as a desirable career that many young people from working-class families could use as their stepping stone into middle-class life and opportunities.

Following Margaret Thatcher's election on the cusp of the 1980s, there was a political and, ultimately, a global move towards what is now known as neo-liberalism. It would define the next half century of social and economic policy, including in education, and would bring populism in its wake – marking the start of another Great Shift that is bringing the neo-liberal era to a close.

The Making of an Educator

This was the end of the innocence. Funding declined. Teachers were criticised and then attacked. Academics in education were blamed for indoctrinating teachers with dangerously radical ideologies. Child-centredness and open education became the targets of concerted assaults. Teacher education and teacher educators were inspected and regulated to patrol their work so that it focused on basic skills and traditional subject content. And the entire language of educational policy, management, and curriculum became infused with, and increasingly oriented towards, new concerns with standards, evaluation, and bureaucratic accountability. This is where and when today's taken-for-granted language of education was first born.

In between was what is called an interregnum or period between reigns. This was a time of transition, uncertainty, conflict, and opportunity. Interregnums are periods when the old order is dying away, but the new one has not yet been born. Often, they are also times of great excitement, of collaborations and partnerships across conventional political divides, and of surges in innovation as new practices and systems are devised to solve the unique problems before them. That is when shift happens!

At their most impactful, the efforts and experiments in an interregnum can influence a new age, and even come to define it. Interregnums also shape the ideas and experiences of young professionals who are in early career at the time. In one form or another, these impressionable young adults then take the transformative experiences they are acquiring with them as they grow into leadership and as they reinvent them at various points throughout their professional lifetimes. In education, the interregnum in England and Wales that spanned the late 1970s and early 1980s led to vigorous activity in three areas in which I became involved and that, in terms of my own and others' generational formation, had major influences on the rest of our work and careers.

Introduction

First, in secondary education, a crisis in youth motivation brought on by rising unemployment led to creative initiatives in vocational education, in expanding and diversifying how people defined achievement and success, and in new forms of assessment that recognised this diversity and supported young people's progress. These alternate forms of assessment have reappeared in contemporary discussions about how to reform tests and examinations in the wake of the COVID-19 pandemic when teenagers' anxieties came to the forefront of public attention. Alternative assessments are also receiving serious consideration in the face of the onrushing opportunities that artificial intelligence (AI) is promising for instant, precise, and differentiated formative feedback. By chance, I was in on the ground floor of alternative assessment reform. What I learned through those years of helping educators to design better assessments for their pupils has stayed with me up to the present day when I have advised governments in Scotland, Ireland, Canada, and elsewhere on moving away from the dominance of traditional tests and examinations.

Second, dissatisfactions with and criticisms of conventional forms of teacher training and continuous professional development led to partnership initiatives between schools and local authorities on the one hand and universities on the other. University departments of education began to concentrate their student teachers in groups in a small number of selected sites rather than dispersing them as individuals across many schools. This new practice established habits of professional collaboration among the students and with the teachers employed in the schools. It also connected the academic interests of the university faculty more directly with the professional preparation of new generations of teachers. The creation of these partnerships started a worldwide movement that would eventually evolve into today's national teaching schools in England, for example. Once more, I found myself working with one of these schools at the very start of the movement's emergence.

The Making of an Educator

Third, dissatisfactions with the quality of professional learning and development (PLD) for full-time teachers also prompted significant rethinking about how in-service education, as it was known, could be redesigned. Traditionally, PLD had been offered to individuals in university courses away from school sites. When teachers took what they had learned back to their schools, it had little impact. Other teachers were usually sceptical, sometimes resented their colleagues taking time away, and showed little interest in what they brought home. For a few years, therefore, government money was given to local authorities to improve the experience and impact of PLD. Partnerships were established with university education faculties where teachers would be given secondments from their regular jobs for a term or a year to conduct research on topics that connected to their practice. Often, this research was undertaken with other teachers who had also been seconded from their authority, with the idea that they would implement what they had learned together.

This initiative was short-lived, but it lasted long enough to fundamentally alter my own approach to working with teachers and schools. I began to relate to teachers not just as research objects or as students taking my university courses, but I learned to engage in new relationships that were mutually respectful. This work with teachers, schools, and school systems laid the practical basis for what would become my lifelong commitment to understanding and creating collaborative cultures in the teaching profession.

In 1927, the Hungarian German (and later British) sociologist Karl Mannheim invented the theory and idea of generations.[1] The things we learn, the generations we are part of, and what he called the crystallising moments in history that we live through in early adulthood shape much of what we believe, fight against, and strive for throughout the rest of our lives. Hopefully, this book will help readers to think about their own generational formations, and how they can build on them as they expand and strengthen their leadership.

Introduction

Divisions and Disputes

Alongside the opportunities and initiatives for innovation and change that flourished briefly in secondary education during the early 1980s there were also bitter ideological divisions and disputes about the quality and character of state education. These were part of my generational formation too.

Education today is no stranger to such conflicts, of course. Arguments have raged about how the curriculum should treat British colonial history and its association with slavery and the exploitation of the nation's conquered peoples. Moves to decolonise British history have been met with countermoves to reassert traditional historical knowledge, even in primary schools. In addition, conflicts among parents and in communities between transgender advocates and gender-critical feminists about self-identification, pronouns, and school toilets have been stoked by government pronouncements and media controversy.[2]

These battles in Britain for the minds of children and their teachers are nothing in comparison to the incendiary conflicts that have raged in the United States over identity politics. By 2024, legislators in 18 US states had passed laws restricting the teaching of race and gender, arguing that these are inherently divisive topics that pit groups against one another.[3] In Florida, Governor Ron DeSantis forbade schools and state universities to teach critical perspectives on race, gender, and social class, while Republicans specified that schools should only teach about Marxism within a mandated anti-communist framework.[4] President Trump himself complained about how US colleges had become 'dominated by Marxist maniacs and lunatics'.[5] On 21 January 2025, President Trump signed an executive order banning all DEI (diversity, equity, and inclusion) initiatives funded by the US federal government.[6] These controversies have sparked heated

The Making of an Educator

debates about freedom of speech, cancel culture, ideological bias, and government interference.

I entered academic life in the middle of another huge national controversy about indoctrination and ideological bias and found myself plunged into the very heart of it. This was a scandal about alleged Marxist propaganda in the course materials that had been produced by the university I had joined, and that was being taken by thousands of teachers. In a review I was called to conduct, I had to address questions of openness, fairness, intellectual balance, and freedom of speech that have helped to form my views about academic integrity in ways that remain important in my research, writing, and stance as a public intellectual today.

A second controversy is one that recurs every decade or two. Educational directions change when governments change, along with their political agendas. They shift when economies move from the optimism of prosperity to the drawing in of austerity. These forces swing the proverbial pendulum of educational change – a pendulum that moves towards progressive education, open classrooms, educating the whole child, and child-centred learning in one direction, and then towards basic skills, a traditional curriculum, prescribed pedagogies, and preparation for the workforce in the other.

I started out on the back end of an educational movement and cultural zeitgeist that touted progressive values of equality and freedom. As a child from a working-class family, I had come by the values of equality honestly.[7] Then, going to university to study sociology during the late 1960s counterculture engaged me with the libertarian values of freedom and autonomy. But the realities of teaching working-class children also challenged me with how to promote autonomy and equality while also establishing structures of safety and control.

I have wrestled with this tension all my career. It has shaped the way that I taught children and that I teach adults now: creating clear, firm frameworks, directions, and protocols that allow, enable,

Introduction

and encourage greater choice and autonomy. It contributed to the framing of my PhD thesis on progressive and traditional middle schools.[8] It has continued to influence my work ever since – in supporting and evaluating the Canadian province of Ontario's policy on outcomes-based education and an integrated curriculum for the transition years in the 1990s, and in my advisory work with governments on introducing alternative educational assessments in the aftermath of the COVID-19 pandemic.

But it is a tension or paradox, not a fixed position. It is more a matter of riding the pendulum to keep it closer to the middle than waiting at one extreme for it to swing back again. Being in the middle is not easy. It involves being unshakeable about values such as equity, dignity, autonomy, and professionalism, yet open to evidence and research about the most effective strategies to achieve them. This book describes two ways in which I took up an aggressive middle position that is strong on values but pragmatic on strategy, and that has come to typify much of my work on leadership, change, and research ever since.

One example was confronting a theoretical field that was split into two camps that mainly ignored each other. One camp was interested in understanding the microworlds of culture, relationships, and interactions inside classrooms. The other addressed how schools were influenced and shaped by the nature of the broader macro society. I was one of the first scholars to try to bridge and integrate these micro and macro perspectives in education because I believed then, as I do now, that to understand what teachers and learners do, and why they do it, we must get to grips with both the cultures and relationships they are part of *and* the kind of society in which their work takes place.

The second example was more political. When and how can we get beyond Left and Right? This was the question that Cambridge University sociologist Anthony Giddens asked in the 1990s, and emerged in the resulting concept and strategy of the Third Way that came to define the political approaches of President Bill Clinton and Prime Minister Tony Blair.[9] This book outlines how I came to my own position on the Left–Right question by figuring out what to make of historical evidence that just didn't fit all my initially preferred theory. Something had to give. At the end of the day, I am a social scientist, and that is your job if you work in a university. We aren't paid to be ideologues, impervious to any disconfirming data. I am not the first social theorist to change my perspective in the face of evidence to the contrary, but we are more the exception than the rule.[10]

Some extreme stances on the cast-iron irrefutability of scientific evidence amount to their own kinds of inflexible idolatry, as we will see. But ever since my own open engagement with theory and evidence, although my values concerning equity, broadly conceived achievement, autonomy, and dignity remain consistent, I now regard theories more as tools at my disposal and resources to draw on rather than as providing me with just one set of tinted spectacles that colour everything I see.

Experience and Research

The relative contributions of evidence and experience are not just an issue for academic researchers. They affect teachers too. A minor part of my doctoral research unearthed an illuminating example of how teachers who were trying to develop a common vision for their school fell seriously short because they relied only on their own practical experiences of teaching and schools to try and come to a decision. Not only did they not consider research, but they didn't consider any other experiences, such as their family experiences outside school, as being relevant either. They just didn't allow any knowledge or the right kinds of knowledge into their discussions that might have helped them. My work was exploratory, but like a

Introduction

lot of small-scale, on-the-ground research, it drew attention to something that wasn't yet on other people's radar – the fact that there was a prevailing culture of teaching in the 1970s where only school experience counted when teachers made judgements to the exclusion of theory, research, and even knowledge from other areas of life.

If only existing experience counts when we make decisions, we all become prisoners of it. We have no way of learning from elsewhere. So, in the last couple of decades or so, people in policy and universities have been right to bring more consideration of evidence and research into professional decision-making. It is commonplace and expected in other professions. Teaching should be no exception. You wouldn't want your dentist to drill holes in your teeth if they had only learned by trial, error, and hearsay. And you shouldn't want your children's teachers to practise on their brains with knowledge gained through experience alone either.

Movements over the last 20 years towards more evidence-based practices and decision-making have been a welcome development in the face of this long-standing culture of teaching where only experience at the chalk face in the school of hard knocks really counted. But the role of evidence in improving and changing teaching has, unfortunately, often been overstated and distorted. It has become absorbed into systems of improvement by numbers, top-down accountability, external control, and exaggerated emphases on statistical effect sizes. Renowned critics of this overconfident stance in Britain and abroad, who include distinguished elected members of their national academies, have pointed out the main flaws.[11]

The investment in evidence-based practices and the organisations that promote it, tend to favour some kinds of evidence, particularly those that meet the purported gold standards of large surveys, blind-controlled studies, laboratory experiments in areas like neuroscience, and meta-analyses that are common in medicine, over others.[12] Practices that get researched are relatively simple ones that are easier to study when they are torn out of their context and treated as discrete variables that are amenable to straightforward measurement. These practices are typically the traditional ones of teaching and behaviour management, which are favoured by policymakers who want a low-cost profession that can manage simple and uncontroversial practices effectively and that promise to improve results on test scores, behavioural incidents, and attendance figures.

Policymakers also use research results selectively, opting for ones that yield quick wins and that do not threaten the special interests of testing companies, technology platforms, and textbook publishers. Evidence that points to the negative impact of achievement tests, conventional examinations, and top-down accountability on young people's and educators' well-being, for example, is ignored or discounted.

In addition, the supposed gold standard of medical research quite often turns out to be fool's gold. Consider the euphoria about new weight loss drugs. For people who struggle with diabetes and other conditions, there is no doubt that they will be a big part of the future of how to treat obesity. But the benefits don't last after people stop taking the drugs, and they may become too dependent on them and abandon lifestyle changes.[13] What a bonanza for the pharmaceutical industry! Meanwhile, in countries like the UK and United States, which are among the worst in the world when it comes to childhood obesity, little effort has been made to curb the big food industry and the quantity of addictive sugar it adds to its products.[14] Narrow solutions, quick fixes, and special interests have put evidence-based pharmaceutical solutions to obesity into overdrive compared to lifestyle alternatives.

Then there is my mother! At the age of 93, in the North of England, she was rushed into her local hospital. I got there as fast as I could from Canada on one of many back-and-forth visits I had made as

Introduction

her primary carer for decades. When I arrived, she was almost unconscious, suffering from multiple conditions and from the disorienting psychological side effects of the drugs used to treat them. As she teetered on the brink of life and death, I met different doctors every day who discussed specific aspects of her condition. But these aspects were disaggregated. They weren't joined up among the medical staff or with each other. Nor were they connected to my mother and her dignity as a human being.

I therefore created a hand-scrawled spreadsheet of my mother – her conditions across the top, her treatments down the side, and the boxes of consequences, including good ones, where they intersected. I presented and explained it to one of the medical team. He looked at it and said, 'This is fantastic. What do you do for a living?' 'I'm a systems theorist,' I lied.

Now that we could start to see the interrelationships of all my mother's conditions, we could also start to talk about her as a human being. For instance, one proposed procedure was out of the question because of a trauma she had experienced as a child. The late psychologist Oliver Sacks, made famous by Robin Williams in the film *Awakenings*, treasured the words of the noted Canadian physician William Osler a century before, who said, 'Ask not what disease the person has, but rather what person the disease has.'[15] When we took all this into account, our conversation changed. The point, we agreed, was not to keep my mother alive. It was to get her back to full consciousness so she could have the dignity to make that decision for herself, which she duly did.

In a less dramatic way, we also cannot fully understand anyone's teaching unless we understand the person the teacher is and the time and place where they do their work. We need to take account of the kinds of research evidence that get at these more holistic aspects of the people we are studying and working with, not just the 'scientific' evidence on bits and pieces of their practice that gets seals of official approval.

The Making of an Educator

In essence, this is what my PhD thesis, the early years of my career, and, indeed, much of my work as an educator ever since have been about. That research, like much of my ensuing work, was and is predominantly qualitative, not quantitative – something that would be dismissed swiftly by some evidence-based advocates. So, what is my response?

All research in the humanities must meet two criteria – validity and reliability. *Validity* concerns whether the instruments, measures, and findings mean what they are supposed to mean. Do they get to the heart of the human experience, or do survey items have respondents scratching their heads and wondering what the questions have to do with them? One of the founders of the discipline of sociology, Max Weber, talked about the importance of the principle of *verstehen* (German for 'understanding') in the human sciences – of taking time to understand the human nature and conditions of the people you are studying if you want to draw valid conclusions from what you are investigating. Weber insisted that historical and cultural knowledge is not like natural scientific knowledge.[16]

Reliability is about whether different people looking at the data will see it in the same way, or whether their interpretations will vary a lot according to their different experiences, biases, and prejudices. Qualitative research tends to score higher on validity than reliability because it gets closer to the people it is studying. Quantitative research tends to score higher on reliability than validity because researchers are working with larger samples and aren't swayed by the people they happen to have met. Qualitative versus quantitative research isn't akin to bad and good research, then. There is simply a trade-off in terms of what we get from it.

Thirty years on, I had a study to conduct in Canada with 10 school districts in the middle of a politically controversial reform. So, as well as doing case studies in each of the districts, I needed to collect some survey data that would have cast-iron credibility. I

Introduction

asked my Boston College colleague, Professor Henry Braun, to partner with me. Henry is a top measurement expert and former vice-president of research for the US Education Testing Services. In quantitative terms, he is as fireproof as you can get. He also joined me and our graduate student team in doing some of the case studies and analysing all the data afterwards. In his 60s, he said this was the first time in his life he had done interviews and observations with human subjects. After many weeks of qualitative data analysis with our research team, he turned to me and said, 'This qualitative research ...' 'Yes,' I replied. 'It's really hard work, isn't it?'

My own research on middle schools contained some quantitative methods, including statistical tests, alongside my qualitative interviews and observations. My highest scoring papers as a sociology undergraduate were in statistical methods. When I choose qualitative methods over quantitative ones, then, it is not a default option driven by lack of expertise. It is a preference. Qualitative research in my case just means using smaller samples – anything from a couple of dozen to a couple of hundred – that provide opportunities to interview people in depth and increase the prospects for validity. This approach also increases the chances of novelty, creativity, and breakthrough. Keep your nose to the ground and stay close to the action, and you will pick up things long before other people notice them in larger patterns or before they surface in official policies. It keeps you ahead of the game and puts other people, especially political opponents and their enablers, off balance and on their toes. To be honest, this element of surprise still gives me a bit of a buzz.

The other point is that if you look with genuine openness and humility at what people are doing from a standpoint of empathy or *verstehen*, then it compels you to consider why people do the things they do before you get on your high horse and start demanding that they do something different or better.

The Making of an Educator

Culture and Strategy

Karl Marx observed, 'Philosophers have only interpreted the world. The point is to change it.'[17] Politicians and bureaucrats have the opposite problem. They are so eager to change the world quickly and claim victory for any improvement that they rarely make the effort to understand it. Sociologists, like me, first want to understand the world and then go on to change it.

There is no shortage of ideas and strategies about how to change teachers and get them to teach differently. Write a new curriculum and issue new teaching guides, then make teachers comply with what they say. Flood teachers with a deluge of data to drive their decision-making. Use research to evaluate the effectiveness of different teaching strategies and impose the results. Make teachers compete with one another to avoid punishment or to receive pay rewards. Scold them about their biases. Introduce digital tablets, laptops, and learning management systems that will prevent teachers using dog-eared textbooks. Or replace teachers altogether with AI.

All these strategies are problematic. They begin from the wrong premise. They start with some idea or assumption about how teachers need to teach differently and better, then line up strategies based on compliance, metrics, extrinsic incentives, or technology to make it all happen. My research starts from a different assumption. Why do teachers do what they are already doing? What purposes does it serve? What problems does it solve in their work, including ones that are not directly concerned with improving learning? To understand and eventually change teaching, in other words, we must first understand the nature of the work in teaching, the people who do it, and the places and conditions in which it occurs.

In my early research, this led me to look at two interrelated factors: strategies and culture. I argued that teachers developed strategies

Introduction

to respond to the situations in which they found themselves – time, space, numbers of children, curriculum demands, building designs, and so on. Over time, these strategies turn into habits and routines, just like the strategies for driving a car, for example. They become so familiar that they often outlive and resist changes in the surrounding environment.

The reason why teachers' coping strategies persist, I realised, is that teachers don't adopt them idiosyncratically. They do it together as cultures and communities. Understanding teaching therefore requires getting to grips with the culture and cultures of teaching. Changing teaching involves engaging with those cultures. It involves working with teachers rather than throwing things at them or doing things to them. My later work, after I moved to Canada, on building collaborative cultures in teaching and the movements like professional learning communities that partly sprang from it, grew out of these initial insights.

Life and Career

The final theme that runs through this book is about the relationship between people's work and their lives. Twisting Oliver Sacks' advice only slightly, we need to grasp what teachers, as people, do for their teaching and not just look at teaching practices in a disembodied way as if the people doing it don't matter.

As this book unfolds, we will see that how teachers approached their teaching in middle schools was shaped in many ways by where and with whom they taught before. The way teachers taught was also influenced by their stage of life, how early on they were in their careers or how close to retirement, and whether they were ready to take a step up or move sideways. All this applies to other kinds of teachers too. For example, innovative schools tend to attract teachers who have been outliers in their previous schools. Teacher

The Making of an Educator

leaders in these schools often have flexible roles that don't involve teaching conventional subjects or don't entail all-day responsibilities for the same class. Or teachers in innovative schools may have space and time in their lives, and enough energy on their side, to take on all-consuming opportunities in their work.

Everything that applies to other educators has applied to me too. Throughout this book, after engaging with my own experiences and my reflections on them as someone starting a career and moving through the early years of it, perhaps you will remember what it was like for you in early career and notice new things about other people's early career issues for the first time. There is a lot in this book about the nature of early adulthood, too, and how it impacts on the work – what it is like to live on a shoestring, to have small children and go endless nights without getting any proper sleep, to not be able to participate as fully in after-school activities as others with different kinds of lives or at different career points, and to come from a cultural or class background that is different than many colleagues. Not everyone's early lives are the same, but they all deserve closer consideration.

The things you start in early career or as a young scholar or both will, in some form or other, probably stalk you and drive your interests for the rest of your life. They will be like young people's author Philip Pullman's dæmons on your shoulder, always reminding you what to take on and what to avoid.[18] So, it is important to choose your professional dæmons carefully, before they 'settle', as Pullman puts it. Otherwise, they will choose you.

My book doesn't begin with finding or facing one's dæmons, though. It starts, instead, with a man in a black suit, in a wheat field, in the middle of England. It is here where the harvest begins.

CHAPTER 1

A Shot at Teaching

A Field, a Suit, a Gun, and a Teacher

It must have seemed an incongruous sight. A young man in a dark suit and sunglasses walking through a wheat field on a hot June afternoon. My wedding suit – £25 from Burtons: The Tailors – was doubling as my interview outfit for a teaching job. The school was in the countryside, on the edge of a sprawling housing estate for coal miners and workers in the nearby claypits. The bus had brought me there a couple of hours early. As I explored my surroundings, I followed the first footpath sign I saw. It pointed towards a pond.

A man in a waistcoat and a collarless shirt with sleeves rolled above his elbows looked over his shoulder towards me. He was holding a gun, an air rifle. 'Eey up,' he called out, 'what are you doin' 'ere?' 'I've come for an interview,' I explained. 'For a teacher at the primary school.' 'Well,' he said, pointing at a tiny object in the middle of the pond, 'I'm havin' no luck shootin' at that. See if you can do any better.'

I had never held a rifle before, even at a funfair. But I was a young man. My hand was steady, my eyesight was good, and the lack of experience that comes with youth was no obstacle to

The Making of an Educator

anything. I lay down on my stomach, took aim, and hit the target first time. 'Right,' the man exclaimed, suitably impressed, 'you'll do!'

It was a ringing if curious endorsement. It is also the only part of the selection process I remember. The formal interview with the head teacher and the local vicar – it was a church school – passed by in a blur. But they gave me the job. Perhaps I impressed them. Perhaps, as the head would later remark, I had the rare (and, of course, unfair) advantage at the time of being a male graduate applying to a small school in a predominantly female profession. Or, given the late stage at which I had entered the job search season, due to my wife-to-be, Pauline, struggling to find a scarce position teaching Latin before me, maybe there just wasn't much competition left by that point. Whatever the reason, like many young graduates then, I was just relieved to get my first job and to have a wage that would pay our rent and help get us started in life.

Work began in the first week in September. Our summer honeymoon was over very quickly. We headed south with our meagre belongings – a metal trunk and a Biba poster from our student years, and, in the days before bridal showers and pre-approved gift lists, a small collection of wedding presents which included an antique shawl from Pauline's nanna, the money to pay for half of a washing machine from her parents, purple blankets from my mum, a set of towels (also purple) from my grandma, and an ironing board from my Auntie Vida. We carried them into our tiny flat behind a TV repair shop next to a noisy roundabout. Like many other graduates in 1973, within just a few short weeks, we stopped being students, got married, moved somewhere many miles away, and started new jobs and careers. I had followed the advice of Cat Stevens' father to his son. 'Find a girl. Settle down. If you want, you can marry.'[1] At just 22 years old, a steady future doing something we liked in a profession with a regular salary and annual increments seemed set for both of us. What more could we ask for?

Primary Responsibilities

Like most new teachers, I suppose, I was excited yet apprehensive about my first job, first class, first lot of kids. I'd had successful experience working with inner-city children on my prior teaching practice placement, so I felt ready enough to teach these children from mining and other working-class families with a few other children from commuter and farming families sprinkled among them. But as the first week of the school year approaches, many teachers still get anxiety dreams in which classes collapse in chaos and children run around refusing to do as they are told. This is particularly true for teachers who are just starting out. Taking a shot at teaching is a lot harder than firing lead pellets at a lily pad.

Pauline had a harder adjustment to make than me. Jobs teaching Latin in state schools were so scarce that she ended up teaching classical studies – Greek and Roman myths and legends – to children in a multicultural school in a poor part of the nearest city. By the middle of August, we were both frantically putting together lesson plans. I painted a life-size Cyclops for her classroom wall. This set the pattern for the year. We spent six or more days a week marking assignments from the previous week and preparing activities for the next on home-made work-cards or on shiny paper for the toxic-smelling Banda machine. On Sundays, we might read the newspapers in bed, then take a country walk. But by late afternoon, we would be back at the schoolwork again.

It was exhausting yet also uplifting. Barely out of my teens, I was now the man that 20-odd children looked to for five days a week. As did their mothers and fathers, all of them older than me. Many of the children saw more of me than their own parents;

sometimes they called me dad by mistake. It certainly helped prepare me for the day in a few years' time when I would become a father myself.

Contrary to what some teachers argue, teaching isn't the hardest job in the world. Try being a paramedic, or an emergency room nurse, or a business manager struggling to meet the targets on which your job and livelihood depend. But there is an intensity to primary school teaching, in particular, that exists almost nowhere else. It is you and the kids together, all day, mostly within the same four walls, no let up. Some days there is not even time to go the toilet. Teachers have legendary bladders of steel.

Every child's triumph, breakthrough, break-up, success, secret, setback, wisecrack, cut and scrape, cuddle and hug, and push and shove belong to you, and make demands on you. The job is never ending. When you really care for the kids and want to do a proper job, evenings and weekends get consumed by developing new materials and devising new strategies to help them. Talk to any primary school teacher's spouse or partner, and they will tell you that at bedtimes and other times, it is almost impossible to find their off switch.

Pauline and I might have taken our Sunday walks to relax, but when we blew a week's rent on the *AA Book of the British Countryside*, this was partly to try and master knowledge of all the birds and flowers that would help me to teach my kids a bit of nature study. The guitar lessons I took up in the evenings were not to pursue dreams of a musical career (the clue was that I was the only one to come to class without a guitar!). I just wanted to learn a few basic chords so I could lead my children in singalongs in class and in school assemblies.

We did manage to take some time off. We periodically visited Pauline's older sister and her husband – Pam 'n' Trev – and their two young children, an hour's bus ride away, when the four of us shared war stories from teaching in the trenches of British education. One night a week I would pop down to the local pub – one of the tiniest in England – to have a flutter on the fruit machine. The barman put my winning tokens in a jug above the bar to pay for my future drinks. We would nip across the road to chat with the sprightly 90-something mother of the black-and-white film character actor Norman Bird. I also bought a racing cycle to explore the country lanes. I even took an epic ride to avoid TV screens on the day off school we got when Princess Anne married Captain Mark Phillips.

In that first year of teaching and marriage, though, 90% of our lives was still focused on our jobs and the kids. Somehow, in our early 20s, like many young teachers, we managed to cram it all in, in ways that were harder for us, and still are for many others, once children come along and caring for elderly parents eat up energy and time.

Psychic Rewards

Two years on, in 1975, one of the most important books about teaching ever written was published. *Schoolteacher: A Sociological Study* by Dan Lortie, a Chicago sociologist, became the most cited text on teaching by a living author until Lortie's death in 2020 at the age of 94.

After interviewing 94 teachers in the Greater Boston area, Lortie concluded that teaching is rooted in what he called 'psychic rewards'. These psychic rewards, he said, are overwhelmingly individual. Teachers 'concentrate their energies at points where effort may make a difference' rather than in vague discussions about how to make things better.[2]

There are some moments of collective success and recognition, Lortie acknowledged – like in the assemblies where my class took its turn to perform in front of the whole school or at the football matches where the boys' team from our little school triumphed over schools twice or three times the size of ours. But these moments are few and far between, Lortie pointed out. The rest of the time the rewards are individual. Sometimes, these are seen in the children who undergo great transformations, like the struggling reader who advanced three whole years in her reading skills in the year I taught her. Sometimes, they are touching occasions that can bring a tear to your eye, like the child from one of the poorest families on the estate who brought me a pair of socks wrapped in newspaper for Christmas that, she explained, her dad had only worn once. Then there are the surreal moments of comedy and surprise, such as the children I came across desperately trying to push the school piano from the assembly hall into the corridor. This was their way of answering my practical maths question: 'Will the piano fit through the door?'

But the failures are individual too – the seemingly scatter-brained pupil I could never really get to concentrate properly or the quiet and gentle girl who, her parents informed me, was sometimes scared by my stentorian male voice.

The key point is that in a world like this, especially as a beginning teacher, you are alone with almost all your successes *and* all your disappointments too. There is no one to validate you when things are going well or to pick you up after a lesson has gone badly. These downsides are part of what Lortie called a culture of *individualism* where most teaching is undertaken alone, in isolation from other colleagues.

Individualism was amplified by *presentism*, Lortie argued. Teaching can often feel like being locked in a perpetual present tense. There is no time to reflect on the past or to plan for the immediate future beyond the next day or week. You are white-water rafting all the time – on the lookout for a tiff or a scuffle before it turns into a fight, keeping an eye open for the quiet ones who are easily overlooked, checking that your more vulnerable kids have had sufficient sleep or enough to eat, listening to two children read at the same time (who came up with that crazy idea?), becoming frustrated that you have to repeat instructions over and over again, and worrying about the noise levels getting too high and attracting unwanted attention from the teacher next door.

Even so, teaching and working with young people still sustains you. They are your psychic rewards. Every day, the children make you feel that you matter. It is not the kids who drive teachers out of the profession and drag down their well-being. It is the adults and their agendas. Schools with great leadership and supportive cultures bring out the best in teachers. Those with poor leadership, bad systems, and toxic cultures make teachers frustrated and anxious as they get distracted into navigating adult issues at the cost of engaging the kids.

The Disintegrated Day

When September approached, I was ready for my first class. I was up for teaching and for being a teacher, completely on my own for the first time. Then, less than a week before the first day of school, the head teacher took me to one side. He was very excited. He and I would be instituting a new system in the upper primary part of the school, he announced. Mixed-age family grouping. Integrated day curriculum and organisation. Teaching in multiple rooms in an old 1870s-era building.

I would have multiple age groups in my class – all the 9–10-year-olds and the lower achieving 10–11-year-olds. That was challenging enough for a first-year teacher with scarcely three days to prepare. This kind of family grouping strategy was also based on the erroneous and now discredited assumption that struggling older learners should be held back to learn alongside and in the same ways as their younger peers rather than everyone moving at their own pace.

The Making of an Educator

The integrated day was an idea that grew out of and followed on from one of the most influential UK education reports ever written – the inspirational and controversial Plowden Report of 1967, titled *Children and Their Primary Schools*. The report became the world-wide, go-to global authority on open classrooms and child-centred progressive education. It revolutionised the look and feel of many primary school classrooms across the UK. In my first ever peer-reviewed article, on the paradoxes and dilemmas of progressive education that I would publish three years later, and that I will return to in Chapter 2, I quoted one of the most celebrated passages from the report:

> The school sets out deliberately to devise the right environment for children, to allow them to be themselves and to develop in the way and at the pace appropriate to them. … It lays special stress on individual discovery, on first hand experience and on opportunities for creative work.[3]

The idea of the integrated day was a spin-off from this report and its overall philosophy. It was first advanced by two school leaders, Mary Brown and Norman Precious, in their book *The Integrated Day in the Primary School*.[4] The integrated day combined children working individually in small groups and sometimes as a whole class – when teachers were reading a story, introducing a topic, or holding a whole-school assembly, for example. The integrated day involved elements of choice but not unlimited choice. Children could choose what to study from topics, themes, or activities provided by the teacher. They could decide at what points in the day or week they undertook or switched between different activities, and they had to organise and monitor how work would be completed by deadlines set by their teacher. Curriculum timetabling for the whole class was skeletal, with many open-ended timeslots during which children organised and pursued their own learning.

A Shot at Teaching

One more feature of this approach to learning is that it often occurs in many places. It is not confined to one classroom. It can happen in a classroom, in the corridor, in the gymnasium, outdoors in the yard, almost anywhere at all, and sometimes all at once. New schools were built with fewer walls than traditional ones. Older schools had barriers taken down. One former colleague boasted that when he had started as a new principal, he unscrewed and removed all the classroom doors over the summer, much to the surprise and consternation of the returning school staff.

Even in the best circumstances, the integrated day demands a lot of teachers and children alike in terms of self-regulation, energy, and expertise. At just three days' notice, however, the whole idea of a newly introduced integrated day using flexible space and family groupings seemed utterly insane – especially to a beginning teacher like me. There was no written curriculum, save for two badly typed pages that passed for 'schemes of work' in maths and literacy. I was completely on my own with this.

On the very first day of school, I lined up my pupils outside against the school wall, with materials in their wooden trays, ready to head indoors. It was a dramatic moment. I had no clue what I was supposed to be doing, but I somehow bluffed my way into getting them to think I did.

I should have been pleased. This new departure that the head teacher was intent on pursuing was aligned with many of my social and educational beliefs. In the final year of my sociology degree, I had read and been inspired by the Brazilian educator Paulo Freire's 1968 book, *Pedagogy of the Oppressed*.[5] Freire decried what he called 'banking education' that treated learners as vaults in which deposits were made. He argued instead for teaching literacy to poor and marginalised adults by connecting texts to the realities of their lives.

Among a shelf of books that I had collected on the need to disestablish schools as we knew them, I had read the thoughts of

The Making of an Educator

Ivan Illich in *Deschooling Society*.[6] I was also fascinated by first-hand accounts of legendary private progressive schools like A. S. Neill's Summerhill[7] and Michael Young's Dartington Hall.[8] These described how pupils directed their own learning, made decisions about school rules and policies together, and embraced cultures of informality that included calling teachers by their first names.

Yet, despite all my theoretical sympathies, on my main teaching practice experience in an inner-city school, I had already learned that if supporting children's choices and interests was not pursued within carefully defined structures, and in a language of clear and precise direction rather than through polite requests or desperate pleas, chaos would rapidly ensue. As I began writing this book, a middle-years teacher in a school adopting play-based learning that I was working with put it well when she worried aloud that she didn't want to be on a bus the kids were driving with no idea of where it would be going!

A few years into our marriage, when our children started attending a famous progressive primary school in Oxfordshire – one that attracted visitors from all over the world – Pauline and I discovered that at the age of 5, our daughter, Lucy, was hiding in the toilet stalls, worrying about what she should choose next. It was as if she had read Barry Schwartz's book on the paradox of choice, in which he argues that excessive choice inflicts a kind of tyranny on people who stress about all the other choices they could have made that might have been better.[9] If, like me, you have ever waded your way through a never-ending restaurant menu and then experienced regret that you didn't make the same choice as your dining partner, or if you have gone shopping for a new pair of jeans and found yourself staring indecisively at vast selections of different shades, cuts, lengths, and waist heights, you will understand how she might have felt. People really can be spoilt for choice.

Within a matter of days, I realised that the integrated day would quickly turn into the disintegrated day unless I imposed some sort of order upon it. So, I established clear times when the whole class would work together as a unit – when I read storybooks aloud at the end of the school day or when I introduced silent poetry writing after energetic physical education classes outdoors, for example. But my main strategy was a home-made monitoring and tracking tool. It consisted of a large chart or grid with the children's names down the side and the activities or assignments they had to complete listed at the top. Every week, I pinned a fresh piece of tracing paper over the chart and the children ticked off when their work was completed. Some activities, like maths, had to be done every day. Others, like project work, were checked off less often. I issued periodic reminders about the deadlines that were looming, glanced at the chart whenever I walked past it to see if anyone was falling behind, and did spot checks to make sure the children's checkmarks were honest and accurate.

The system was effective, but I also felt uneasy and sometimes conflicted about it. First, it was all supposed to be about what we now call student choice and voice. But I seemed to be spending inordinate amounts of time zipping backwards and forwards between different rooms and spaces, making sure that the kids were up to date with their work assignments and meeting their deadlines. Tellingly, when the children were given an assignment based on Edward Blishen's book, *The School That I'd Like*,[10] about how children imagined school might be, one boy wrote, 'In the school that I'd like, all the teachers would be old.' I was intrigued. 'Why is that?' I asked him. 'Because they wouldn't be able to keep coming round checking up on us like you do,' he replied.

Second, after I had talked with several parents, I also learned that some children were only meeting their deadlines by completing lots of their work at home to make up for lost time after they had been socialising with friends in their groups in school.

Last, even the original idea of the integrated day is not all about free and open choice. There was little choice and not much voice.

The Making of an Educator

Many of the projects and activities were chosen by me, not my pupils. These included practical maths puzzle cards, science activities urging children to explore how things like zips and ballpoint pens worked, an overly ambitious project that involved mapping and looking at the history of the local community, producing colourful collages to illustrate a contemporary folk song, and carrying out an investigation into various aspects of transportation. This investigation comprised assorted work-cards featuring pictures of steam locomotives cut out from my old railway magazines and a vast classroom mural complete with a cable car mounted on a wire and operated with the assistance of a cotton bobbin.

In hindsight, while some of these project activities were potentially interesting and relevant for all the children, others were clearly not. Transportation, for example, was an interest of mine, and of some of the children too, such as the farmer's son who loved agricultural machinery. But was it really the most suitable topic for the girls as well as the boys, I should have asked myself. And what was I thinking when, for religious education, a subject in which I had little knowledge and for which I had even less aptitude, I chose an in-the-news topic for the children to study of Padre Pio, an Italian priest who claimed to have manifested the crucifix signs of the stigmata on his hands and elsewhere? Their little drawings of this kindly priest in which lines of red wax crayon depicted blood dripping from his hands might have traumatised them for years!

The Music and the Words

One of the most frequently mentioned reasons why educational innovations fail is that teachers don't really want to implement them. The innovation is someone else's passion, not theirs, and so they resist it. They just go through the motions. If the head teacher or inspector walks in, they will teach the way they are supposed to

A Shot at Teaching

for a few minutes, then shut the door and revert to the old ways when the visitors have gone. Children might be seated *in* groups, for example, but they don't work together *as* groups. They just carry on working alone, side by side.

University of Toronto Professor Steve Anderson has a different explanation. Educational change often fails not because of insufficient implementation, he says, but because the new practices are poorly understood.[11] Enthusiastic adoption does not always lead to effective implementation.

For instance, around 2010, when I was studying approaches to inclusion in 10 school districts in Ontario, Canada, which involved differentiating instruction for diverse learners, the schools created flippable menus of strategies that were now, literally, at the teachers' fingertips. But when one school came up with its own alphabetically organised list of 26 strategies, teachers tended to turn to them for variation or novelty rather than to make more precise decisions about how best to match specific strategies to different students' needs. This could stave off boredom and inject more fun into the teaching and learning, but it didn't necessarily lead to greater depth of understanding.

It wasn't just the hasty introduction of an integrated day that suggested my head teacher might not fully grasp what he was doing. There were many other indicators of his misunderstandings of teaching, learning, and curriculum content.

One concerned a new approach to mathematics that was based on understanding mathematical principles as a foundation for arithmetical procedures like addition and multiplication. In the 1960s, not far from where I was teaching, a Hungarian-born professor had been pioneering part of this new approach to mathematics that embraced play, discovery, and manipulation of materials. Zoltan Dienes helped transform approaches to young children's acquisition of mathematical concepts. His greatest and most tangible legacy was his invention of wooden blocks that taught children the nature

The Making of an Educator

and arbitrariness of base 10 as a counting system, along with the meaning of place value.[12]

I employed the eponymously named Dienes apparatus, which had similarities with the more widely adopted Cuisenaire rods of today, in my mixed-age classroom. In base 10, the apparatus began with little wooden cubes or units. Ten of these would make a 'long' or 'ten'. Once you added one more unit to your nine, you had to exchange these ten units for a long. Placed side by side, ten longs then eventually made a 'flat' or a hundred. Ten hundreds stacked on top of each other made a 'block' or a thousand.

Base 10, the one that is used in modern society, it is believed, comes from counting systems that use our fingers and thumbs. There is a reason why we work in tens, hundreds, thousands, and millions, and it is historically and biologically arbitrary. But suppose, by a quirk of nature, most of us had been born with eight digits, not ten. In this case, we would get as far as seven and be able to go no further. So, whereas in base 10, nine would be the highest digit you could have, in base 8, it would be seven. In the case of base 8, then, after seven, eight would now be the new long, or ten, as you wouldn't have enough fingers and thumbs for more. In base 8, nine would now be eleven, ten would be twelve, and so on.

The point of Dienes apparatus was to introduce the children to these other bases before they got to base 10 and thereby take away the mystery of working in tens, hundreds, and thousands. An obituary on Zoltan Dienes when he passed away in Canada in 2020, just short of 100 years old, reported him as saying, 'How could a child learn what the base 10 is if he is not familiar with other number systems?'[13] Playing around with base 6, say, and realising the highest number of anything you could have would be five before exchanging it for a long, flat, or block conveyed a deep understanding of the place value that is otherwise so hard for many children to grasp. Tackling addition problems using work-cards in different bases is how I introduced my own class to the principle of place value.

A Shot at Teaching

My head teacher saw it all a bit differently. One Wednesday morning a month, he used to drive off to the local city on the dubious pretext of collecting crisps (chips, in the United States) for the school. Incredulously, this left me, a first-year teacher, with my own class of children plus his own class of 10–11-year-olds. This amounted to 58 mixed-age children for the entire morning.

On one of these days, he left his class with some multiplication problems in different bases. The children were stuck, so they came to me. The biggest unit in Dienes apparatus was a large block. There was nothing greater. But the head teacher had set problems that led to answers involving say seven, eight, or nine blocks, even though the base was 5 or 6.

The pupils realised that mathematically, and practically, they couldn't have seven or eight blocks in base 5 or 6, just as you couldn't have twelve or thirteen blocks in base 10 without going up another level to a unit of tens of thousands. What should they do, they asked. It was a teachable moment. We discussed it together and concluded they needed to invent another unit, draw it, and give it a name, like a giant block, giant long, or snake. Indeed, what they drew would provide an insight into their mathematical reasoning.

It made perfect sense, but not to the head teacher. Next morning, before school started, he stormed into my classroom and hurled a pile of exercise books onto a desk. They spilled all over the floor in disarray, like discarded tablets.

'Mr Hargreaves,' he raged, 'I would appreciate it if you would *not* interfere with my children's work! I have had to mark all of it *wrong!*'

I was a first-year teacher. It wasn't just his children who were sometimes operating in a culture of fear. I had joined them. I knew I had to stay calm. I asked him what the problem was. He described what the children had done – drawing and naming new units, so that no answer had a figure that exceeded the base in which the problem was posed. It was nonsense, he insisted.

The Making of an Educator

'But their answers are mathematically correct,' I pointed out.

'No, they're not,' he retorted.

'Yes, they are,' I replied.

This was beginning to feel like Monty Python's 'Is this the right room for an argument?' sketch.

I slowly walked over to the blackboard and carefully, but a bit condescendingly, set out in my slightly too-clever-by-half tone of voice why their answers were indeed correct. He looked at my working out, turning beetroot red as I explained the reasoning. After a brief silence, he then conjured up a justification for having large numbers of blocks beyond the permitted base. It was beyond ridiculous.

'Look,' he fumed, 'just because it says base 10 on the card, doesn't mean it *all* has to be in base 10! You have pounds, shillings, and pence. They're all in different bases. Why can't these be too?'

I was at a loss what to say next. Had he not even noticed that UK currency had converted to decimalisation two years previously? At this moment, for the first time, I seriously started to think about leaving the school. But the point for now is that his own understanding of the new mathematics that he was introducing was plain wrong.

This was not the only instance of poor judgement. Consider his choice of music for whole-school assemblies. After I had led my own class, at the time of the school fair, in a guitar-accompanied performance of Simon and Garfunkel's 'Scarborough Fair', which had apparently impressed him, he began his own assembly a few days later by playing another Simon and Garfunkel song that he wanted to share with everyone because of its 'catchy beat', as he put it. The lyrics to this song are far from innocent, though, and it quickly became obvious he had not really listened to them beforehand.

'Cecilia' describes how the singer was 'making love in the afternoon with Cecilia up in my bedroom' and how, after getting up to wash his face (we didn't ask why!), when he came back to bed, someone had taken his place!'[14] As the head teacher's posterior

A Shot at Teaching

wobbled back and forth in time to the music, these racy lyrics put smirks on the faces of the oldest children, drained the blood from the cheeks of the local vicar, and provoked painfully stifled belly-laughs among all the teachers standing round the side.

It wasn't just in this assembly where the head teacher heard the music but didn't really get the words. It applied to many other aspects of his and others' approach to the integrated day that were being adopted at the time. My excuse was that I was a first-year teacher. Like a pedagogical autistic savant, I handled some things like storytelling, creative writing, 'boys' games', and art with flair, imagination, and relentless dedication. Yet in other areas, without any kind of guidance, I was clearly floundering – in religious education, in my over-ambitious community project, and, most obviously and literally, when, as a 100% non-swimmer, I was placed in charge of swimming lessons!

My head teacher had less excuse than me to introduce innovations he did not yet fully understand. But although his transgressions and indiscretions were side-splittingly funny in some cases and disgracefully unprofessional in others, the example he represented of poorly understood innovation was and is far from being an isolated one.

In 1976, a young professor from Lancaster University, Neville Bennett, published the results of an extensive research study that raised many questions and advanced serious criticisms about progressive or open education. His book, *Teaching Styles and Pupil Progress*, attracted controversy and received widespread attention in the national press.[15] As he drew together his research conclusions, Bennett quoted from a book on the integrated day. The integrated day, its author argued, 'can be outstandingly successful; and it can be dismally bad … when it does not work, the results can be almost totally unprofitable for the children, and demoralising and exhausting for the teacher.'[16]

The integrated day, open classrooms, and progressive education seemed to be able to succeed spectacularly in a few cases, Bennett and others concluded, but most often, they fell short. I had encountered my own successes and failures. I was living the conflicts and tensions of the integrated day every day. In just a few months, I would start analysing and engaging with these paradoxes of progressive education that I was feeling in my bones in a very different way as a researcher in a university.

The First and Last Time

About three years before I retired from full-time work and teaching in a university, a colleague offered a profound insight. 'The classes you will always most remember,' he said, 'are your first classes and your last classes.'

This really made me think. How did I want my last classes to be? Did I want to succumb to the temptation of repeating what I had already planned for the previous year and not expend any more energy on creating anything new? I had always got good evaluations. Should I just cruise into retirement? I wouldn't be the first! No, I thought. I want my last classes to be truly memorable. I am going to teach out of my skin. I decided to experiment with digital technologies in my in-person classes. It wasn't always successful, but my students, especially my younger students, loved it, and two years before I retired, they successfully nominated me for the university's Excellence in Teaching with Technology Award. My colleague proved to be right. I can vividly remember every detail of my teaching and my students in those last years.

When I look back on my brief school teaching career, my colleague's insight has also given me pause for thought. Many people remark on how much I remember from my time in teaching. There is a reason for that. My first class was also my last class. It was alpha and omega, all at once.

A Shot at Teaching

But why did I leave teaching so soon, after just one year? I truly loved my work with children in the classroom and often felt successful at it. My initial plan had been to teach for at least three years and then move into teacher education, to train and inspire new teachers. But, as you have probably already gathered, the head teacher at our tiny school of barely more than 100 children was emotionally volatile, to say the least. One minute, he would be fulsome in his praise for my dramatic storytelling style, for my success with the boys' football team, for the art class that had given the school inspector cause to hand me great compliments, or, more dubiously, for simply being another man in such a little school. He even offered me a promotion and a pay rise to stay on for another year.

But he also picked fights about issues that, Dienes apparatus notwithstanding, had nothing to do with my actual teaching. These dramas and disputes were not just restricted to me. The deputy head, an inspiring and super-efficient silver-haired leader of the infants department, was regularly at loggerheads with him, for example. She reported countless examples of his eccentricities and unreasonable conduct, including the time he instructed her to tone down her classroom displays and performances because they were showing him up by comparison.

Touchline gossip at football fixtures with other schools also drew scathing comments from other head teachers. These included the time when, at an athletics event involving local schools, the heads had looked behind them to see my own head painstakingly undoing all the knots on the rope they were using to measure out the track. When I asked one of the heads how they coped when my own head had been the deputy at his school, he answered by saying, 'Well, we sent him off to you, didn't we?' He had calculated that by writing a good reference to get him a job as the head of another small school, he would do less damage than continuing to be deputy head at his own bigger one!

The Making of an Educator

Things came to a head, as it were, for me during a six-week argument about cutlery. My head did not approve of how I was eating my dessert, or pudding as we then called it, during school lunches or dinners. I should be using a fork, not a spoon, he insisted. I was setting a bad example to the children. It began as a small request but quickly escalated into a heated and protracted dispute. They were working-class children, I pointed out, who almost certainly did not use forks for dessert at home. Making them eat pudding with a fork was a social class insult. It also cast aspersions on my own working-class upbringing. When there were no signs of getting beyond this impasse, I began to throw in bits of satire. Did he want me and the children to eat *all* puddings with a fork, I ventured – even rice pudding and semolina?

In the middle of one of these arguments, he paced back and forth in his office, ranting about how I was a constant thorn in his side. I took this as a compliment. But when he threatened to report me to the local authority for refusing to comply with his dessert-eating policy, matters took a more serious turn. I decided to head him off. On the deputy head's advice, I reported him to the regional branch of the teachers' union. They were extremely helpful, and I have been a strong supporter of teachers' unions ever since.

The union representative interviewed me, the head, and the deputy. I recall listing the bizarre issues that had brought us into conflict and apologising for how ridiculous, trivial, and hard-to-believe they must have sounded. Only the Dienes apparatus incident had any connection to my teaching, I pointed out. Yet, cumulatively, what we would now call harassment or workplace bullying was having a profound impact on my health. I knew I could win many of my battles with the head, and I refused to allow his intimidation to subdue me. But every day, I came into school 'on pins' that he would provoke yet another argument. By a few weeks into the second term, I had developed a painful stomach ulcer.

A Shot at Teaching

The union representative was very supportive and, at the end of his visit, informed me that he had issued the head with a stern warning. This was just desserts, you might say. I was offered a transfer to another school, but I refused it on the grounds that this would imply the problem was with me, not the head. I loved the actual teaching. The children liked me and worked hard for me. As a first-year teacher, I had my blind spots to be sure, but I was also having a lot of success. I worked relentlessly hard, as a kind letter from the school governors acknowledged on my departure. The inspector gave me a positive report. The deputy head also offered me reassuring feedback. And the parents approved of me too. Part of the reason may have been that when all the school teams in the B league of little schools we were in refused to play us any more because we were winning too heavily, we then got promoted, mid-season, to the A league of larger schools, where we reached the cup final.

So, I made two decisions. First, I would stick things out until the end of the school year. Fortunately, after the union's intervention, the head did indeed back off and the stress eased up. At the same time, I started to pursue the idea of a research degree, ahead of my original schedule, with the intent of returning to teaching after that. This would give me the opportunity to investigate more deeply the 'open classroom' regime and whole progressive movement that I had, in my own way, become part of.

CHAPTER 2
The Paradox of Pupil Autonomy

Open Season on Open Classrooms

I had left my teaching job with unanswered questions about efforts, including my own, to give children a voice and some choice in their own learning and to grant them autonomy in what they learned and how they learned it without havoc ensuing. I remained inspired by my teacher at the end of primary school, Mary Hindle, who, as I describe in my memoir of my early life, *Moving*,[1] was magnificent in her ability to be organised and authoritative, yet also inclusive and innovative in the ways she embraced group work, projects, nature study, and creative dance. Why couldn't there be more teachers like her?

By the early 1970s, though, after a long honeymoon in the previous decade when visitors from over the world came to visit the purported miracle of English primary schools, progressive education in general had started to come in for a bit of a hammering. It was open season on open classrooms.

Failed Implementation
In the United States, case studies surfaced showing that most innovations didn't get implemented properly.[2] Success depended on the

degrees of understanding and commitment of individual teachers whose approaches and responses varied a lot within a largely unregulated profession.

Flawed Implementation

Neville Bennett's highly publicised book, *Teaching Styles and Pupil Progress*, indicated that only a few truly exceptional teachers seemed able to pull off open education methods and get results too.[3] For every Mary Hindle who understood the deep principles of curriculum integration and group learning that engaged the whole child and their interests, many later converts implemented the principles superficially or badly. Like my head teacher, they heard the music but didn't get the words.

Years later, my colleague and research partner, Dean Fink, conducted his own analysis of how an innovative Canadian secondary school slowly lost its edge over time. The hand-picked teachers who founded the school grasped the progressive message in depth, but succeeding generations only noticed the surface features of the school's approach and thought it was mainly about students calling teachers by their first names and doing pretty much what they liked. Fink recalled confronting one youth wandering on the school corridor and asking him what he was doing. 'We're doing a walkabout,' he said. 'What's that?' Fink asked. 'Oh, you know,' said the student, 'Walkabout, talk about, f*** about!'[4]

Left-Wing Indoctrination

In the 1970s, a notorious collection of critiques of progressive education was published under the title of the 'Black Papers'. The critics argued that progressive education was undermining the moral fibre of the nation and producing under-educated future generations, ill-equipped for economic competitiveness. 'If the non-competitive ethos of progressive education is allowed to dominate our schools,' the editors of the fourth paper claimed, 'we shall produce a generation unable to maintain our standards of living when opposed by fierce rivalry by overseas competitors.'[5]

Whenever child-centred education moves from the periphery to the mainstream and becomes part of policy, in English-speaking countries at least, there is always a backlash that complains about fuzzy maths, mishmashes of subjects, manipulation in social and emotional learning, neglect of the 'basics', and, most recently, blurring of gender identities in literary texts and pronoun usage – all examples of deviating from the basics. The British sociologist and curriculum specialist Basil Bernstein offered one explanation for this reaction – boundaries. 'Any attempt to weaken or change' boundaries between subjects or between teachers and children, he argued, threatens people's identities and the privileged gateways to success that traditional knowledge and examinations provide.[6]

Weakening or changing boundaries threatens many areas of privilege – in the mixed-race relationships that challenged the black-and-white order of slavery and that threaten to corrupt royal bloodlines even today; in non-binary gender identities that question conventional conceptions of what is male and female; and in upward mobility from the working class that prompts elites to try and put striving interlopers back in their place. Likewise, the dissolution of conventional boundaries in the curriculum or in teaching, Bernstein asserted, threatens 'the distribution of power and the principles of social control' in schools *and* societies.[7] Backlashes against progressivism are, from this standpoint, also rearguard reactions in defence of privilege.

Fascist Brainwashing

The opposite of the argument that progressive education is moving children's minds towards the Left is that child-centredness, and letting the self and its ideas unfold, is a form of emotional manipulation that grooms young people for totalitarianism. After looking

The Making of an Educator

at the United States' Dalton Plan in the 1920s, which involved children moving between projects and learning centres within a 'block' timetable, Italy's education minister under Mussolini, for example, boasted that from Italy's progressive schools would issue the nation's fascist citizens of the future![8] The Marxist Antonio Gramsci, who was imprisoned by Mussolini, wrote in one of his legendary letters from his *Prison Notebooks* that educating children's emotions at a critical time of their young development would not let them emerge as human beings, but would stunt their critical powers and rational thought processes and make them easy meat for autocrats. Anticipating many later criticisms of block timetabling, or the integrated day, as it was later called, he advanced concerns that constant choosing (or dithering about choosing) would detract from more rigorous study:

> The pupils are free to attend whichever lessons ... they please, provided that by the end of each month they have completed the programme set for them; discipline is entrusted to the pupils themselves. The system has a serious defect: the pupils generally postpone doing their work until the last days of the month, and this detracts from the seriousness of the education and represents a major difficulty for the teachers who are supposed to help them but are overwhelmed with work.[9]

Here, elements of both Right and Left seem to be in some agreement: that excessive emphasis on personal and emotional development will inhibit serious study that, from the conservative standpoint, prevents the elite getting and staying ahead, and that, in the Left's perspective, undermines the critical thinking necessary for democracy. Indeed, in 2013, former UK Conservative Minister of Education Michael Gove mischievously channelled his newly acquired inner Gramsci to justify a move back to structured disciplines and basics.[10]

The Paradox of Pupil Autonomy

Capitalist Control

In 1975, after doing fieldwork in three infants' schools, two young University of London academics, Rachel Sharp and Anthony Green, developed an interesting if somewhat contorted analysis of child-centred education in their book, *Education and Social Control*. 'The rise of progressivism and the institutional supports it receives', they claimed, 'are a function of its greater effectiveness for social control and [for] structuring [children's] aspirations.'[11] Right at the outset of their school lives, apparently, little infants, according to Sharp and Green, were already being prepared by misguided progressive educators to take up their places in the social class system of capitalist society. Among people in my discipline, the book garnered great attention.

Sharp and Green produced one of the most detailed descriptions of school life that had been seen up to that point, at least in the UK. Their observations of children in classrooms, as well as their interviews with the head teacher, three teachers, and a group of parents, produced a rich seam of data. They depicted educators who passionately believed in and were even a bit beguiled by the progressive education movement and its elements of child-centredness, choice, and discovery at key moments of readiness within an overall curriculum of the integrated day.

As in many other cases, including among proponents of child-centred methods and within my own teaching experience too, Sharp and Green noted that teachers find themselves struggling to know when children are 'ready' to move on, and to reconcile when to intervene and when to let the children's explorations flow. As the head teacher himself remarked, the best teachers know how to figure this out somehow. 'The integrated day serves to make children reasonably independent and self-reliant,' he said. 'The strongest principle of growth is freedom of choice ... every time you choose you grow up a little bit [...] if there is a need to divert the child from something then the best teachers do it.'[12]

The Making of an Educator

The head teacher also worried that many working-class children 'who are not wonderfully stable ... find this kind of thing rather difficult because many of them are crying out for more direction'.[13] Yet teachers tended to spend more of their time in this fluid atmosphere supporting and stimulating more motivated middle-class children with whom they had more immediate rapport rather than with children who were 'dull' or 'peculiar'. These other children were instead engaged in 'busyness' – tasks and activities that kept them occupied but didn't really advance their learning. The 'bright' children from more advantaged backgrounds could somehow negotiate their way through this web of implicit cues and the approach of 'leading from behind' because they 'know what the teacher wants' and they rewarded the teacher with interactions that were intense and affirming.[14]

The problem with Sharp and Green's take on their data was that they stretched their argument beyond any evidence or plausible bounds of belief to argue that these patterns were the results of power relationships in a stratified social class society of which teachers were unwitting bearers. The researchers had no evidence on or insight into the policies in local or national government that reflected these structural inequalities. They merely took a leap of faith, or despair, into asserting it was these forces that explained teachers' beliefs and actions. Teachers, they said, are confused, inadequate, and contradictory in their efforts to explain terms like 'readiness' and 'needs'. In Karl Marx's terms, they would be victims of false consciousness about the inequalities they were perpetuating. Teachers responded to structural constraints with individualistic psychobabble, the authors seemed to be saying.

David Hargreaves, who had cut his own research teeth on the impact of streaming in secondary schools, launched into a vitriolic critique of Sharp and Green's book. Their efforts to turn their case study into a neo-Marxist exposé of how dumb teachers were oppressing working-class kids through fake and flawed uses of child-centredness, were, he wrote, 'arrant nonsense'.[15] If the teachers seemed confused, he argued, it was because the researchers' highly abstract questions lured them into an academic trap in which practically any answer would be found wanting.

To sum up, Sharp and Green's critique of progressive education for perpetuating social class power relations, of which infants' teachers were the bearers, was not only an outrageous leap from three classrooms into the intellectual and ideological stratosphere. It was also an insult to the teachers themselves and to their dignity as professionals and human beings. They were falsely accused of doing bad things because they didn't have the wits to know any better. They were pulling the progressive wool over their own eyes.

Inescapable Dilemmas or Paradoxes

Sometimes, if you don't know when to leave people alone or when to intervene, it isn't a plot or a conspiracy. It is just a tension or a paradox. It happens in many areas of life. In a football or ice-hockey game, when should you defend deeply and when should you go on the attack? In leadership, when should you express your opinion and when should you hold back so that others can express theirs? How can you trust people and leave them alone, yet also check up on them to make sure nothing is being neglected?[16]

Teaching is no different. Only in the most autocratic environments is there little ambiguity and one approved way to teach – the three-part lesson or the scripted approach to literacy, for example. But even here there are still tensions, like whether to reward the enthusiastic pupil who keeps raising their hand versus calling on all the others who also want to participate.

All professions require judgement that goes beyond compliance and rule-following. The more complicated teaching gets, like it is in open classrooms, the more paradoxes and tensions there are to make judgements about. In the mid-1970s, two US academics, Ann and Harold Berlak, studied three British primary schools to try to figure out what was going on in 'open' education.[17] They came up with a framework of dilemmas to explain the kinds of actions and choices they witnessed among the teachers they observed. The apparent inconsistencies that were labelled by Sharp and Green as confusion or contradictions were, according to the Berlaks, more a result of teachers feeling drawn towards the opposite poles of common dilemmas and trying to find ways to resolve them. Four of these dilemmas of open primary education were:

- Treating children uniquely *as children* or interacting with them seriously *as young adults*.
- Cultivating *intrinsic motivation* by providing an environment where children can follow their interests, or using *extrinsic motivation* like treats, praise, and threats when the intrinsic impulse was not enough.
- Getting the *holistic* or big picture understanding of an idea compared to accumulating *incremental* knowledge, one small piece at a time.
- Learning what is *personally interesting* up against needing to learn what is *publicly important* in terms of facts, skills, and disciplines.[18]

In the Berlaks' view, the apparent contradictions of open primary education do not come down to failed or flawed implementation. Nor are they conspiracies of the Left or the Right. They are simply practical instances of how educators can work with young people who deserve to be treated with dignity and empathy as autonomous human beings on the one hand, yet whose (literally) immature minds call for adult guidance and intervention to protect them against harmful or frivolous choices and to prepare them with the knowledge and skills they will need for a future they cannot yet grasp on the other.

The Paradox of Pupil Autonomy

Technically, their use of the term 'dilemma' – which means a choice between two undesirable alternatives – is not quite accurate. They might have better referred to tensions that call for efforts at balance, or even paradoxes, where two seemingly contradictory positions are both true and call for creative solutions that combine them. But the important implication of their work remains: that contradictions need not be the result of failures or power plays but can be inherent to the nature of practices, such as progressive teaching, that are under consideration.

Progressivism and Pupil Autonomy

My own enquiry into the paradoxes of progressive education began theoretically in 1976. We had moved north in 1974, so I could start a graduate degree in sociology at Leeds University. I commenced fieldwork in schools – I say a lot more about this later – and began to reflect on what I was learning and what it meant for the field of educational research in which I was working.

My first effort at a publication was a critique of one of the most prominent figures in British educational studies at the time. University of London Professor Basil Bernstein, who made an appearance earlier in this chapter, was famous, and even notorious, for his research in linguistics, which argued that the language in middle-class families was more 'elaborated' than in working-class families in which 'restricted' codes of communication limited children's cognitive development.[19] In the United States, William Labov, one of the founders of the discipline of sociolinguistics, who passed away in 2024 at the age of 97, launched a scathing attack on what he took to be Bernstein's deficit theory of lower-class language, saying that Black nonstandard English (and, by implication, working-class English) wasn't grammatically inferior at all; it was just a different style.[20]

The Making of an Educator

In the UK, Bernstein went on to develop theories of curriculum and pedagogy which received broader and more lasting acclaim than his research on language. In a key paper on visible and invisible pedagogies, he described open classrooms, or invisible pedagogies, as places that used 'implicit control' of children's learning, where the child '*apparently* has wide powers' and '*apparently* regulates his own movements'.[21] This classroom regime, he went on, favoured children from families in the 'new middle class', which worked in symbolic professions like teaching or advertising and communicated with its children indirectly in ways that relied on *personal authority* ('Would you?' 'Could you?'). This contrasted sharply with children in working-class families whose parents relied on the *positional authority* of adult–child power differences to direct their children explicitly and demand their compliance ('Do as you're told', 'Because I say so') with their instructions.

My paper was original and clever, but also, in hindsight, incredibly convoluted in its exposure of a contradiction between Bernstein's theories of language and his theories of pedagogy. In the end, though, our eventual positions were not all that different. Within invisible pedagogies, I argued, middle-class children could weave their way through the labyrinth of apparent choices and indirect requests to figure out what it was they were expected to do and to get their work completed effectively. Working-class children, by contrast, took the requests and suggestions at face value and became lost as a result. This is how I expressed my point in one of my less constipated sentences:

> Though control is present and still depends upon status position, and though it ultimately reflects the asymmetry of the teacher–pupil relationship, difficulties are nevertheless created by the fact that it is implicit, that rules are not obvious and require discovery yet are not discovered easily, and that some children originate from a family background where such control forms are not in use.[22]

The Paradox of Pupil Autonomy

In years to come, writers across the ideological spectrum would argue that minoritised students in Black or working-class communities achieve better when discipline is firm, and communication is direct and explicit. Whole chains of schools, like the Knowledge is Power Program (KIPP) and Uncommon Schools networks in the United States and beyond have built their philosophy on more direct forms of instruction and expectation. The point that I and others were making in the mid-1970s was that progressive approaches and open classrooms were giving pupils only a sense of autonomy rather than actual autonomy. This caution needs to stay on the radar in modern pushes for student voice and choice and for more project-based and self-determined learning in the curriculum.

My paper on 'Progressivism and Pupil Autonomy' was my first publication. It followed on from an invitation, in the middle of 1976, to contribute to a seminar on classroom decision-making at Keele University, run by Professor John Eggleston. I was the youngest person there, just 25 years old, and the only graduate student. Everyone else turned up with a few notes on the back of a postcard. By comparison, as a working-class striver, I overachieved and came with my own pile of 25 copies of the only paper that had been written in full. I felt like I had shown up to a barbecue in a tuxedo!

My presentation began well. The argument was new. People listened intently. They were clearly impressed. 'Who was this new person on the scene?' their faces seemed to be saying. But at around 45 minutes, the paper was showing no signs of coming to an end. I was barely halfway through. People started looking at their watches. As I hit the hour mark, other members of the seminar began shuffling their chairs and scraping them across the floor. I was flustered and embarrassed but didn't know what to do. There was still such a lot to say. So, I just kept on reading every word, only faster. What was already an intellectually dense paper must, at this pace, have now seemed utterly impenetrable. Eggleston himself yawned aloud. Mercifully, at around 1 hour 20

The Making of an Educator

minutes, I finally stopped. It was awful. I just wanted the earth to swallow me up.

At the end of the meeting, I was offered a ride home by David Hargreaves, one of the more senior scholars in the room and already an intellectual giant along with Bernstein. I had been warned about his driving, which had not improved even by the time I was writing this book. In his mid-80s, he drove me from his home to the train station, which included multiple circuits of the same roundabout before he found the right exit. On our way back from Keele, as this other Hargreaves crunched through the gears and wrestled with his clutch control, I unburdened myself about what I felt had been a dreadful academic debut.

'No, it wasn't awful,' he responded. 'It *was* a bit long,' he conceded, with disarming understatement. 'But it's a very good paper.' He went on to invite me to submit it to one of the world's top three sociology journals, which was encouraging contributions from new scholars and where he was a member of the editorial board. This was gold standard mentoring. And so, by 1977, my argument about progressivism and pupil autonomy, which was also my first ever publication, saw the light of day in one of the leading journals in social science. As Steve Munby would say many years later when he was director of England's National College for School Leadership, it is OK to get off to a bad start!

Who was the most impressed? My grandmother, Grandma Kenyon. She was a huge figure in my life. A working-class woman, brimming with kindness towards me and others, she was an immense support in my early teens when my mum, who had just been widowed at 43, had a physical and mental breakdown. This suddenly left me with a lot of emotional and household responsibilities that had a substantial impact on my schooling, including extensive absenteeism. My grandma stepped in and stepped up a lot during this time, so I didn't have to struggle with it all alone. When I showed her the offprint of my article, she picked it up, and with the one eye that could still see, through a telescopic lens that was attached to her spectacles, she read every single word of my tortuous prose. At the end of more than an hour, she lay the article down on her lap, looked across at me, took a deep breath, and announced, 'Well! That's something!'

Time and Freedom

I had made a start in understanding the paradox of progressive education. I had felt it in my bones, and I had picked it apart in theory. I needed to go deeper now. What I especially needed was evidence. After my first few weeks as a graduate student, I came up with a proposal to compare the pedagogies of teachers in progressive and traditional primary schools. With the support of my supervisor, Dennis Warwick, I located two middle schools about 40 minutes travel outside Leeds – close together and starkly contrasting in their philosophies of curriculum and teaching. I spent all the summer term of 1975 taking two bus rides a day each way, for five days a week, to observe classrooms and to interview the teachers and their heads. It was exhausting listening and watching attentively every single day with no time to reflect or recoup my energy. Ever since, I have recommended no more than three days per week of fieldwork for anyone, including myself. Even so, it was all undeniably stimulating. Sharp and Green, Neville Bennett, and both Berlaks – none of them had published their research yet. I didn't know of their existence. I truly believed I was breaking new ground and making my own original contribution to knowledge.

Through the rest of 1975 and into the spring of 1976, I spent endless hours transcribing nearly 30 interviews. There were no digital ways of processing data then, and I couldn't afford a transcriber of my own, so this work consumed weeks and months of my time. I began analysing what I had collected, and I also read around the topic a lot to help me make sense of what I had seen and heard. By the time of Eggleston's second seminar, in the spring of 1977, I was starting to produce papers organised around the data from these two schools as well as from a third one that had served as a pilot project. Towards the end of the year, I put together a paper that included data on the more progressive or informal of the two middle schools I had been studying.

This paper, on 'The Significance of Classroom Coping Strategies', would turn out to be a bit of a launching pad for me when I presented it at a national conference in January 1978, as we will see in Chapter 3.[23] The important point here is that it included new evidence on how teachers and pupils managed and controlled their time in a choice-based system within the integrated day or block timetable environment.

Time, I once wrote, is the enemy of freedom.[24] Freedom is essential to human dignity. There is no autonomy when your time does not belong to you. When I started my first job in teacher education, straight out of graduate studies, in 1977, my grandma asked me what I did. I spent a few confusing minutes trying to describe classes, meetings, and so on. Clearly, my efforts were not successful. So, she posed a more precise question. 'Look,' she said, 'do you have to clock on and clock off?'

In the mills and factories where she and members of our hometown community had worked, workers were required to punch in a card with their name on it in the morning and punch it out again when they left at the end of the day. The punching in and out was timed to the minute, by the clock. Workers' time was not their own. It belonged to the factory owners and managers. When I assured my grandma that no, I didn't have to clock on and off, she said, 'Well, that's a wonderful thing.' For her, that was everything my education had been about – to get a job where there was no clocking on and off, no serving your time for an owner or a master. One of my mother's more memorable sayings when holidays came

The Paradox of Pupil Autonomy

around every year was, 'I'm not going to be ruled by a clock on my holidays.'

Time matters. If your time does not belong to you, if you are using it to make money for someone else, if other people are monitoring and measuring your time in minute detail, if your keystrokes are being tracked and timed when you are working from home, then you are not free, you have no autonomy, and your relationship to your work becomes alienated or estranged. For these reasons, giving people control over their own time can seem like an act of liberation from micromanagement and control.

The open-plan, progressive school that was part of my fieldwork officially treated time as something that pupils could manage for themselves as they undertook and completed work that was inherently satisfying. If the work engaged them, the head teacher said, he encouraged them to take it home and continue it there. This kind of intrinsically motivated learning was meant to break down the boundaries between home and school.

But in the way that this school implemented its block timetable, time put both the teachers and pupils in a bind. Instead of being a source of liberation and autonomy, it became a mechanism of power and control. Contrary to Sharp and Green's analysis, and my own earlier speculations, nobody was confused or misled by how the school used this time. And whatever their social class background and identity, all the pupils seemed to have a good idea of how this system of apparent choice operated and what was at stake. Together, though, they had to figure a way out of the bind they found themselves in. The answer was *homework*. It was a safety valve for a system under pressure.

The children grasped the fact that time did not belong to them. It was teachers' time.[25] One pupil commented that 'You're just getting in your flow then you get dragged off somewhere. It's better not to start anything at all, just to play noughts and crosses [which he had been doing] ready for when anybody comes.' At this point, with a perverse sense of timing, a teacher walked across and asked his group to clear up the art area. With a shrug of the shoulders and a knowing look, he muttered, 'See what I mean?'

Another pupil remarked how, 'You think "I'll leave that until tomorrow," and then when tomorrow comes, you find you have a film and you don't know about it, then you can't get it done.' Workflow was unpredictable, and the sheer number of tasks imposed by the teacher could feel overwhelming sometimes. As one child complained sarcastically, 'We get three months' work a week!' Time for these pupils was controlled by their teachers who could manipulate it, extend it, or contract it without warning and at will. And it was mainly allocated for completing work that the teachers had set, instead of pupils pursuing projects they had chosen themselves. A giveaway sign was that when pupils discussed work in which they were currently engaged, their remarks were almost always prefaced with phrases like, 'We've got to ...' 'We have to ...' or 'She said we had to ...'

Pupils in this block timetabled system were not engaging in what is now called *self-determined learning*, where they pursued and took responsibility for their own learning in their own way. Instead, they worked within a system of *self-regulated learning*. The learning tasks were imposed. What pupils were supposed to do was manage their own time to make sure the tasks were all done and duly delivered.

Yet even this modest system of self-management was undermined by other aspects of the curriculum, timetable, and organisation of the school. One of these was the distracting influence of noise in an open-plan environment. Children complained that 'There's too much racket in here.' 'They should have doors on the classrooms.' 'In the cookery area, you have wood shavings from the craft area, and also in the library you get smells from the cookery area.' 'They've got the woodwork area next to the library area. You can't think.'

The Paradox of Pupil Autonomy

Work was imposed but time was allowed for avoiding it. A teacher set out what the problems were: 'One of the things that we fall down very badly on is having the children organise their own time during the day when they have choices.' Instead of giving them choice in what work they did, their choices about time were restricted to *when* they do the work'. 'They're given a lot of free time,' he pointed out, but there were 'many, many children who can't see more than a little time ahead'.

In a system like this where there is no autonomy in designing or selecting tasks, but where there is high autonomy over the scheduling of time, there is a real danger that by the end of the week, teachers will be confronted by long queues of children holding out their uncompleted assignments. Homework, defined as 'taking work home' as a freely chosen extension of schoolwork, provided the system with a release mechanism.

'I prefer working at home because it's quiet and I've got my own room,' one pupil said.

'Do you usually finish all your work during the week?' I asked.

'Sometimes.'

'But I always take my English home and do it on a Tuesday night,' another child added.

'So, is that the only thing you take home, then? English?' I prodded.

'Sometimes you take topic work home.'

'That's when you're getting really keen, is it? Really interested?'

'Or when we've got too much to do!'

One of the children said that although they were allowed to do homework, but didn't *have* to do so, they still took a lot of work home. 'You take homework if you haven't finished anything. You take it home over the weekend or something, and then if it's done on Monday morning, you're OK,' he said. Officially, there wasn't supposed to be any homework. But unofficially, everyone knew it was going on. A tell-tale sign of this accepted practice was expressed in the words of one child who, when asked if it was easy to avoid working, responded that, 'Yeah. It's easy to avoid it because *you can keep saying you left it at home.*'

'Everybody knows that the dice are loaded,' sang the late Leonard Cohen.[26] It might not have been possible to connect how the school was outsourcing responsibility for supervising pupils' learning to the home to any overarching structures of capitalist domination, in Sharp and Green's sense. But the teachers and the children, and likely their parents too, were all in on the secret.

We know for sure now that when responsibilities for learning and schoolwork are relocated to the home, achievement gaps between social class groups get wider. Homework that attracts active parental support in some families and that leaves children to their own devices in others exaggerates existing inequalities. The necessity of working online at home during the COVID-19 pandemic created profound increases in achievement gaps between higher and lower socio-economic groups, as some pupils raced ahead with the extra time and help they got from their middle-class parents, while children in poverty struggled to keep up without the same supports, at the same time as having to endure countless disruptions in crowded home environments. Part of the global crisis of student absenteeism after the pandemic is not just a result of mental health problems among poorer students. It is also a consequence of parents in more privileged families taking their children out of school and using the online curriculum, along with their own support systems, to accelerate their children's learning and to find extra time for other enriching family activities too.[27]

There is nothing deliberate about this perpetuation of social class differences in schools. But the paradox of progressivism is that when it doesn't offer real choice, or when its teachers are not skilled or fit enough to manage a curriculum of authentic choice that engages with young people's interests, then it gets left to other systems and processes such as 'homework' to fill the gap. It is this that perpetuates inequality, albeit unintentionally.

The Paradox of Pupil Autonomy

The key question is how can we realistically retain a curriculum and way to organise schools that has significant elements of choice and autonomy for young people, without this becoming unmanageable for teachers, lowering standards of work in schools, and amplifying social and educational inequalities?

Three Ways Forward

The problem with over-enthusiastic adoptions of progressive, open-plan, integrated, or problem-based learning systems is that they take an all-or-nothing approach. The conventional wisdom of educational change experts doesn't help. Unless everyone implements everything all the time, they believe, innovations are failing. But especially where teaching and learning is complex, as it is in progressive, open education environments, this kind of full-scale adoption is neither realistic nor desirable. So, here are three ways to make hope practical in the innovative and progressive efforts of today.

1. Don't Innovate in Everything

Making progressive teaching styles and philosophies effective requires considerable effort and significant expertise, as we have seen. Younger teachers in earlier career can sometimes squeeze it all in for a while. But as time passes, and when, for many people, children and other responsibilities start to come along, working in top gear all the time can be too much. A LEGO Foundation-funded project that I co-led in 2022–2023 on supporting school teams to develop innovations after COVID-19 revealed that most innovative teams are led by educators such as counsellors, learning support teachers, or teacher-librarians who don't have full-time classroom responsibilities.[28] So, while it is important to value and be grateful for educators who can commit whole-heartedly to major innovations when they are young and energetic enough, or when their jobs give them priceless relief from being full-on with the same group of children all day, *we cannot and should not expect all teachers to be teaching in open classroom, integrated day, problem-based environments all the time.*

2. Protect Time for Self-Determined Learning

Some tasks in education need to be assigned. Some knowledge needs to be given. This can be done in engaging and culturally responsive ways, but it may still need to be taught directly sometimes rather than being left to be discovered. Not everything can or should be chosen. And if some of the curriculum is determined by the teacher, it is insensitive and even cruel to insist that pupils must then take responsibility for organising the imposed work all in their own time. In-school resistance, work avoidance, and time mismanagement should not come as a surprise in these circumstances. The answer is not just to make innovation optional, like in electives outside the core, but to allocate protected time within the regular curriculum for self-determined learning. For instance, pupils can pursue their own passion projects like in the 'Genius Hour' that some schools have borrowed from Google, or they can sign up for classes in half-day-a-week sessions based on teachers' passions and interests, such as cooking, knitting, decorating the school, or doing magic tricks, as I witnessed in the LEGO Foundation-funded project on innovation networks.[29] *Innovation and project-based learning may work best when it is a part-time engagement, not a full-on commitment.*

3. Use Innovative Schools as Incubators, not as Blueprints

Beacon schools or lighthouse schools that recruit and draw together teachers who believe in and are relentlessly committed to child-centred education practices can be an inspiration for others, but they should not be a model that other schools are then expected to replicate. In terms of age, life circumstances, or role responsibilities, the teachers in these schools are often atypical. In time, many of them get burned out from being 'on' all the time. The innovative schools that do endure tend to be the same very few that international visitors come to see or that researchers write about repeatedly. *Innovative schools make their best contribution not as blueprints or models for others to follow but as incubators for teacher leadership in early career.* These evolving leaders can then take all they have learned to other schools in the system where they can implement changes in a lesser way. This brings some innovation to lots of places rather than lots of innovation to a few.

Progressivism with Pragmatism

Education cannot be based solely on visions or ideals, on scaling up what the perfect parent would most want for their individual child to whole classes and systems, or even on what scientific evidence indicates are the most effective approaches to learning. Teaching and learning must somehow be workable and doable by less-than-superhuman teachers in busy, crowded, diverse, and inclusive classroom circumstances. Teaching, in other words, cannot just be understood or developed in terms of scientific theory, idealistic philosophy, or exemplary experiments. It must be squared with practical and realistic strategies. This requires a different understanding of teachers and teaching than most people have today.

CHAPTER 3
Classroom Coping Strategies

A Lucky Break

Our Trimphone rang in its distinctive trilling tones. The call was from a detective in the West Yorkshire Police force. He wanted to interview me in connection with one of the most notorious serial killings in British history: the 13 murders committed by the man who came to be known as the Yorkshire Ripper. I wasn't a witness. I had no connection to any of the victims. I was, it seemed, a potential suspect.

The detective explained that they were interviewing all the owners in the region of 'Farina'-type cars, 1960s-made Morris Oxfords, Austin Cambridges, and, as in my case, Wolseley 1660s. They had already completed hundreds of interviews. But they had made a mistake – one of many egregious errors by the investigation team, it later turned out – and had missed a few vehicles on the first sweep. They were now following up. How many were in this final round, I asked. The number he gave was disconcertingly small. Twelve!

The Yorkshire Ripper had committed many of his murders in the Chapeltown area of Leeds, a neighbourhood used by sex workers. This part of town was also on my direct route home from the city centre to the suburbs, beyond the ring road, after we had gone shopping or after visiting my supervisor or doing research in the

The Making of an Educator

university library. My licence plate had been recorded when I had been driving through. Understandably, I began to feel uneasy.

The detective came to our apartment and sat down. He took out his notebook and enquired if I could account for my whereabouts on several dates – the days and nights when different murders had been committed. I kept no diary. I had no written record of my movements. I was just a research student, and now a junior college lecturer, with no unusual meetings or out-of-town appointments that might provide me with an alibi. The dates went back over several years. Each one drew a blank. As I became increasingly nervous, I even misremembered a time when my wife and I had (not) gone on holiday.

By the time we were getting round to the fifth or sixth date, I was sweating. Even as a child, I had often felt anxious or guilty when announcements were made in school assemblies about hunts to find culprits of vandalism or other misdeeds. Then, thankfully, to my immense relief, the detective came up with a date in the late summer of 1977. On that very day, I recalled, I had been kept overnight in hospital with a broken wrist, my arm encased in plaster up to the shoulder. They would need to check out my alibi with the hospital records, of course, but I never heard from them again. It was a very lucky break.

The injury was a severe one: a double fracture and dislocation. I had sustained it in a high-velocity collision playing football for the college where I was starting work. My team-mates called the ambulance as soon as they saw that the end of my arm had assumed a gruesome 'S' shape. It was just three days before starting my first job in higher education at a teachers' college on the outskirts of Leeds. My teaching schedule was very demanding – 18 hours a week of student contact hours, including several lectures per week, many of them on subjects that were completely new to me. I had written some of them out in advance over the preceding summer, but my detailed notes only took me through the first few weeks. I didn't type, and I couldn't write at

Classroom Coping Strategies

all with my injured arm and hand. All I could do was scribble a few words on yellow paper with my non-dominant left hand.

This is how I learned to lecture and speak for long periods without notes – a skill that has stayed with me all through my career. No more reading out my papers head down at high speed, but just speaking extempore around a few headings and trusting that I had command of the content and flow of it all in my head. I wouldn't recommend this for anyone else, but this coping strategy would set me up for life. My injury, and how I had to deal with it, had been my second lucky break.

A Few Firsts

I moved into my first higher education job, as a lecturer at Trinity and All Saints College, a Catholic teacher training college, in the autumn of 1977. It represented a significant change of life and career plans. The college had offered me some part-time lecturing while I was still doing my PhD. They were pleased with what I had done and approached me when a vacancy for a position came up at the end of my studentship. It was a paid full-time job after three years of being a student, I knew and liked the people who would be my new colleagues, and it was local, so we wouldn't have to move to another city. But by accepting the job, I would not now return to school teaching as I had originally planned. It was a big fork in the road. The path I chose would have lifelong consequences for my career. It also had immediate implications for both of us as a family.

While I was still a student, Pauline and I had decided it was time to start a family. Our intent was that since I was on a research grant and she was making the larger income in teaching, I would stay at home, look after our first child, and somehow synchronise this with working on my PhD thesis. The plan was not so much radical – although househusbands in the 1970s were a pretty rare

The Making of an Educator

phenomenon – as wildly unrealistic. If we'd had the slightest inkling of just how hard taking care of a baby would be, we would never have imagined I could do this at the same time as continuing to work on my thesis. We envisaged long nap times and protracted periods when our infant would agreeably go back and forth on his baby swing while I wrestled with data and theory. What on earth were we thinking?

Fortunately, after a longer period trying for our first child than we anticipated, I had already secured this first job, and so our parenting plans switched around. On 2 January 1978, while I was having morning tea with my colleagues, in the days when higher education lecturers still had time for morning tea, someone came in and said my wife had just phoned. She had gone into labour. After a few encouraging smiles and a bit of 1970s male backslapping, I shot out to the car park, drove home, and took Pauline to the hospital.

She had a brutally long labour. It went on for 24 hours until, after a long night, the doctor eventually came in to conduct a forceps delivery. We were both up all night. Pauline was going through constant pain and trauma, and it was with immense relief that the delivery in the end was successful with no lasting harm.

The next day, I was due to give my first major presentation to one of the largest academic education conferences in Britain. At this three-day event, all the papers were delivered to the entire assembled audience. Everyone else was famous. I was the youngest there, barely out of grad school – a late stand-in for someone who had dropped out. Pauline and I discussed what to do. I had already missed the first day. We decided I should go and then come straight back after my talk. It was 120 miles away and the middle of winter.

I went home from the hospital, snatched a few hours' sleep, and got the early train to Birmingham. I arrived at the conference at lunchtime, grabbed a quick bite to eat, and accepted a pint of beer from my colleagues in celebration of my son's arrival. I was the first

Classroom Coping Strategies

Tuesday 3rd January.

Arrival and Registration	9.30-11.00
Coffee in Teaching Centre	11.00-11.30
Opening Remarks	11.30-11.45
1. I. Reid Past and present trends in the Sociology of Education - A plea for a return to Educational Sociology.	11.45-12.30
Lunch	12.30-1.30
2. D. Hargreaves Whatever happened to Symbolic Interactionism?	2.00-2.45
Coffee	2.45-3.15
3. S. Delamont Sociology and Classroom Research.	3.15-4.00
Seminars	4.00-5.00
Dinner	5.30-6.30
4. V. Furlong Language and Classroom Interaction.	6.45-7.30
Open Forum	7.30-8.15

Wednesday 4th January.

5. R. Meighan Consultation, Teaching Style and Educational Ideologies: some issues raised by research into Childrens' Judgements of Teaching Performance.	9.15-10.00
6. G. Vulliamy Culture Clash in the Classroom: Music Teaching as an example of Liberal and Radical Alternatives.	10.30-11.15
Seminars	11.15-12.15
General Feedback	12.15-12.30
Lunch	12.30-1.30
7. A. Hargreaves Towards a theory of Classroom Coping Strategies.	2.00-2.45
Coffee	2.45-3.15
8. P. Woods 'I do not like to see her bottom.' How teachers turn the other cheek.	3.15-4.00
Open Forum	4.00-5.00
Dinner	5.30-

Thursday 5th January.

9. G. Whitty The Politics of School Knowledge.	9.15-10.00
Coffee	10.00-10.30
10. O. Banks School and Society.	10.30-11.15
Seminars	11.15-12.15
Lunch	12.30-1.30
11. G. Bernbaum Schooling in decline: A crisis for the Sociology of Education.	2.00-2.45
Final Open Forum	2.45-3.15
Coffee	3.15-

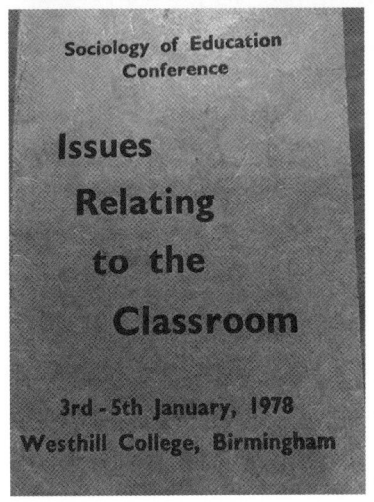

Sociology of Education Conference

Issues Relating to the Classroom

3rd - 5th January, 1978
Westhill College, Birmingham

I arrived at the conference at lunchtime, grabbed a quick bite to eat, and accepted a pint of beer from my colleagues in celebration of my son's arrival. I was the first lecture after lunch.

lecture after lunch, just before Peter Woods, a more senior figure who ended up having a significant impact on my work and career, as we shall see. His talk had what would now be viewed as a very ill-advised attempt at a humorous title. It was '"I Do Not Like to See Her Bottom": How Teachers Turn the Other Cheek'. Bottom, in this very-much-of-its-time double entendre, referred to being bottom of the class, of course!

The Making of an Educator

I entered the lecture hall. It was packed, like nothing I had ever faced before. Everyone was older, more experienced, and, in many cases, with big reputations already behind them. I took the stage, looked at them all, and then I began. The paper – on classroom coping strategies – was theoretically sophisticated, but it also had data that I could weave stories around.[1] I strode back and forth across the stage without looking at my notes, tried to communicate in a manner that was as close to everyday language as possible, peppered the presentation with extracts from my data, and finished after 45 minutes, right on time.

I stopped, looked at the audience, and experienced what felt like an eternal silence. My first and overwhelming thought to myself was, 'Well, that was completely common sense, wasn't it?' And then they stood. And clapped. A standing ovation, almost (no one gave standing ovations in Britain then!). It was an extraordinary moment that somehow combined the first public launch of a new theory about my research findings with feelings of utter euphoria about the safe arrival of our first child, along with some kind of out-of-body adrenaline surge that came from the alcohol-enhanced effects of sleep deprivation. If I could have bottled all that as the secret of how to make a great presentation, I would have done. As it was, though, I had no time to meet all the other famous speakers whose work I admired and even revered, and no time to soak up any glory. Instead, I came off the stage, took a taxi (it may even have been a bus) back to the station, and headed straight home.

We'd had our first child, I had taken my first academic job, and I had made my first big presentation – all within weeks of each other. It was a lot of firsts. The work, the idea, the contribution to knowledge on which the culminating presentation was based was a theory of teachers' classroom coping strategies, including how teachers used their experience to respond to the situations in which they found themselves.

Evidence or Experience

When people ask how teachers should teach these days, one common answer is that what they do should be evidence-based. Teaching should be in line with scientific research findings on what works and what doesn't, they say. Data from large surveys, blind-controlled studies, or meta-analyses of studies over long time periods, irrespective of context or circumstance – this is the sort of evidence that overrides professional judgement. Evidence doesn't merely inform judgement. The data drive it. Only evidence counts. Experience doesn't.

The evidence-based education position is based, in many respects, on the medical model of decision-making with its blind-controlled studies and large-scale epidemiological data about the spread of disease. However, this evidence-based stance can be overstated. It fails to account for dissimilarities between surgical practice and classroom practice. Teaching is more akin to complex human conditions in community medicine, eldercare, or mental health, for example, where the evidence base is much less clear than in clinical, surgical, or pharmacological practice.

Overconfidence in the medical model also overlooks areas that are disputed within medicine itself. For instance, cancer treatments for individual patients are often contested between surgeons, radiologists, and pharmacologists. And in everyday life, medical opinion has changed, and sometimes even reversed, over time on matters varying from the risks of hormone replacement therapy as a treatment for menopause to the health benefits and drawbacks of using standing desks. One of the most telling sets of studies concerns the startlingly different rates at which tonsillectomies were once recommended for children with chronic sore throats depending on where the children lived and the social class of the patient's family, for example.[2]

The Making of an Educator

What works in any one classroom at any one time rather than for large samples, on average, is at least as uncertain in behaviour management strategies or choices of pedagogy than it is in medicine concerning any individual patient's treatment. Scientific evidence should not be ignored, but it should not be obeyed unquestioningly either.

At the other extreme from excessive dependence on research evidence is a long-standing work culture in teaching which has discounted theory and research in favour of teachers' individual and shared educational experience. In a paper I turned out a few years later, I described my data in the more progressive middle school in my doctoral study on how teachers planned a curriculum together for the following year.

'Experience Counts, Theory Doesn't' documented how teachers didn't draw on research when they were discussing children's moral development, or on how philosophers and sociologists had analysed the relationship between different school subjects, when they were planning units of curriculum integration.[3] Apart from a teacher who was studying sociology of education with the Open University and two others who made passing references to things their partners had told them from their standpoint of being teachers' college lecturers, these teachers informed and justified their planning by drawing on their own past, present, and shared experiential knowledge of teaching.

Sometimes, teachers referred to individual children, especially ones who figured among the more colourful characters in the school. The mere mention of some of these pupils' names incurred laughter, such as the boy in science who 'can't make paper and he probably doesn't know it, but he's doing various experiments and learning far more because he's following his own line of thought than if he was guided more strongly on what to do next'. A child's name was all that was needed in some cases to make a point, as when one teacher said that 'Schools ought to teach manners, but you can't teach them to children like [pupil's name], for instance.'

Classroom Coping Strategies

Experiences with children might be couched as almost natural laws of pupil behaviour. 'Kids are going to be kids. I mean, no matter how hard we try, they're still going to be cheeky to the dinner ladies at the end of the day,' one teacher remarked. Another teacher supported her argument against free choice for pupils by appealing to the common knowledge that 'You'll all know that there are some girls who, every term, would do a project on horses.'

Examples from other schools that teachers had worked at or visited were sometimes treated as sufficient to justify how choice should be handled. One teacher dismissed another school's efforts to introduce topic work when the children 'would choose any old thing and very soon they would realise that what they've chosen is beyond them or it's not interesting enough for them'.

What was it that influenced how these teachers taught? In interviews, they referred to 'sheer, hard experience; the hard graft of doing the job', 'tips from other people that I've watched teaching', 'force of circumstance', 'the other teachers you're working with', 'observation of other teachers at my last school', and 'variety of experience'. This wasn't just a question of limited vision or lack of access to other ways of thinking and making decisions. Even the two teachers with indirect access to more formal educational study scarcely mentioned it in their curriculum discussions. And while the teacher doing a degree would introduce some of what he had been studying into meetings, he offered only short snippets and even these provoked opposition.

Teachers clearly knew more than they were letting on sometimes, but in discussions with their colleagues they kept this knowledge to themselves. This didn't just apply to formal, theoretical knowledge. It applied to other experiences with the children too. One teacher, for example, felt that having had children of her own made her appreciate that 'children can be absolutely horrible and nice at the next moment'. She added, 'I don't expect them to be on a level all the time.' Others referred to something we all have in common – having once been a child. One teacher had been raised in a strict Christian family and grew up questioning everything – an approach she felt now served her well in teaching middle school pupils. Another reflected on how she had not been naturally 'brilliant' in school and had to work extremely hard to overcome her difficulties, which now made her 'understand that there are a lot of children who are also like that'.

The teachers I had observed and interviewed didn't only give little credence to formal educational research. In curriculum planning discussion with their colleagues, they also excluded other experiences outside the classroom that might have been relevant. It was as if there was a tacit norm that only experience with pupils counted. Restricting the basis of discussion to classroom experiences meant that the planning sessions were quite unproductive, and teachers complained to one another in their meetings that the process was 'vague', 'inconclusive', and had them 'going round in circles'. As the end of term approached, even the deputy head was getting worried that he didn't 'know what level of curriculum integration there's going to be. Are they going to have class teachers or what?'

Unease was mounting, so the head teacher panicked. Just a few days before the end of the school year, he came into the staffroom, placed a pile of papers on the table, and announced that these were the teachers' timetables for the following school year. The teachers were outraged at this betrayal of their inclusive and democratic curriculum planning process. 'I wanted to integrate more. I thought we were, but that's been stamped on,' one teacher complained. 'I've been given all science throughout the school. I wanted at least to retain some maths,' an infuriated colleague added. 'You never know where you are. The timetable's changing all the time,' said a third. 'What was the problem?' I enquired. The teacher who was doing his Open University course thrust two raised fingers towards the head teacher's office and summed it all up in one word: 'Autocracy!'

The paradox of autonomy and autocracy where the efforts to grant autonomy end up in impositions of autocracy can afflict the adults in schools as well as their pupils. Several years later, I would come up with a new term to describe this phenomenon: *contrived collegiality*.[4] This process of going round in circles until the leader had to impose their authority to reach a conclusion was not helped by a culture with a knowledge base that was insufficient for the task of curriculum planning: relying on past and present examples and experiences with pupils.

All this might seem to support a case for introducing research evidence into the professional learning and planning practices of teachers by imposing evidence-based policies. However, at the end of the article, I argued that any attempt to disrupt the experience-based nature of the culture of teaching would meet with little success if it ignored the conditions, demands, and constraints that give rise to and provide continued support for that culture of teaching in the first place. Changing the culture of teaching could not happen without changing the structure of teaching, I concluded. Time for shared decision-making, opportunities to visit other schools, and increases in professional learning – all within regular teaching time – would be some of the structural changes required for a cultural shift. If teachers didn't change because they fell back on experience rather than evidence about children's learning, it was important to find out why. My work on teachers' strategies, along with that of one or two peers, suggested some new possibilities.

Coping Strategies

Most discussions about how to improve teaching and learning involve trying to get teachers to do things they are not currently doing or getting most teachers to do what only a few of them are doing. Everything but the kitchen sink has been thrown behind these efforts – analysing data, top-down standardisation, professional development, market competition between schools and teachers, coaching and mentoring, and, most recently, AI.

The Making of an Educator

My own theory of classroom coping strategies flipped the question. Why do teachers do what they are already doing? The theory was based on a sociological framework first developed in Chicago in the 1930s known as symbolic interactionism, in which people do what they do, even when it can seem irrational to an outsider, not because they are stupid or lazy but because their actions make sense to them and the people around them in the circumstances in which they find themselves. If we want to understand the ways that teachers teach, I argued, we must address the conditions, constraints, and opportunities that define teachers' working environment and the sense that they make of it.

I wasn't the only researcher who was thinking this way. There are times when you believe you have invented something completely new, and then you come across someone else who, quite independently, has created almost the very same thing. We imagine we are the authors of our own fate, but in many ways the world is writing us. I showed up at John Eggleston's second seminar along with a newcomer, Peter Woods. In a couple of years' time, Woods would offer me a job, but for now, we both arrived having never met each other before, and were astonished to find, when we collected all the printed papers together, that we had written very similar pieces. My paper was on teachers' coping strategies in a middle school. His was on teachers' survival strategies in a traditional secondary school.[5] We even started from a similar source point – a 1973 paper by an American scholar, Ian Westbury.[6]

Westbury explained why coping strategies that teachers took for granted – like introducing a topic, then having pupils raise their hands in competition to answer the teacher's questions, followed by individual seatwork – originated in the 19th century. Then, the strategies had evolved so that teachers could manage large classes, motivate pupils to compete for the teacher's attention, and complete the curriculum. Over time, these strategies became functional, traditional, and taken for granted as the normal or accepted way to teach – what US

Classroom Coping Strategies

historians David Tyack and Daniel Tobin would later term an unquestioned 'grammar of schooling' that became very hard to change.[7]

Woods went further than Westbury, and in the challenging secondary school for non-academic students that he studied, he argued that mere coping, in some ways, turned into a business of grim survival. Teachers who, mainly, did not have other career options that might offer them an exit if they wanted one, quickly accommodated to the very demanding constraints on their work by necessity, such as working with large classes or with teenagers whose difficult behaviours could even turn aggressive. Woods listed eight survival strategies used by these teachers – domination, punishment, negotiation (lowering expectations in exchange for compliance), fraternisation with the enemy (especially by younger teachers), avoiding teaching the most challenging classes, using ritual and routine to eliminate shocks and surprises, employing occupational therapy to keep kids busy even though they might not be learning much, and, more positively, engaging in morale-boosting efforts through praise or humour.

In a rather cynical passage, Woods observed not only that short-term survival strategies tended to persist until they had outlived their usefulness – like many people now say about the traditional grammar of schooling, but also that these strategies didn't free up teachers for more teaching or better teaching. Instead, 'they expand into teaching and around it, like some parasitic plant', so that they present themselves *as* teaching, however strangled or corrupted that version of teaching might be.[8] The strict and draconian teaching approaches and behaviour management strategies that have been adopted by 'no excuses' schools today have not only accepted the necessity of such extreme survival strategies. They have turned them into profitable business brands.

My own version of classroom coping strategies did not limit them to only the more challenging conditions of schooling that Woods described. All teaching, whether progressive or traditional,

The Making of an Educator

with younger children or older pupils, resulted from the ways that teachers developed coping strategies to respond to their environment. In my paper for Eggleston's second seminar, and in the more extensive presentation I gave at the Birmingham conference a few months later, on the back of first-time fatherhood and a glass of beer, I set out what this wider theory of coping strategies looked like.

All teachers use coping strategies as creative ways to make sense of and respond to the constraints and opportunities that exist in their work situation. They are 'creatively articulated solutions to recurring daily problems'.[9] In this respect, coping strategies are a way of explaining the work cultures of teaching, just as they explain work cultures in other occupations. How do gravediggers cope with the fact they are doing 'dirty work'?[10] How do female dancers who get paid for keeping their male dancing partners company maintain their sense of dignity?[11] How do detectives cope with crime victims who tell them to do things like test for fingerprints because of all the cop shows they have watched?[12]

All people, in all occupations, construct their work through the coping strategies they use. This doesn't mean that detectives and doctors, for example, don't treat evidence seriously. Nor does it suggest that workers' own goals, purposes, or beliefs are unimportant. But the circumstances and conditions of every job significantly affect what teachers and other workers decide to do.

Coping strategies are employed in both traditional and progressive, 'closed' and 'open' school environments. And each, in their own way, becomes the accepted approach to doing schooling – the control and domination or question-and-answer strategies of traditional schools, or the use of busyness and homework outlets in more progressive ones.

Like Rachel Sharp and Anthony Green, I argued that the constraints under which teachers work ultimately have their origin in the wider society, but I expanded how these might be interpreted. With them, I pointed to the contradictory goals of state-provided education to develop the whole child on the one hand and prepare children for an economically stratified society on the other. Yet I also discussed the material constraints of class sizes or of school building environments that are the result of public policies and expenditure levels. This second set of material-constraining conditions marked the beginning of a longer term effort of mine to go beyond Sharp and Green's improbable leap from the micro world of teachers to the macro world of society by setting out intermediary or middle-range influences that connected the macro forces to micro-level interactions – an issue we will come back to in Chapter 5.

Coping or Transforming

How can looking at teaching through a lens of coping strategies guide future reform strategies? What can a coping strategies perspective move us towards?

Confront the constraints
In life, we sometimes talk about beating the odds. Whatever the constraints of teaching – large classes, low resources, no time away from class responsibilities – there are always some teachers with boundless energy and unrelenting commitment who can achieve extraordinary results even in the most challenging circumstances. But not everyone can beat the odds – due, perhaps, to their age, their life circumstances, or their concerns to have some work–life balance. So, as well as finding ways to beat the odds, it is time to start changing those odds.

One of them involves time. Outside Asia, several higher performing countries, such as Finland, allocate more time out of class for teachers to plan, prepare, think, reflect, collaborate, and relax than their lower performing counterparts.[13] Time that is over-scheduled for mandated training days or for imposed professional learning communities dedicated to raising short-term results is not what is required. It is time to collaborate on teachers' own terms that really matters, in line with the school's direction but still in ways that leaves considerable scope for teachers to think, read, and innovate together. Time is money, of course, which is why reformers try to consider almost any other initiative to change things up, but few things beat investing in more and better quality of time. As musician Dave Crosby wrote after a life-saving liver transplant, 'Time is the final currency / Not money, not power.'[14] It is time.

Get the Big Picture
Teachers are intellectuals. At least they should be. You can't be very good at helping kids to think if you don't get enough or give yourself enough time to think. If you teach literature, what kind of books are you reading for yourself? And if, as we often say, part of the job of teaching is preparing young people for the world beyond school, how are you engaging with and thinking about that world – in the news, in what you read, in what gets your attention? Doctors and dentists make it their business to keep up with research on and advances in their practice. Teachers need to do that too. But there is no point just badgering them into doing better.

The problem is that, too often, we infantilise teachers and teaching. Head teachers, principals, and perhaps a few teacher leaders get the big picture in their own reading, in their studies for a post-graduate degree, or in listening to thought leaders talk about learning, well-being, change, leadership, racism, or climate change, for example. Then they pass on a watered-down version of what they have learned to their teachers or introduce some new initiatives based on that learning. It is the leaders who get the big picture. Teachers just get the big binder of plans, activities, and colour-coded exercises.

Time is part of the answer to this, of course. It is hard to step back and see your reflection if the water is always rushing past you.

Classroom Coping Strategies

But self-motivation and self-regard within the profession matter too. In 2024, I turned down a professional development opportunity to work with teachers in a US school district on student engagement and well-being. It was just before the start of the school year. I had co-authored a short book on this and tried to make it accessible, practical, and even pleasurable to read without compromising the big ideas. It is why the leaders of the event approached me.

As we started planning, I asked if the teachers could be given a copy of the book ahead of time, so that instead of me delivering ideas that were already in print, we could discuss and think about them together. There would be no fee, I explained. But I had the expectation that if I was going to work with them, then perhaps they could take some time to read what I had written. I was told that the teachers' contract wouldn't allow any reading to be required outside the scheduled two days. How about a chapter, then, I suggested. This, apparently, was still not possible unless they did that in the allocated time. The best the professional development leader could offer was that she would prepare a two-page summary of the book's key points. But the book is a narrative that is meant to inspire people and not just inform them. It is written to engage its readers intellectually, emotionally, and morally. It is not just a set of bullet points. Teachers' unions and school administrators alike all need to help teachers look up and see the big picture that they are part of and contribute to, and teachers themselves need to go above and beyond their contract provisions to expand their own knowledge too.

When we look up, we can see what is behind the constraints, what is responsible for them, and whether they can be changed by others and sometimes by ourselves. In 2017, I studied a school in Norway that had a strong reputation for promoting collaboration among its teachers. I watched them engage in multiple intersecting activities to plan a new vision for the school – not in tiresome and inconclusive meetings but through varied, stimulating interaction, so that, in the principal's words, everyone could see the big picture of where the school was going and be part of it.[15] In schools like this, everyone gets the big picture. They see it, live it, and create it together.

Change the Game
Big classes, old buildings, conventional classrooms, no time – no wonder coping strategies that seem to work get widely adopted, deeply ingrained, and passed on from one generation of teachers to the next. But once we look up and see the big picture, we may notice that there are ways we can change the game. Football (soccer) has 11 players on each side, a goal net at either end of the field, and each half lasts for approximately 45 minutes. But in living memory, when teams got a lead and started to waste time by passing the ball back to the goalkeeper, which made the game extremely boring to watch, new rules were introduced to prevent goalies picking up the ball when it was passed back to them, and coaches developed strategies to press the opposing goalkeeper and defence and make them panic. The game got faster, riskier, and more exciting. It was still the same game, but changing it, at no cost, made it better.

We can change the game in teaching and learning more often than we imagine. If you are short of time to meet and collaborate, you can bank time by lengthening the school day for four days a week, then start the fifth day of classes later so that teachers have had time to work and think together before that. Team teaching arrangements or giving small teams of teachers the responsibility to manage their own curriculum with larger groups of students mean that when the work the students are doing doesn't require too much teacher attention, one member of the teaching pair or several members of the teaching team can leave the class to observe other teachers, catch up on their professional reading, or collaborate with each other.

Classroom Coping Strategies

Space can be changed as well as time. If the available space is old-fashioned and uncongenial, you can get children or adults to sit and talk in circles or ellipses, rather than in rows and rectangles, to make discussion more intimate and inclusive – just like indigenous communities do. You can even take the children into nature and teach them outdoors, like many schools did during COVID-19 when they needed to reduce the risks of infection. Going outside is very good for people's physical, emotional, and intellectual well-being, and it doesn't cost a thing. And if you have a one-on-one meeting with a colleague and don't need tools or devices, you can have a walking meeting outdoors, so that you are literally as well as metaphorically moving forward together.

Last, great potential is emerging for technology to transform many of the working and learning conditions in school. Sometimes, of course, digital technology can be oppressive and create neverending work – more emails to parents, more messages back from them at all times of day and night, and more learning management systems to download material from and keep managing in real time. But technology can also liberate teachers and learners, especially AI.

- Stuart Hargreaves, who is a law professor (and also my son), has been developing ways for AI to manage formative assessments with classes of over 100 students in the middle of lectures, so he can adjust his teaching in response to real-time feedback on how much and how well those students are learning.[16]
- Yngve Lindvig, who manages an international network of system leaders with me, heads a company that has created AI tools to support, streamline, and enhance teachers' curriculum planning. AI doesn't replace teachers here. It doesn't do the planning for them. But it can draft a curriculum plan within parameters that teachers create,

such as the age group of the class, the goals of the course or unit, and the cooperative learning activities they want to use. Teachers can then develop this draft, so the learning is deeper and richer. With the time saved, they can advance their professional learning in other areas too.[17]

- Tom D'Amico, director of one of the school districts in my own community in Ottawa, engages all his leaders and their schools in developing the use of AI in curriculum planning, project-based learning, and educational assessment. Someone is not developing AI strategies for them. They are creating AI-based learning innovation together.[18]

Beyond Coping

Sometimes, though, you just can't cope any more, however hard you try. You may not be able to accomplish your goals or having to juggle too many priorities can just be exhausting. In their book on *The New Lives of Teachers*, Christopher Day and Qing Gu point out that the teachers they studied were highly effective if three things were going well and aligned – their day-to-day work, their lives outside their work, and their sense that their careers were progressing. If all three were going badly – the job was too hard, the career was going nowhere, and their life was a struggle – then they were likely to be ineffective.[19] Even if two out of these three factors were problematic, they were still at risk.

How did this apply to me? I loved my work as a college lecturer. I enjoyed my students. I was barely three or four years older than most of them. They were enthusiastic about becoming teachers and excited about the ideas I introduced them to. We laughed, we fraternised (especially through lunchtime five-a-side football), and I

Classroom Coping Strategies

was part of their generation, in tune with what they thought and how they felt. Indeed, I was quite often mistaken for being one of them, which eventually prompted me to grow a moustache.

The staff, too, was one of the most collegial and collaborative groups I have ever worked with. We planned our courses together in sociology of education and debated the ideas and perspectives in the field intensely at morning tea and other times. One of them would sometimes work with me in his driveway at weekends, teaching me how to do my own car repairs as I couldn't afford the garage bills. And the football games were not just with the students. They involved the staff too. It was a Catholic college, and it lived up to the best of the denomination's ethos – intellectual, collaborative, and, among the men, who mainly made up its staff at that time, it bonded us through sport and physical activity.

Home life, though, was something else, as it often is for the young parents of tiny children with no grandparents or aunties and uncles at hand to support them. After Stuart, our son, had been born, we imagined it would take just as long to try for a second child. However, the first time we got a babysitter and went to watch the dance moves in *Saturday Night Fever* that theory went belly up. We had, it turned out, a bit of Night Fever of our own happening, and Lucy Gemma Hargreaves duly arrived just 13 months after Stuart.

We lived in a 1970s professional middle-class world of natural childbirth, gender-neutral toys and clothes, and fervent beliefs that you should never leave your child to cry alone in their cot. One or the other of our two children always seemed to be waking up. Eventually, Pauline and I took to separate beds. She would take Lucy in with her, and I would lay the couch cushions on the living room floor and bed down with Stuart. My most intense fantasies at this time revolved around sleep. I had two options of driving to work – quickly on the ring road or slowly on a country lane. I often took the backroad and pulled in by a farm gate so I could tip my seat back and get the only 20 minutes or so of uninterrupted sleep I could guarantee.

Of course, there were many great pleasures of being the parents of tiny children, which we still remember fondly, but with the extensive parenting demands and the long hours of the job, I had no time or energy left to work on my unfinished PhD, which was now into its fifth year. Even when I went into the portable cabin that was my office to work on my dissertation for half a day at weekends, I frequently ended up spending more hours falling asleep than I did working. In baseball terms, I was two for three. In career terms, I was about to strike out.

This was not helped by my continuing obsession with reading, knowing, and trying to master every possible theory that might have relevance to my study, as well as many other theories that didn't. I just wanted to know everything about everything, and I probably just needed someone to tell me, as I tell students now, to not take too much on and just get the dissertation finished. But this combination of a heavy teaching schedule, family demands, and my over-ambitious approach to my thesis made me fear for my career as an academic. These days, if you are a junior scholar, you need to produce several papers a year to get promotion. I was lucky if I was managing two. I loved the college, but from a career standpoint, I needed to get into a university. So, my coping strategy was to find an exit door.

CHAPTER 4
How to Build a Theory

The Loneliness of the Long-Distance Thinker

If you think teaching condemns you to isolation, try doing a PhD. UK graduate school in social sciences and humanities in the 1970s was a strange existence. Sometimes, it still is. Apart from my relationship with a single supervisor, a few seminars from visiting scholars, and chance encounters with a motley collection of fellow students, graduate school was an intense and rather lonely life. I had to be very comfortable in my own head to live with it because, basically, I was alone with my thoughts and the pretty dense and intense ideas of the people I was reading, hour after hour, week after week, for months and years on end.

When I moved to North America, there were times when I could be critical of and even somewhat snooty about Canadian and US graduate degrees in education. All the required taught courses students had to do before they embarked on a much shorter and modestly defined doctoral study than ones in the UK and Europe led to a lack of intellectual depth and to excessive dependency on their professors, or so I felt. Conversely, many of those professors encouraged hierarchies of fealty to them and their ideas in university departments that were run like intellectual fiefdoms in some cases.

The Making of an Educator

Yet, taking courses together does give graduate students more of a sense of belonging and being part of a community, which provides stimulation as well as moral support when things get difficult. In this sense, Americans especially have mainly been better than Brits at groups, teams, and ceremonies, beginning with summer camp in school, extending to the graduations and prom nights that are now a permanent fixture in Britain too, and then, in the country's more elite institutions, moving on to the fraternities and sororities of college life. It can all be a bit suffocating sometimes and delay young people's intellectual independence, but there is no doubt that it helps to improve thesis completion rates, which had been dismally low when I was doing my PhD.

Over the last 20 years, UK doctoral programmes, in education at least, have added supervisors and training courses, especially in research methodology, so it is less lonely and not so intense now, although some older professors, with a bit of nostalgia or anti-nostalgia for their own past struggles, are inclined to feel that increased community and support has come at the cost of intellectual depth and rigour.

The Leeds University sociology department, which accepted my application to study for a graduate degree, was very theoretical. Its chair, the late Zygmunt Bauman, was a Polish émigré who had a monumental command of social theory. Criticised for working for the secret services in communist Eastern Europe when he was a very young man, and the target of a suspicious burglary in 2015 when his papers were ransacked and his laptop stolen, Bauman nonetheless became one of the greatest intellectuals of the last 30 or 40 years, with more than 300,000 citations to his name. When I turned in my first paper reviewing the state-of-the-art of the sociology of education to my supervisor, he suggested that I transfer to Bauman given what he saw as my potential as a social theorist. Bauman was a formidable figure, even then, and in the years to come I would be very moved when, in his 2004 book on *Identity*,

How to Build a Theory

he quoted a paragraph of my work on the same subject and honoured me as 'a uniquely perceptive observer of the contemporary cultural scene'.[1] It was, one of my Boston College colleagues said to me, 'like being anointed by God'.

But while I loved social theory, and although I consumed the books of every great 'grand' theorist, living and dead, that I could at the time – Jürgen Habermas, Michel Foucault, Antonio Gramsci, Erving Goffman, and more – in the end, social theory was a means to feed my greater passion for understanding education. In many respects, though, I was still fortunate to be doing my PhD on sociology of education in a sociology department where I encountered the authors and works of some of the greatest minds of the time rather than consuming them in derivative form within an education faculty. Sociology gave me frameworks to look at the world and things to think with which were not tied to one idea or paradigm to which I would subordinate myself, but that enabled me to move between one perspective and another then back again, and to forge my own intellectual pathways and build my own theories.

Anyone and everyone of distinction in British social theory came through our department. Ralph Miliband, firebrand father of the two Blairite Milibands – David and Ed – had us hanging on his every word when he taught us, as he did in his 1975 book on *The State in Capitalist Society*, that inequality and power weren't just theoretical questions, as they were for the ill-fated French philosophers of the day, like Louis Althusser, who strangled his wife, and Nicol Poulantzas, who threw himself out of a window.[2] Rather, you could use evidence to map the interests and interconnections of the ruling class throughout the state in its exclusive networks, elite private schools, senior echelons of the church, and cabinet membership of Conservative governments.

Future BBC Radio 4 presenter Professor Laurie Taylor modelled how sociology needn't always be earnest but could be entertaining and playful too. He came to deliver a memorable talk on his

The Making of an Educator

research on long-term, maximum-security prisoners where he compared his qualitative approach that tried to get into prisoners' minds and experience with more traditional psychological testing that did no such thing. One of the most outrageous standardised test items administered to these lifers and murderers, he pointed out, was the question, 'Do you feel you are able to liven up a rather dull cocktail party?'[3]

The most impressive and, for me, influential presenter to come through was Anthony (Tony) Giddens. Giddens is listed among the top five most cited authors in the humanities and has published more than 30 books. With ambitious titles like *The Constitution of Society*, Giddens' works accomplish what practically no others have been able to do – brilliant integrations and syntheses of contrasting and sometimes conflicting theoretical perspectives.[4] Giddens has brought together Left and Right, macro and micro, old and new ideas that almost everyone else has kept apart to deepen our understandings of the world we are in, free of ideological zealotry.

In a remarkable range of analyses of subjects as diverse as society, intimacy, modernity, and identity, Giddens laid the foundations for a theory of the Third Way that would provide intellectual underpinnings for the political strategy of Prime Minister Tony Blair in the UK, President Bill Clinton in the United States, and Chancellor Gerhard Schröder in Germany. This Third Way, Giddens argued, did not overly invest in the institutions of the state (First Way), and nor did it overcommit to the free market (Second Way). Instead, it forged a path between and beyond these alternatives, such as in dealing with crime as well as the causes of crime.[5]

Giddens was not yet 40 when he came to deliver a public lecture at Leeds. In one hour, with no notes, he took us on a tour and critique of classical and contemporary social theories, showing the strengths and weaknesses of each before masterfully bringing

How to Build a Theory

them together. His talk was deep, lucid, organised, and completely original – a thing of intellectual beauty. He never faltered or hesitated, and he finished, to the second, right on time. The moment he stopped, I recall thinking, 'That's what I want to do!'

I was too overawed to approach Giddens at the end, but some years later, when I had become a lecturer at Oxford University, he wrote to me, by hand, to let me know the high regard in which he held my work, and to ask if I would write a book on social theory and education for his Social Theory series. It was a huge compliment that, of all the people he might have approached to master this field and explain it to others, he had turned to me, still one of the youngest around, even though we had never met. One of my small regrets is that I turned him down. In my view, Margaret Thatcher's policies in education had swept away most UK education scholars' interest in anything that had theoretical depth. My book would have no readers, I felt. It was some compensation when, more than 20 years later, in 2009, Tony Giddens graciously endorsed 'the unique and excellent text' that Dennis Shirley and I wrote on *The Fourth Way* by saying, 'It is high time for a Fourth Way of social and educational reform,' which, he noted, we had outlined for the first time.[6]

Big Things and Small Things

What do you do when some young up-and-comer takes a piece of your best work, one of your finest accomplishments, and rips it to shreds in front of everyone else, before your very eyes?

As a 1980s chart-topping song said, 'every generation blames the one before'.[7] Young scholars tear down old icons so they can make space for their own work. They kill off their mothers and fathers and make orphans of themselves. Modernists are superseded by postmodernists. Class inequality is displaced by gender equity. Both are surpassed by researchers of gender identity and critical race

The Making of an Educator

theory. Quantitative researchers give way to qualitative ones, then quantitative methods make a comeback again.

As a professor, I have encouraged these generational challenges and successions, even in relation to my own work. Unlike some of my colleagues, I can't stand intellectual disciples. If, by any chance, I ever was to get disciples, I would banish them all, and Judas would be the last of them. I want people to be independent thinkers, read widely, respect what they learn, confront any misconceptions and shortcomings, challenge their leaders, keep them honest, and forge their own path through it all. Apart from hate towards others and unquestioning idolatry of one's own paradigm, I want intellectual breadth and freedom. It is far better to engage with the work of previous generations instead of cancelling or ignoring it. The sunshine never stays in one place. Those who now bask in its glow will find themselves back in the shadows soon enough.

In September 1978, while I was still working at the teacher's college, I was short-listed for a job at the Open University, one of the world's first distance learning institutions that was already a leader in my own discipline – the sociology of education. The head of department was the same Peter Woods who had authored 'Teaching for Survival'. He was also the organiser of a small annual conference at St Hilda's College, Oxford, to which I had been invited, and which was taking place just a short time before my upcoming interview. I was presenting a paper in the presence of my potential future employer. Almost everyone else in the room – many of them leading lights or future leading lights in the discipline – knew this. In a way, I was pitching for a position right in front of them. How would I play it?

By late 1978, I had written and thought about my case study data and built the rudiments of a theory around it. It took a few speculative leaps beyond all the micro data into the theoretical stratosphere, but the most convincing parts of my arguments were

How to Build a Theory

about the interactions and perceptions of the teachers themselves. I felt dissatisfied not only with my own shortcomings in trying to connect my schools to the wider society. I was also impatient with how the field itself was failing to address this question. Sociology, as a discipline, was abundant with Grand Theory, and I read as much of it as I could get my hands on. But the micro theorists of everyday interaction and the macro theorists of social order and conflict were mainly ignoring or talking past one another.

Just as Anthony Giddens had done so brilliantly in the world of general social theory, I wanted to see how I might connect not just macro theory to micro data, but also how I could integrate macro theories of big things with micro theories of small things in education too.[8] I guess I was trying to do my own sociological equivalent of integrating theories of relativity with quantum mechanics in physics! Before I even knew about my upcoming interview, I had already begun to construct my paper as an attempt to create an ambitious theoretical synthesis.

The presentation began well enough. It cited one of my favourite sociologists, the American C. Wright Mills, who, in his 1959 classic, *The Sociological Imagination*, argued that the purpose of sociology was to show the relationship between the self and society and, specifically, to connect personal troubles, such as being out of work, to public issues, such as the conditions that create unemployment.[9] This, I began, was what we should be trying to do in the field of education.

In an overly complicated effort to connect just about everything of note that had ever been written in the sociology of education up to that point, I then took on the macro theorists of society and the implications that their work had for education. After critiquing two of the commonly agreed founders of the discipline, the conservative Frenchman and former teacher Émile Durkheim and the more centrist German sociologist Max Weber, who popularised the concept of bureaucracy and invented the idea of the Protestant work ethic,

The Making of an Educator

I turned to the modern heirs of a third founder of sociological thinking, Karl Marx.

The hottest text in my field at the time was by two US Marxist political economists, Samuel Bowles and Herb Gintis. It was titled *Schooling in Capitalist America*.[10] One of the most central and contentious concepts in the book was what they called a 'correspondence thesis'. Schools, they argued, reproduced in microcosm the social relations of capitalist production. For example, streamed classes in high schools mirrored the class system of society. My paper pointed to how these claims were oversimplified. It also described clear exceptions that more micro studies were revealing. These included the fact that some of the lower streams or tracks in secondary schools had incorporated elements of project work and curriculum integration to motivate students, contrary to what the correspondence thesis might have predicted in terms of low-level, draconian regimes of rule-following.

Earlier in the paper, I had abseiled theoretically down to the micro level where scholars were researching the fine-grained details of classroom interaction. They came off little better in my critique. Micro and macro alike, I visited a plague on both their houses. The micro researchers, I argued, lived a life of splendid isolation. They acknowledged there was a place for a macro theory of schooling and society but disavowed wanting anything to do with it. I challenged this view and pointed to several examples of how what went on in the everyday world of schools couldn't be understood properly without some grasp of the social context surrounding those schools. It would be untenable, these days, for example, to interpret classroom interactions involving Black or Brown pupils without some grasp of the meaning of race and the nature of racism within the wider society.

My St Hilda's presentation was going well, and although the written version was, again, far too long, I had learned to emphasise key points more effectively in my oral deliveries by this time. Everyone remained attentive. They all looked like they were with

How to Build a Theory

me. I returned to my case for the importance of a micro-macro synthesis in the sociology of education, and then I homed in on one of the few scholars who had attempted it – Peter Woods. At this point, as they told me later, members of the audience thought, 'Well, this is going to be an interesting approach.' Eyes turned towards him, then back to me.

I started off by giving a précis of what his theory offered. He had provided what I called a split-level model. Some influences and controls on schooling, pupils, and teachers were social, he said, in how schools socialised pupils into capitalist society through the behaviour they expected and the curriculum they imposed. But, harkening back to his earlier work on survival strategies, Woods then also claimed that some controls were not social but products of how teachers and others responded to constraints in the immediate situation – like class sizes, school buildings, or the recent raising of the school leaving age. Basically, both the micro and the macro people had a point, in Woods' view.[11] They could simply coexist, side by side.

Woods was wrong, I argued. If elements of the situation were to blame, according to Woods, then schools could be improved by fixing the situation without attending to the society. For him, the situation stopped pretty much at the school gates or, at the most, at the doors of government policy. But these constraints did not come from nowhere. Factors that are ostensibly situational in nature, I said, 'may well have their origins in the changing social, economic and political conditions of capitalist society'.

I turned to a current example – an economically induced Great Education Debate in 1976, which had spawned a 'new rhetoric' of education and educational change. The thoughts that came next turned out to be chillingly prescient of what would happen to state education, and the changing situations that would define the new educational world of pupils, parents, and teachers, over the next half century.

The Making of an Educator

> There has been a gentle, if rapid, filtering of the new rhetoric and its accompanying practices of 'assessment', 'evaluation', 'standards' and so on into the everyday working assumptions of the advisory service, the Department of Education and Science, colleges of education, and so forth. A new context is being shaped, a new set of situations is being framed, in which present and future teachers will find themselves. The language and practice of 'accountability' is so quickly becoming a part of college curriculum courses and of educational practice in general, that its political and economic origins will soon be lost sight of. It will become just one more set of elements to be considered as part of *the situation,* and to be taken into account by the teacher when formulating his [sic] survival strategies. The split-level model will, I fear, direct us away from rather than towards these extremely important issues.[12]

The culminating part of my paper was brilliant, I thought. It was also relentless. It gathered momentum and did not ease up for a moment. I had seen the future, and Woods' model lay broken in pieces before it. Like the singer in Coldplay's lyric, it seemed, 'I was born to kill any angel on my windowsill'![13]

Peter Woods sat there in his chair at the head of the group. Everyone looked on. And I felt a surge of regret. I had gone too far. I may have hurt the man I most respected. Instead of being a stimulating intellectual critique, the presentation could now have turned into a career train wreck or, to be more precise, a hot mess in a train wreck inside a hurricane.

My peers turned out to be less harsh on me than I was being on myself. My future employer paused. His eyes scanned the room. He took a deep breath. Then he spoke. 'Well,' he said, 'I suppose that's back to the drawing board for Woods!'

Everybody laughed, including me. The sense of relief was palpable. The intellectual father had not been slain. No one would let me become an orphan, least of all him. From that moment on, Peter Woods commanded my unswerving support. Irony, humility, and a little self-mockery are among the greatest intellectual leadership skills there are.

Round the Mulberry Bush

I joined the Open University in January 1979. I didn't fully realise at the time what a remarkable institution it was. Along with Canada's University of Athabasca, it was established in 1969 as one of the world's first distance learning institutions using technology rather than just being a postal correspondence course. The brainchild of Prime Minister Harold Wilson and Minister of State for Education Jennie Lee, it became known to many as the university of the second chance for members of a post-Second World War generation that had never been able to study for a degree in residence first time around.

The OU, as it quickly became known, initially had its headquarters in London. In the early 1970s, it moved to the new town of Milton Keynes, supposedly a model Garden City, but quickly derided for its 130 roundabouts, for its Brutalist architecture which included roads with unromantic names like the V (Vertical) 7, and the H (Horizontal) 5, and for a cluster of controversial concrete cows that have, over the years, been vandalised, beheaded, and even taken hostage. By a quirk of fate, the principal planner for Milton Keynes, John de Monchaux, would later become the Aga Khan Professor of Architecture at the Massachusetts Institute of Technology, as well as a neighbour in and fellow trustee of our small condominium association in Boston, to which my wife and I moved in 2002.

The OU is now the largest university in the UK with approximately 200,000 students. Its alumni include prominent figures and celebrities, such as the entertainer Lenny Henry, celebrity chef Nadiya

The Making of an Educator

Hussain, TV adventurist Steve Backshall, and the late TED Talk superstar Sir Ken Robinson. The OU took its first students and launched its first modular programmes in 1971. The education courses helped get the OU off to a racing start by recruiting thousands of teachers who wanted to upgrade their qualifications from their three-year teacher training college certificates to a recognised degree, and thereby also increase their salaries. Courses consisted of printed correspondence materials (course units), occasional TV programmes, a one-week summer residency, and local evening classes, popularised in Willy Russell's play, *Educating Rita*, which were taught in regional centres by academics from other universities.

I was told that the sociology of education discipline group was divided into two camps, micro and macro. The hope was that I could create some kind of bridge between them. One of the key education courses was called *School and Society* – a sociology of education course that included a 40-chapter course reader.[14] The chapters encompassed a wide range of materials including micro-level ethnographies of classroom life, studies of school culture and organisation, and macro-level perspectives authored by theorists as varied as Karl Marx and conservative cultural critic F. R. Leavis. By 1976, this reader had expanded into a 50-chapter, two-volume compendium, *The Process of Schooling* (predominantly micro) and *Schooling and Capitalism* (mainly macro).[15]

After a delayed house move, I arrived in the spring to see a campus centred around a blossoming mulberry tree outside a practically empty university library. The campus was almost completely devoid of physical students. My task of bridging the micro and macro communities was decided at the first lunchtime. One group of course writers and editors, including well-known academics like Roger Dale, future Cambridge University professor Madeleine Arnot, and Leon Trotsky lookalike Ben Cosin, had lunch together at the university bar. The micro-oriented writers, including the head of department Peter Woods and Martyn Hammersley, who would write one of the most cited ethnographic research methods books of all time, went for lunch in the coffee lounge. Who did I really belong to?

Like Hammersley and Woods, I had small children and I didn't drink alcohol at lunchtime. And there my perceived ideological fate was sealed. To all intents and purposes, I was not a macro theorist, and I was patently not a Marxist (the most popular macro theory at the time). I was one of the interactionists. Instead of building a bridge, I was just one more academic fruitlessly going round and round the theoretical mulberry bush. In schools and universities alike, educational subcultures are determined not just by what people believe but also by who they befriend.

A Cock-and-Bull Story

I was appointed in the same year that Margaret Thatcher won her first election. Her assault on university funding, especially in social sciences, would mean that temporary contracts like mine would not be renewed. So, my time at the OU would be short. But it was far from uneventful.

Milton Keynes was where we purchased our first home. We were already behind the rest of the middle class in house-buying because I had been a research student for three years. We moved into a little terraced house, a fixer-upper, round the corner from Martyn Hammersley and his family in Wolverton, just up the street from the old railway carriage works and on the edge of the new town. We quickly bonded with a marvellously supportive community. We were all young professionals. The mums hung out together with their tiny tots during the day. Because the OU campus had no students, I could often work from home, so I was able to have lunch with the family on many days, and I was always there for bath-time and bedtime. We had a baby-sitting circle, and both mums and dads took their turn in each other's homes. The dads formed a small running group, and every Sunday morning I would also turn out for the OU Reserves football team in the Fifth Division of the Milton Keynes and District Sunday League.

Money was perilously tight. Inflation was running at 13%. We struggled to pay bills. At Christmas, we bought almost all the children's toys second hand through newspaper ads. Pauline took on part-time work in the evenings. First, she tried selling Avon cosmetics door-to-door – a product in which she had no interest and a line of work for which she had little talent. Then, in the evenings, she became a waitress at the Cock Hotel in nearby Stony Stratford, 100 yards down the street from the Bull Hotel – the two pubs being the origin of the phrase 'cock-and-bull story'. We kept a little lined notebook of weekly expenditures, and if we had five pounds left at the end of the week, I could go for a beer with a friend at the bottom of our street. Many times, I couldn't. I continued to do our own car repairs, which now extended to patching up rusting bodywork and replacing rear axles and braking systems. Our experience may have been a bit extreme financially, but whenever we review young colleagues' promotion and tenure cases, and their portfolios of accomplishments today, it is important not to be oblivious to the life circumstances that many of them are dealing with and how this affects their performance.

Our children were tiny and took up much of our emotional and physical energy. Through all this, my unfinished PhD chapters stared down at me from our bookshelves like disapproving albatrosses. All this took an undoubted toll on my health. I plunged into a depression, triggered by job insecurity, overwork, family demands, and the punishing intellectual standards I often set for myself. It lasted all through the winter as I sat in my pyjamas for many hours each day.

There was more behind it than this, though. In hindsight, I had had my first depression when I was preparing for the selective 11+ test at the end of primary school when I had no energy, wouldn't

How to Build a Theory

play outside, and my parents kept dragging me to the doctors for tests for leukaemia and other suspected ailments. Depressions would continue to stalk me every few years, like Winston Churchill's metaphorical black dog, until, in my mid-50s, a life-changing diagnosis for adult attention deficit hyperactivity disorder (ADHD) and a few sessions of priceless counselling equipped me with strategies that have thankfully spared me from further episodes.

New Tricks

The work itself was quite different from my previous job, and indeed from the work of most academics. It took me on a rapid learning curve. I am an old dog now. But then, I was not much more than an intellectual puppy. And I had to learn a lot of new tricks, not just because I was starting a new job, but also because it was unlike almost any other in higher education. We didn't have any in-person students but, somehow, over the miles and mainly through written texts, we had to devise ways to engage our students in what they were learning. We also had to collaborate a lot with our fellow course writers, and to learn to accept what could be very challenging public feedback from them. Furthermore, we had to master the arts of scriptwriting, reading autocues, and even appropriate studio wear.

To outsiders, making TV programmes might have seemed like the most glamorous aspect of the job, but anyone looking back at those early video cassettes will realise that glamourous is the last adjective you would assign to famed and, in comedy sketches, defamed OU lecturers' selections of sartorial dress when unkempt hair, scraggy beards, and scruffy sweaters dominated the airwaves.

I co-wrote and presented a programme to support a course unit I had written on 'Teaching and Control'.[16] Interspersed with archive film material from secondary school classrooms were studio segments where I walked in front of and between three large circular

The Making of an Educator

boards, each demonstrating a particular type of classroom control. I practised finding my chalk marks on the floor where I had to plant my feet. I walked between them as I read my lines from the autocue. I gained confidence. I even began to feel a bit like Robin Day, the noted presenter of the BBC current affairs programme *Panorama* as I strode purposefully from one illustrative board to the next. There were a few retakes, but in general I felt I was handling it rather well.

The only problem was that I got no advanced coaching on what I should wear. These days, when I make a TV appearance, I am advised on what *not* to wear – nothing jazzy, no fancy ties or patterns. I go into make-up, and they powder the bald spot on my head. But in 1980, on low budget OU TV, there was little make-up and not much coaching.

Our struggling finances left me with few wardrobe options, so my ill-fitting rust-coloured sweater looked like it had been purchased

I witnessed my terracotta torso float across the studio like Banquo's ghost in Shakespeare's *Macbeth*, invisible from the waist down.

How to Build a Theory

from a thrift store that had acquired its inventory from another thrift store. But the biggest mistake was my pants. I was clearly wearing the wrong trousers. My choice, I thought, was quite smart for the period – brand new black corduroy. But I had not been forewarned that, apart from the white boards hanging behind me, the rest of the studio would be in complete darkness. When the programme had been edited and was finally broadcast, I switched on my TV one Wednesday afternoon and, to my horror, witnessed my terracotta torso float across the studio like Banquo's ghost in Shakespeare's *Macbeth*, invisible from the waist down.[17] Still, I was not yet 30, I was on TV, and I had already acquired some basic skills of scriptwriting, run sheets, and on-camera presence that would set me up for media appearances in the years that awaited me abroad and ahead.

The other big learning curve was collaborative course-writing. A course consisted of up to 30-something course units for students to read and respond to. As a course member, you might be responsible for writing three or four of these units. Each unit would go through up to four drafts. The drafts would be circulated to the course team who, in a meeting of a dozen or more members, were gathered round a huge rectangular table. One by one, each of them delivered their feedback to you. The protocol was to listen to all the feedback before responding. It was a rigorous process, and sometimes also an intimidating one. This was Britain in the early 1980s. There was honest praise where it was due but no gratuitous flattery, no gilding the lily. When a dozen people in succession said your unit was too long, or unclear, or didn't contain enough ways for students to engage with it, it was hard to dispute what you heard or to duck responsibility for acting on it in your next draft.

Thinking Together

Collaboration is not a norm in much of academic life, certainly in the arts and social sciences. I have worked in faculties and departments, some of them quite recently, where junior members tell me that it isn't accepted practice to read each other's work. So, they learn to keep their heads down and get on with things by themselves, as one of them put it. But in my teacher's college job, I had already gained immense fulfilment from discussing and debating the core ideas on which our courses were based with people who were my colleagues, peers, and football team members. And now, at the OU, Martyn Hammersley, a colleague, neighbour, friend, and fearsome table tennis opponent, would respond to any draft article that I or anyone else sent him with margins full of scrawled comments and feedback that were as incisive as they were hard to decipher. The OU course design process institutionalised collegial feedback and turned it into an expectation and a ritual. In terms of an academic career, I had been gifted an extraordinarily lucky start.

Today, I try to give substantive feedback on any assignment, chapter, or paper that people send me. I never provide a foreword or an endorsement for someone else's book without reading every page of their manuscript first. Being an intellectual requires me to treat my students' and my immediate colleagues' work with respect, including when I am less than fully satisfied with it. If I am a discussant for a conference panel, I will try to weave a narrative through all the closely read presentations, and then say something of substance about each one. And if I am to be honest and critical about what I have heard, I spare the most junior members of the panel from public rebuke and save my toughest comments for those who are, professionally speaking, big enough to take it. Working collaboratively should not be a new trick for our emerging scholars. We need to make it the oldest trick in the book.

How to Build a Theory

Creating a new theory is not as dangerous as firefighting or law enforcement. Unlike surgery, it doesn't immediately save any lives either. But connecting what happens in schools every day to how the society works around them is no mean feat. Make no bones about it, this sort of intellectual work is hard. It makes your brain hurt sometimes. And it matters. As psychologist Kurt Lewin, who invented action research in the 1940s, put it, 'there is nothing as practical as a good theory'.[18] But creating and combining new theories doesn't have to happen in the long shadows of loneliness. It should be an experience of living colour rather than feeling like having to perform in cinema noir.

We all need to get out of our own heads sometimes. A community of scholars that respects each other's work, is curious about what it means, and is open to reciprocal influence can turn doctoral study and scholarship, at all levels, from being an accumulation of individual papers and metrics into a shared experience of intellectual stimulation and accomplishment. Long-distance thinking doesn't have to be an isolated endeavour. It can be pursued as a great intellectual adventure with others.

Six Secrets of Theory Building

If you are conducting your own research or enquiry, you don't always have to build your own theory. You can test, apply, or refine another one in relation to new data that you collect. But if you want to make an original contribution to knowledge, to come up with an important idea or insight that no one has really thought of before, then, at some point, you will, in effect, be building a new theory. Drawing on my own experience during and after the period covered in this book, here are six things – or what, in one of his books, Michael Fullan calls 'six secrets' – that might help you in that process.[19]

The Making of an Educator

1. Read Books
Read books, not just articles or abstracts of articles. There is an increasingly popular practice in graduate social science programmes to conduct literature reviews only of peer-reviewed articles. And in the age of online literacy and short attention spans, there is a tendency to fall into the TLDR (too long, didn't read) trap and avoid anything that isn't quick and easy. As a researcher, just reading scholarly articles can make you current. And it is quicker to read articles, or sometimes just abstracts of articles, of course. This can be helpful to highlight new evidence and to get work completed faster when deadlines are looming. But there is no opportunity to get to grips with arguments in depth, see how they flow, discover what their foundations are, and flex one's intellectual muscles. Try to immerse yourself in big ideas. Read the originals, not summaries or derivatives of them. In fact, originals are often easier to understand. Find the source point of a concept – who invented it, what it originally meant. This helps you to understand what is in the baggage that ideas carry. Don't be academically shallow. Be bold and delve deep.

2. Respect Evidence
One of the best ways to develop a theory is to build it inductively from the evidence by looking for patterns, and then test existing theories with the evidence you have.[20] When it looks like a finding is taking shape, one of the best intellectual disciplines is to look for evidence that might dispute it or disconfirm it. The result is rarely to disprove the entire theory but to elaborate it, so that it can accommodate the exceptions you have discovered. Induction, deduction, looking for patterns, and seeking out exceptions – this is the essence of theory-building.

3. Combine Contrary Theories
Creativity arises from putting together things that, from other people's point of view, don't really belong. Micro and macro theories

or theories from different ends of the political spectrum offer opportunities to explore and integrate unusual combinations. Then, it is a case of working with the creative intellectual tension that all this produces. Sometimes, opposites really can attract. And when it happens, creating something new can be utterly exhilarating. This is how I felt about integrating micro and macro perspectives. And imagine the thrill that Michael Fullan and I felt, years later, when we put together the ideas of profession and capital to make *professional capital* and then discovered that almost no one had ever thought of this concept before.[21]

4. Assign Analytical Time

Time for analysis is often the most neglected feature of project timelines. In research grant proposals, most time is assigned to conduct literature reviews, construct samples, collect data, and then write everything up. Time assigned for analysis is almost always insufficient because it can look like time that is poorly spent where nothing is really happening. But this is priceless thinking time – time to explore unexpected leads and unearth new literature that is related to what you are discovering. Analytical time requires time not just to process data that has already been theorised, but also to be surprised by the data, to follow unanticipated directions, and to search for new theoretical frameworks when the data cannot be explained by the frameworks you started with. In addition to induction and deduction, it can therefore be useful to indulge in a little abduction – time to wander away from the data, take a walk, mull things over, or engage with other literature.[22] Don't think doing all your reading ahead of data collection and analysis absolves you from further reading that helps you to understand and explain what your data show once you have analysed it.

5. Transpose Theories from Other Disciplines

In my research on the emotions of teaching, which I conducted after I had moved to Canada, I took and applied theories from sociology, social psychology, anthropology, and geography to develop a theory of 'emotional geographies' of distance and closeness in teachers' interactions with others in their workplaces.[23] Similarly, in my research on long-term change in education that led towards concepts of sustainability, my co-researcher Dean Fink and I drew on environmental theories of biodiversity and the physics of energy renewal to enrich our own contributions to theories of sustainable leadership.[24] My doctoral thesis was informed by sociology, social psychology, and sociolinguistics – three different disciplines. Be curious about exploring other disciplines. Don't be intimidated by them.

6. Create Diverse Research Teams

Building great theories can come from building great teams with common values and interests but that also include different skills and perspectives. Creative combinations of disparate ideas can arise from the diverse personalities recruited to the team. I learned how to ground my theories more effectively by writing with practitioners like my co-author teachers at Oxford. In later years, I would come to appreciate the contribution of management theory to leadership and change by collaborating with Michael Fullan. Effective, diverse teams can create breakthrough ideas together.

CHAPTER 5
Bias and Integrity

Scholarship or Propaganda?

What happens when those who hold to one theory ignore or insult all the others, or when subscribers to an ideology pay no attention to any evidence that might challenge their allegiances and beliefs? In today's universities and schools, this takes us into the realms of book banning, cancel culture, decolonisation, the handling and mishandling of controversial political issues, heated debates about race and gender identity, and more besides. It takes us into the worlds of critical race theorists, J. K. Rowling, Jordan Peterson, and other controversial figures who have preoccupied school district offices, university campuses, government legislation, and national political campaigns. These controversies are not unique to any one period in history. We can learn a lot from how they have been experienced and handled in the past.

In the 1970s and early 1980s, Marxism and neo-Marxism provoked national scandals to a similar extent as critical race theory and decolonisation do today. Suddenly, almost without warning, I was plunged right into one of them. What I learned then still influences how I think about the bias and integrity of ideas and opinions in schools and universities now.

The Making of an Educator

Less than two years before I joined it, the OU found itself at the centre of a news storm that had links to an international intelligence agency. An education course, E202, 'Schooling and Society', was the target of an article published by the Institute for the Study of Conflict, a right-wing UK think-tank that received funding from the CIA. The author of the article, Professor Julius Gould, accused the editors of one of the two course readers, *Schooling and Capitalism*, of being part of a 'self-justifying web of Marxist faith' that perpetuated 'shameful' and 'shady' critiques of capitalist inequality. Realising that the course would be studied by thousands of teachers pursuing professional upgrading for increased pay, Gould was concerned that Britain's young people would be in the hands of educators who would indoctrinate them with one-sided presentations of extremist views. Gould's paper, titled 'Scholarship or Propaganda?' first published in the *Times Educational Supplement*, was quickly taken up by *The Times*, *The Observer*, and *The Telegraph* newspapers in commentaries that were also highly critical.[1]

We may not always like where critiques come from or approve of the interests or identities that underpin them, but it is important not to let these considerations blind us to the possible validity of any points they raise. We need to listen to our opponents. So, the question, then and now, still matters: was E202 prone to Marxist bias?

When I arrived at the OU in early 1979, Peter Woods informed me that my opening assignment would be to contribute to an enquiry into whether E202 contained the alleged bias. My brief took me over some of the same ground as other reviews of course materials, but it also factored in observations of evening and weekend in-person sessions taught by regional course tutors across the country. Some of these tutors were also the authors of course readings, several were famous figures in the field, and all of them were more experienced than me.

Bias and Integrity

My judgements, then and now, would mainly align with a retrospective analysis by Martyn Hammersley of this extraordinary historical episode and its implications for academic freedom and integrity today. Hammersley, one of E202's course designers and a co-editor of the other course reader, *The Process of Schooling*, concluded that 'it is disputable whether E202 was or was not biased – in terms of coverage, the prominence given to Marxism, or the failure sufficiently to encourage a critical attitude on the part of students'.[2] A lot depended, he said, on 'what standard of evaluation is used'. Even so, when all things were considered, his original and continuing judgement is that there were clear grounds for legitimate criticism.[3]

The position on how schooling reproduces capitalism and its interests is overt and transparent in the introduction to *Schooling and Capitalism*. 'This collection of papers is assembled to show how the capitalist mode of production influences ... schooling,' it stated. Schooling, it argued, is 'the most important institution' in reproducing the social class relations of capitalism. The purpose of the reader was to challenge liberal assumptions that schooling had been a force for 'progressive social change' in terms of fuelling economic growth and technological development, promoting meritocracy and social mobility, and advancing knowledge through a curriculum that was neutral or benign.[4] The course text advanced a viewpoint that was politically controversial and one-sided, but there was nothing 'shady' about how it did so. It was doing what it said on the tin.

However, the other course reader, *The Process of Schooling*, edited by Hammersley and Woods, was organised mainly around micro theories of symbolic interaction.[5] It included little or no material on the role of schools in society. At least half the course content, therefore, was not concerned with capitalism or critiques of liberalism at all. No charges were laid by anyone about symbolic interactionist bias. The point at issue was not one of intellectual imbalance in general, but of an imbalance that tilted towards one politically controversial perspective: Marxism.

There are other reasons why the accusations of political and intellectual bias can be taken with a pinch of salt.

- Significant parts of the critical stance adopted in *Schooling and Capitalism* that were then considered extreme are a normal and prominent part of educational and social debate today. For example, many mainstream thinkers and writers now accept that schools alone don't create social mobility, and that meritocracy is therefore a flawed aim of state education.[6]
- Not all critiques of liberal democracies are Marxist. In *Schooling and Capitalism* itself, later chapters argue that state school systems have been suffocated by bureaucratic control. The very idea of the 'iron cage of bureaucracy' originates with a different sociological founder, Max Weber, and modern versions of it apply more to accusations about the influence of excessive centralisation than about Marxist economics.[7]
- Many other courses and intellectual fields provide one-sided coverage in universities but are (regrettably) not subject to public scrutiny because of it. Classical economics, for example, omits the environmental costs of economic policies and calculations, and as a new and influential generation of women economists points out, it also conceives of national economic outcomes in terms of gross domestic product and 'growth' rather than quality of life.[8]

My own perspective on intellectual bias is not that we should be merely tolerant of free speech and diverse perspectives, but that we should make every effort to include contrary perspectives

Bias and Integrity

in our courses and encourage students to consider, compare, and debate them. For example, when I have listed my work on teacher collaboration for a class reading, I have also set a vigorous critique of my perspective by one of my opponents. Critical race theory is an important theory of racial inequality and oppression, but not the only one, and not all criticisms of this perspective should be dismissed because of the identity, privilege, or politics of those who advance them. Intellectual freedom should be about including adversaries, and unless their work is deeply racist, misogynistic, or hateful in other ways, it should be about treating those opponents with dignity and respect, even when we profoundly disagree with them. And we shouldn't wait until young people get to university for this to happen. It should all start in school with debates considering contrary perspectives, making sense of original historical documents, and so on.

Once course content has been decided, the key question then is how that content is taught. What is the pedagogy like? Hammersley reflects honestly on this issue. 'If one examines the first block of the course there is little encouragement of students to critically engage with the arguments being presented,' he notes. Both course blocks, he continues, the one on *Schooling and Capitalism*, and the one co-edited by him, 'did not sufficiently facilitate critical engagement on the part of students'.[9] This, in a nutshell, was my own conclusion. The presence of bias was at least debatable. But, whatever the content, the one-dimensional, one-directional nature of the pedagogy was unarguable and indefensible.

I handed in my report to my head of department, Peter Woods. He was pleasantly surprised. The report was, in his view, a politically shrewd document. The course did not get off scot-free. It had major shortcomings, but these were pedagogical, not political. And no one was going to raise a national scandal about old-fashioned and ineffective pedagogies. Once you start to shine that light, it can bring all kinds of perspectives and practices out of dark corners that others would rather were left there.

Contortion or Complexity?

In a very short time, neo-Marxism moved on. And so did my relationship to it. From embodying somewhat simplistic explanations of correspondences between schooling and capitalist society or grafting theories of capitalist control onto classroom teaching strategies, Marxists and their followers in education began to take up more complex and nuanced positions. They didn't accept the Bowles and Gintis correspondence principle any more. Education and the state had a degree of autonomy from the capitalist economy and its power structures, they argued. They referred to this as 'relative autonomy'.[10] Picking up on a statement by Friedrich Engels, Marx's co-author, neo-Marxists began to argue that the state superstructure, including education, could act back upon and influence the economic base. Yet somehow, 'in the last instance', to quote a famous phrase of Louis Althusser, capitalist interests still exerted their interests even if, to add to the complexity, that 'lonely hour of the last instance' never completely arrived.[11]

Inconvenient Truths

I invested a lot of energy in trying to get my head around these incredibly contorted arguments. I was drawn to these kinds of Marxism partly because of my concerns about social injustice and inequality. Also, in terms of macro theory in education, if you had an interest in educational and social inequalities, it was almost the only show in town. Then, a chance conversation set me off in a very different direction.

Bias and Integrity

Around the time of my impending move south to the OU, a historian in the Leeds University education department drew my attention to an archive in the Leeds Education Museum of policy letters and memoranda relating to the establishment of middle schools in the West Riding (of Yorkshire) Education Authority. My thesis had already been slowly changing shape. From comparing progressive and traditional primary schools, it had turned into a study of English middle schools (the selected primary schools happened to be middle schools that had not been studied in detail previously).

By 1980, I had published my first edited book, *Middle Schools: Origins, Ideology and Practice,* which included my own chapter on 'The Ideology of the Middle School' that discussed how English middle schools, like their US counterparts and predecessors, were founded on an ideology of providing early adolescents with a smooth transition from the one-teacher class system of nurturing primary schools to the more impersonal subject-based system of secondary schools.[12] Yet, in the United States and England alike, I observed, it often seemed that as school populations changed, middle schools were established more as a way of providing an administratively convenient way to reuse existing buildings. Their romantic ideological rationale was, in this sense, perhaps little more than a cover for a more basic and brutal economic reality.

The administrative convenience argument seemed to offer an opportunity for me to bring in neo-Marxist theory to explain the on-the-ground realities in the schools. Middle schools, I could argue, were 'overdetermined'.[13] Perhaps a liberal and romantically inclined ideology which drew on educational progressivism was masking an educational reform solution that minimised the costs of public expenditure in a capitalist economy.

However, access to the treasure trove of historical data that took me more than a year and many library visits to explore prompted me to trade the philosophical speculations of French theory for a full-on Miliband-like engagement with actual evidence. The West Riding had been responsible for persuading the Ministry of Education to change the existing law, written in 1944, that transfer to secondary education could only occur at age 11. In the early 1960s, the region's chief education officer, a charismatic champion of open education named Sir Alec Clegg, persuaded the ministry to change the law to allow transfer to secondary schools at ages 12 or 13, and thereby permit the creation of middle schools. This happened after he had communicated with his 28 different school divisions on how best to change from a selective system of secondary education to a non-selective comprehensive school system in ways that would make the most efficient use of existing school buildings.

The solution to the educational reorganisation problem was not the same for each division, though. So, as an evidence-based test, I decided to select three divisions that implemented different strategies. Could my hitherto preferred neo-Marxist theory of over-determination explain these three different outcomes, separately and together?

The truth is that no matter how I manipulated the neo-Marxist framework of overdetermination, it could not explain all three different policy outcomes. So, I scouted around for other theoretical alternatives and came upon pluralism, which argued that there were often multiple causes behind social changes. In the pluralist stance, different pressure groups and status groups with varied goals and vested interests compete, collaborate, and compromise to bring about changes that are favourable for them.[14] Some divisions in West Yorkshire, especially those in traditional coal-mining communities, were driven by a strong egalitarian impulse, for example, while others, more inclined towards meritocratic arguments, wanted a system that could provide Latin teachers for pupils from age 11, so they would have a chance of getting into Oxford and Cambridge universities.

Bias and Integrity

In view of these multicausal factors, I argued, policymakers like Clegg 'have to exercise strategic dexterity in order to devise proposals for change which are acceptable to the various groups who voice their competing demands in any particular locality'.[15] The diverse outcomes of comprehensive school reform were, in other words, a result of multicausal interactions. Pluralism was a better fit for my evidence.

Where did this leave neo-Marxism? Well, although Marxism couldn't explain what the different divisions did, it could help to explain what they *didn't* do. It couldn't show how different divisional policies were determined or even overdetermined by capitalist forces, even in the last instance, but it could show how they were delimited in the range of options that were available to them.

I cited a neo-Marxist theorist who was popular in the sociology of education at the time – an American, Erik Olin Wright. Wright talked about a boundary-setting process of structural limitation in which 'some social structure establishes limits within which some other structure or process can vary, and it establishes probabilities for the specific structures or processes that are possible within those limits'.[16] In short, capitalist requirements might not be able to explain what was on the table for different school divisions, but it could help people to see what was off the table. Policymakers like Clegg and ministry officials preferred incremental change that fitted local circumstances and economic restrictions here and there rather than transformational change that might overturn the entire educational order.

Where did this leave things? First, it brought together two traditions that had mainly ignored each other: Marxism and pluralism. It was a Giddens-inspired moment for me – a combination of Left and Right or at least Left and Centre. The engagement of Marxism and pluralism could be a rapprochement, not a win–lose battle. 'It is difficult, and perhaps futile,' I concluded, 'to propose that the limits to change are more significant than the different possibilities contained within them, or vice versa.'[17]

Second, my paper and the research on which it was based introduced a new way of approaching the micro-macro problem. No longer was it a question of grafting Grand Theory onto evidence of micro-level interactions. The realm of society, or at least of educational policy, could now be treated as a question of evidence about micro-interactions. It wasn't just teachers and pupils who interacted. Policymakers did as well. For obvious reasons of political discretion and secrecy, there is little documented evidence on how policymakers, and especially politicians, make educational decisions. But I had struck it lucky. An entire vault of historical data had become available to me.

Third, my obsessive quest to know everything about everything, to combine different theories, and to connect ethnographic evidence collected from two schools with historical data sitting in the archives of Leeds Education Museum delayed the completion of my PhD by at least two more years. I knew all too well that my thesis continued to be an albatross around my neck, but I was now falling tragically in love with it.

Distortion and Frustration

As I sat for days on end in the archives, and struggled some more with mastering new theories that could help me make sense of what I was reading, I began to become frustrated and impatient with other scholars who hung on to their closed ideological positions without looking at the evidence or opening themselves to other theoretical alternatives. My frustration turned into a kind of resentment, and this led to two or three explosive papers that were, essentially, attacks on my neo-Marxist colleagues. As someone who had been closely allied to neo-Marxist theories, I must, in

Bias and Integrity

sociological terms, have seemed as annoying as a born-again evangelist or reformed smoker.

Looking back on the titles of my papers in the early 1980s, it is hard to deny that I wilfully attracted controversy. I published a critical review of education books by the prominent US neo-Marxist Michael Apple under the very naughty title, 'Apple Crumbles'.[18] With Hammersley, I wrote a critique of the work of the University of Birmingham Centre for Contemporary Cultural Studies (CCCS), which had become an icon of more complex Marxist thinking. This review used another eye-catching pun for its title, 'CCCS Gas!' (CS gas is a weapon used by law enforcement to control and disperse protests).[19]

The full force of my critique of neo-Marxism, though, was contained in an article under another title that was also lacking in understatement: 'Resistance and Relative Autonomy Theories: Problems of Distortion and Incoherence in Recent Marxist Analyses of Education'.[20] I laid my charges concerning obfuscating relative autonomy theories against notable Marxists in the field – namely, Michael Apple and Henry Giroux in the United States, and Roger Dale, Geoff Whitty, and Madeleine Arnot in the UK. All these academics were already prominent figures at the time and went on to have impressive careers.

To the *contortions* of relative autonomy theories, I added the charge that theories of pupils' resistance produced *distortions* of what they did and why they did it. Resistance, I argued, became an attractive narrative for neo-Marxists because it expressed the hope that through their unwillingness to comply with the dictates of state control, young people embodied the possibility of radical transformation towards equality and social justice. They weren't fooled by capitalist oppression in this view. In their own inarticulate, sometimes maladroit, and often self-defeating ways, they saw straight through it.

Neo-Marxist observers of pupil resistance were so driven by their political agenda to bring about social transformation, I said, that they overextended what counted as resistance to make it seem a much bigger deal than it really was.[21] Minor infractions, pranks, episodes of boredom, withdrawals of enthusiasm, and general disengagement were all evidence of young people's working-class insight into and refusal to comply with capitalist state control. The 'indiscriminate application of the category "resistance" to almost all pupil actions that do not count as absolute and willing compliance with teachers' demands' was an ideologically driven distortion of the evidence, I concluded.[22]

When word got around that I would be presenting this paper at the annual Sociology of Education conference in Birmingham, in January 1981, in advance of its publication, I came onstage to see several subjects of my critique in the front row, arms folded, facing me down, waiting with their challenges. It was a stern test.

It is not clear what contribution, if any, this presentation made to subsequent movements in the field away from the dominance of neo-Marxist perspectives at the macro level. I couldn't hang around after my speech to discuss people's responses in depth. We had two children under 3 years old. Pauline was alone with them, in the depths of winter, without a car, and I needed to get back home as soon as I could.

Within a few years, though, many of the targets of my criticism had also moved on as the field embraced new perspectives, like postmodernism, which addressed the world's complexities differently. And in most cases we reconciled. Intellectual battles that seem so big when they occur diminish greatly in importance with the passage of time.

Integration and Integrity

What have I learned from this moment in my work, my career, and the evolution of the field that has lasting value for education and academic research, and for my own contributions to it? Three issues stand out.

1. Evidence
Evidence matters. It isn't the only thing, and we shouldn't be uncritical about 'what works', how we collect data, and what it all means. Evidence is rarely self-evident. But this is no reason for ignoring or dismissing it. Without evidence, we just make stuff up and end up spinning around inside our own collective echo chambers of shared delusions. In the resistance and relative autonomy paper, I argued that many Grand Theorists, Marxist or otherwise, 'are simply more at home with imaginative conjecture and assertion than with the unavoidably messy world of empirical research'.[23]

Respect for evidence should sometimes challenge what we have passionately believed to be true. My analysis of historical evidence changed my own relationship to neo-Marxism. This has not been my only pivot. For example, in the early 2000s, I thought that large-scale literacy reforms in Ontario, Canada, would repeat the errors of literacy reform under the Blair government in the UK. But through observing the impact of reform in 10 school districts, I discovered that teachers rather liked the new approach to literacy. It was the high-stakes testing that was the problem.

What is your relationship to evidence? Have you ever changed your beliefs about something because you were interested in and open about what the data showed – perhaps about the best way to teach, about how to deal with behaviour, or about approaches to inclusion? Or if the evidence seems to challenge your beliefs, do you, like 1970s neo-Marxists, climate change deniers, or doomsday cults that are faced with the fact that their prophecies about the end of the world have failed, generate more and more contorted rationalisations and circumlocutions to justify your existing position and keep on doing exactly as you please?

2. Openness

Bringing together Marxism with pluralism, and micro- with macro-perspectives were attempts at the appeal that Hammersley and I made for a 'genuine spirit of intellectual openness'.[24] A basic course about 'school and society' should never have been rewritten so that the societal aspect of education was largely expressed as a narrow neo-Marxist analysis of 'schooling and capitalism'. The fact that this was not the only example of closed-mindedness in university life is not, in the end, a sufficient defence. Educators especially need to model curiosity and humility about the value of other ways of thinking. In the words of the writer Graham Greene in his classic novel, *Monsieur Quixote*, 'I hope – friend – that you sometimes doubt, too. It's human to doubt.'[25]

In the late 1970s, it was neo-Marxism in sociology and education that bordered on intellectual fundamentalism. Almost 50 years later, academic self-righteousness manifests itself in other ways. Gender-critical feminists have been harassed and cancelled for claiming that biological sex forms part of the definition of gender. Critical race theorists who attack inherent White privilege have been less prepared to criticise extreme wealth privilege that sometimes includes people of colour. Purging the curriculum of historical controversy, of gender issues, or of culturally diverse materials to protect and perpetuate an overly positive view of the British Empire or colonialism in general is equally unacceptable too.

Intellectual freedom is about tolerance for multiple voices and perspectives, even if all they create is a cacophony of opinions. Intellectual integrity is about exercising openness to, curiosity about, and engagement with those other perspectives, even and especially when they challenge one's own existing commitments and beliefs.

3. Left Back

By the early 1980s, rock and roll was over. Punk was going full steam ahead. Margaret Thatcher was laying waste to manufacturing jobs and the labour union movement. More women were finally starting to appear as presenters on conference platforms. Gender equity, followed by anti-racism, and then LGBTQ rights replaced concerns about economic inequalities with cultural ones. This shift was overdue. But the cost was that social class and economic inequality became passé. Marxism went out of style.

Cultural politics gathered pace and identity politics took the stage. Meanwhile, a wealth gap was growing that was the greatest for 100 years, social mobility and equal opportunity were sinking like a stone after their brief flourishing in the 1960s and 1970s, and postmodernists were saying that none of this, and indeed none of anything, was really happening. Material reality was unknowable. Life was all just words. This was easier for philosophers to say than it was for people like my working-class mother to accept when local government wouldn't, under Thatcher's economic austerity, provide her council flat with a new door to keep out the cold in winter.

In recent years, though, and especially during COVID-19, Karl Marx's warnings have come back to haunt us as vast wealth has been concentrated in the hands of fewer and fewer people – over half of it belonging to just 26 people worldwide – with less than 50% remaining for everyone else.[26] Some governments are considering doing what was, just a few years ago, unthinkable – introducing taxes on the very highest earners to fund public investment and provide resources to combat climate change. And in 2024, the socialist president of Brazil, Lula da Silva, started a global movement to tax extreme wealth.[27] In all but name, Marxism is making a comeback.

Marxist economics doesn't explain everything. But for almost 40 years, it was set aside and allowed to explain nothing, as identity politics took its place. The consequence was deepening economic and educational inequalities and growing resentments among all those who were being left behind. In Brexit Britain, Trump's America, and countries across Europe, populists capitalised upon people's sense of loss and their frustrations about being ignored, took up the reins of power, and created culture wars that have been tearing our schools apart. It is high time to put some aspects of Marxist-informed thinking back on the table, so that we can address the serious consequences of extreme economic inequality for everyone.

Postscript

By 1984, after I had left the OU for a lectureship at Oxford University, my former course team colleagues asked me to write a unit on 'Marxism and Relative Autonomy' for E352: Conflict and Change in Education.[28] The unit expanded and developed many of the arguments I have presented in this chapter. By now, following on from the spirit of my review of alleged Marxist bias, it also included activities that would help students to engage critically with what they were reading. These activities asked students:

- To review criticisms of Marxist theories in earlier course units and provide counter-arguments where appropriate.
- To consider whether capitalism and patriarchy exhaust all the limits to educational change.
- In two contrasting readings about pupil resistance, to ask who was doing the resisting, who was not engaged in resistance, and what was being resisted in the examples that were presented.

In other words, course design now included deliberate strategies and directions to encourage and even expect students to take a critical stance towards what they were reading. A clear anti-bias orientation in the pedagogy was adopted in these and other course materials.

Bias and Integrity

The OU paid me £300 as an external consultant to write this unit. It bought us a new settee. It was marketed as an American colonial-style couch with a high back, edged in cherry wood. We called it our Marxist settee. We took it with us to Canada, the United States, and then back to Canada until, after 40 years, it eventually decolonised itself and fell to pieces. This sort of metaphorical irony seems to express the story of my life.

CHAPTER 6

Cultures of Teaching

From the Sewers to the Spires

It was bath-time. Just like every other day. Our baby boy was running around naked when the phone rang. On the other end of the cream-coloured handset affixed to the bare plaster of our dining room wall was David Hargreaves. There was a job coming up in Oxford University's Department of Educational Studies. He couldn't invite me to apply, he said, as he pirouetted around the academic protocols of the time. But he wanted to let me know it was being advertised, that it could be a good fit for me, and that it was something that might be of interest. As he carefully explained this extraordinary opportunity, our son pooped on the carpet, right by my foot, where I duly trod in it.

Kids keep you grounded. While I was being offered the prospect of working among the dreaming spires of Oxford, I looked down to see the most basic excretions of humanity and humility that define everyday life in young families. The intellectual heights of academic culture and the most basic elements of mundane existence were there together, in a single moment, as they seem to have been all my life.

It wasn't the first time I had experienced this unlikely juxtaposition. When I had been a sociology undergraduate, I spent my summer holidays on a team of four university students compiling a map of the underground sewer system of Accrington, my hometown, in the North of England. It was as graphic an example as you could get of what the American symbolic interactionist Everett Hughes called 'dirty work'.[1] Dressed in overalls, with no harnesses or hats (this was the early 1970s!), we clambered down deep shafts and crouched in tiny chambers, measuring inflowing and outflowing pipes among earwigs, rats, and toads, as the human effluent of the townsfolk went past the toes of our boots on its long downhill journey. But dirty work was not the high-flown intellectual subject matter that drew my attention to this subterranean world of waste matter. It was the broader *culture* of the unusual work we were all doing that interested me.

We worked together in rotating teams. One pair would survey the heights above sea level of manhole covers (the entry points into the sewers), as they were then called, and the other pair charted the directions of flow of the sewer pipes underground. The teams were given almost complete autonomy and there was no intruding supervision. For my university undergraduate dissertation, I collected quantitative output data from the teams on numbers of manholes surveyed per day per team, using a cover story that I was doing a statistics assignment for my degree. I also undertook covert ethnographic observations (almost certainly ethically unacceptable today) on the patterns of interaction among these teams who were all in different stages of friendship – friends, potential friends, and antagonisms (pairs who actively disliked each other). Who would be most productive, I asked – friends, antagonisms, or the ones in between? My supervising professor warned me that my project was too ambitious and that it would probably fail. Like Michael 'Eddie the Eagle' Edwards, the unlikely British ski-jumper at the 1988 Calgary Olympics, I love to prove people wrong![2]

There was already a literature on the connection between workplace relations and organisational culture on the one hand and productivity or output in work teams on the other. One of these was a classic text on what became known as the Human Relations School of organisational management. In their 1939 book, *Management and the Worker*, Fritz Roethlisberger and William Dickson investigated the effects on productivity of attempts to vary the conditions of workers at the Western Electric Company's Hawthorne Works in Chicago.[3] What is now well known is that the physical environment was less important in determining productivity than the social relations among the workers. Even when experimenters made the room considerably colder and turned down the lights, so that it became almost impossible to see, productivity still went up because the workers appreciated someone genuinely taking an interest in them. Indeed, this phenomenon of improved results being an effect of the human act of research interest itself became known as the Hawthorne or halo effect.

My own study discovered that the pair with the highest productivity was, curiously, the antagonism.[4] It had the highest mean because work partners kept to the task whenever they could to avoid social interaction. But it also had a high standard deviation, as the proximity that the work required provoked disruption through argument and conflict.

The pair that had the strongest friendship had the lowest mean combined with the highest standard deviation. Its members would work when they wanted to, sometimes take very long lunch breaks at one of their homes, then try to compensate later by accelerating their rate of production. A key insight here, as in the early human relations studies, was that greater friendship does not always lead to better collegiality or improved performance.

It is a long way from the Victorian sewers of Accrington to the dreaming spires of Oxford, in more senses than one, but what connects these two worlds, as I encountered them, is the importance of workplace culture.

The Making of an Educator

High Culture in Low Places

The OU had been a world without in-person students. I had also been going through a phase of focusing my intellectual energy on high-level theory. Aside from course team planning and writing, I was still living in my head for much of the time. Indeed, over two years, I never went into a single school, a pattern that was also par for the course for my colleagues. Oxford University offered something else altogether.

The 40-mile drive from Milton Keynes to Oxford was, in cultural terms, like crossing a continental divide. Most obviously, it was a journey from one of Britain's newest new towns to the oldest university in the English-speaking world. Still only a few years out of my working-class upbringing, I was moving into one of the most elite and privileged institutions on the planet. It was a massive existential shift as well as a professional one.

I gained many positives from my five years at Oxford. I didn't really feel at home or at ease with the university itself, though. I never truly belonged. In important respects, this may have been because I didn't really want to. This may come down to the experience of social mobility. When you have upward mobility, there is a push to move up in achievement but sometimes also a discomfort with the company you are in when you get there.

Some people who come from working-class origins or other lowly beginnings don't have this experience. Like *Hillbilly Elegy* author and US Vice-President J. D. Vance, who went to Yale University from poverty in Appalachia, or Tara Westover, who wrote the bestseller *Educated* and found her way to Cambridge from an abusive family of scrap metal dealers in rural America, they embrace their elite opportunities wholeheartedly and are grateful to leave the dysfunctions of their upbringing behind them.[5] For them, belonging was about fitting in with what was already there. David Hargreaves,

Cultures of Teaching

who grew up in Bolton, Lancashire, and who had an even more solidly working-class background than mine, loved every minute of his time in a selective grammar school, and he took to Oxford University life like a duck to water.[6] I was deeply ambivalent, though.

Oxford University life sometimes felt like being in a spy movie about the 1950s, a world of emotional repression and understatement, where scholars still referred to their colleagues as 'chaps' (even when they were women!), and where, as David revealed, it had only been a few years before that, after dinner at high table, the men would have brandy and cigars while the women retired to another room. One of our colleagues, the philosopher John Wilson, commenced all his 9 a.m. classes with glasses of sherry. High table itself was an intimidating ritual of multiple courses, complicated cutlery arrangements, and conversations across disciplines that were often interesting but also felt like tests of cultural scrutiny where, any second, you might be exposed as an intellectual fraud. Bananas and all other fruits were eaten with a knife and fork, and pudding was certainly never consumed with just a spoon.

Perhaps if I had been at a different stage of family life, this characterisation of Oxford University culture might have ended up sounding less ungrateful. When we moved house after a few months, we couldn't afford to live in the city, so we bought a small modern terraced home about six miles out. It was in a little development, across from a council estate, and backed on to a main road. After a couple of years, the children started school, and it was my job to walk them there, through the estate, every morning. Instead of dining in college, I ate at home. Our after-school babysitter came from the estate. So did the typist for my PhD thesis. Typical family meals were fish fingers or cheese on toast and jelly and blancmange (eaten with a spoon) – not a lot like high table. Wine came out of a box, not a bottle. Pauline took another waitressing job on the other side of the village. Social life consisted of Sunday nights with a friend who taught in further education down at what used to be the working men's club, playing snooker and Space Invaders. Although I had encountered the high culture of Oxford University, I continued to value what country music star Garth Brooks ironically celebrated when he sang about having 'friends in low places'.[7]

On weekends, we took our toddlers in their pushchairs for walks along the Thames. Still short of money, I was continuing to do our own car repairs, cannibalising used parts from a local wreckers' yard, and, when a second royal wedding came up, I decorated the living room as another monarchical avoidance strategy. Christmas toys were still a make-do-and-mend endeavour. I carpeted and wallpapered an old doll's house from my brother's family which, to our daughter's astonishment, Santa had decorated in just the same way as our living room. At midnight one Christmas Eve, to my visiting mother's consternation, I was still fitting a second-hand bicycle I had restored for our son with new pedals and stick-on transfers – in exactly the colours he wanted, it turned out. Pauline used to complain that after taking rubbish to the dump, I had come back with more items than I went with!

There wasn't really any time for all the opportunities that college life could have offered, even had it been more available, or for the museums, concerts, public lectures, and other cultural events that Oxford academics with different family circumstances and at different life stages were more able to enjoy. I went to work, came home, pitched in with the family, and had a few hours a month out here and there. It left very little time for anything else. Home life and university life were worlds apart. So, although I came by my inclination to inverse snobbery honestly, in truth, some of my churlishness was probably down to my life, which was just a very poor fit for the more ethereal existence of Oxford University culture.

Even so, the exclusionary elitism of the university and its arcane rituals of academic gowns and college life, which continue to this day, should be neither underestimated nor excused. As a mature academic who has given keynote addresses and run international meetings in castles and palaces all over the world, I still feel unease about the extreme privilege of these surroundings. And the sight of an academic gown, which our masters wore when I went to a selective grammar school, should still probably come with a trigger warning for me!

The other reason I felt like an outsider within the university had to do with the nature of my job and the department it was in. Most scholars who joined the university faculty were appointed as members of a department, like classics or medicine, and as members of a college where students and faculties across disciplines had rooms, dining rights, and other privileges. At that time, before the first competitive research assessment exercise in the UK ranked universities and departments against one another, the field of education was regarded by the university as little more than a place to prepare its many graduates for teaching careers. This was expressed very clearly by the fact that the university appointed Harry Judge, a former secondary school head teacher rather than an accomplished academic, to be the head of department. The education department had very low status in the university, and, at that time, only the most senior members of its faculty, like David Hargreaves, were awarded college fellowships. The experience of college life for the rest of us was occasional, extraneous, and, from time to time, embarrassing when a colleague from within or outside the university would enquire about which college we belonged to.

In truth, the marginal status of the Department of Educational Studies at Oxford is an extreme case of the marginality of most departments or faculties of education. Education is perceived as an applied field, mainly staffed by former teachers, rather than a pure discipline made up of lifelong scholars. Many education schools were upgrades from former teacher training colleges. For this reason, they are still often housed on the periphery of universities, away from the core of academic life. They are geographically as well as professionally marginal.[8]

All my career, in interdisciplinary environments, I have observed a tendency among academics in other disciplines to see education scholars as lesser beings. While you, as an educator, might ask them intelligent questions about their field in astronomy or medieval history, say, they are more likely to discuss their own children's education, as if you are still a teacher. Sometimes it is as if they think academics in educational studies are lepers who should carry a bell!

In hindsight, David Hargreaves has wondered aloud with me whether I might have stayed if the department had been more successful in arranging a college fellowship for me. If that had happened, and perhaps once my family grew up a bit, we became more financially secure, and we carved out more adult time for ourselves, my relationship with the university and my feelings about it might have changed. It is a hypothetical sliding doors question to which I will never truly know the answer.

But I am more than grateful for the experience I had. It gifted me with several legacies, both small and large. Interdisciplinary exchanges equipped me with a lifelong ability to strike up a conversation with anybody, on almost any subject, anywhere. I acquired the obscure skill of punting up and down the River Cherwell without falling into the water (the secret is to *steer* with the pole, more than *push* it), which enabled me to entertain and impress friends and colleagues on international conferences at Oxford for many years to come. But the most important legacies came not from the wider university but from establishing relationships with local schools and from co-teaching classes of teachers and school leaders within the department. In the end, it was these engagements that began to loosen and eventually untie the knot that had been holding my albatross thesis around my neck.

Cultures of Teaching

Back to School

Oxford, oddly, was where I got back into schools and all things to do with schools. First, I became a school governor. Within days of starting my new job, I got a call from someone on the governing body of a middle school on a large council estate near the car factory on the opposite side of the city from the university. They knew my work on middle schools, had heard of my appointment, and invited me to become a governor with them. My first meeting was to interview candidates for the role of head teacher. The next ones were to plan an amalgamation with another middle school. All this drew on and used not just my knowledge of middle schools but also my organisational knowledge of different school cultures and how to integrate them. We discussed measures like having common pupil activities before the amalgamation took place, holding preparation meetings on both school sites rather than just one, and considering how to distribute leadership responsibilities carefully and fairly across the two staffs, for example, rather than favouring one school over the other. I was no longer just a pure scholar. I was using my scholarship to help a real school now.

Second, my wife went back to school too, full time. When Lucy, our younger child, was about 4 years old, Pauline found a job teaching French, which was quickly followed by another job in a middle school, where one of her colleagues down the corridor turned out to be none other than Philip Pullman. Both schools were unreachable by public transport from our village, and we couldn't afford another car yet, so we purchased a second-hand Honda 50 motorbike. Because neither of us had ever ridden a motorcycle before, it spent its first weeks in perpetual second gear!

Once Pauline started teaching 9-year-olds, our professional worlds and perspectives began to converge. We saw children, teaching, and learning in very similar ways now, and the research and

The Making of an Educator

practice began to intersect and influence each other in our everyday conversations. My head was coming down from the theoretical stratosphere and getting right back into where this all mattered – schools.

The third factor that drew me into the practical world of schools and teaching sprang from the work of one of the most legendary figures in British education in the past half century, the late Sir Tim Brighouse. Over his career, Tim occupied several prominent positions in English education, including director of education for Birmingham and schools commissioner for London.[9] In the early 1980s, he was chief education officer for Oxfordshire Education Authority. Sir Tim was committed to continuous professional learning for head teachers and middle leaders. He established a system of year-long teacher secondments to the Department of Educational Studies. Many of the teachers at the time did not even have university degrees – they had qualified through teacher training colleges. But Tim was a believer in teaching as a profession and in the capacity of all educators to learn, grow, and move further into leadership.

The secondments were designed to stimulate teachers' professional learning, refresh them professionally and personally, connect their dissertation studies to the needs of their schools, and figure out how to improve their practice when they returned. One result of this ingenious programme was the arrival at my office door of five diploma students; neither they nor I had any idea what they would be doing. I was totally responsible for them. All were older than me. I was still barely 30 years old.

I designed the curriculum for the first term – a smattering of curriculum theory and studies of schools. Like characters in a post-Second World War novel, we sat in moquette-covered chairs discussing readings around a gas fire in my office overlooking the university parks. In the second term, I said that *they* would design the curriculum, based on common interests rooted in our readings and their roles in school.

Cultures of Teaching

Our focus became personal and social education. We went to one of the group's schools to observe and discuss their social education course. We brought in trainers of a life-skills programme, so we could engage in and reflect on their learning activities. We spent a day in Peers secondary school, a famous innovative secondary school where the head teacher was Bob Moon – a leading light in British education, who would go on to become a trailblazing professor of teacher education at the OU.

The work of the diploma students in these classes and in their dissertations was impressive. They matched many doctoral-level theses I have supervised since. These educators manifested Sir Tim's belief that if you give teachers time and space to engage collaboratively in high-quality professional learning linked to practice, they will achieve far beyond the initial expectations that levels of certification might have suggested.

Halfway through the second semester, I suggested to the group that 'there might be a book in this!' So, through the rest of the course and for more than a year beyond it, far beyond their period of secondment, we met every few weeks to co-author what became *Personal and Social Education: Choices and Challenges*.[10] They went back to their schools, implemented what they had learned, and, in some cases, went on to become school leaders, national level directors, and senior local authority advisors.

It was a transformative experience for us all. Sir Tim had the vision. He believed in the power of his middle leaders and fledgling academics like me to create something magical and practical together. And he established the structure and culture that made it possible.

The experience lasted a lifetime for me too. I began to see teachers and leaders not just as objects of research, or even as students in my adult classes, but as partners in creating new knowledge and practice together. Working with educators in relationships of mutual respect brought together the culture of commitment and impact in schools with the culture of curiosity and questioning in educational research. It formed a new culture, a bridging culture, in which both commitment and doubt could prosper together.

Appreciation of this culture and relationship, which spans the theory-practice divide, has stayed with me until the present day as I have done collaborative research with schools, school systems, ministers, and governments around the world. This commitment, this respect for people in school systems as professional equals and for the professional culture of teachers and school leaders, all began with Tim Brighouse, who I only met a few times during my early career but who, through what he set up, was more of a mentor for me and many others than he could ever possibly have known.

Mentors and Tormentors

In 2000, Michael Fullan and I wrote a paper on 'Mentoring in the New Millennium'.[11] It described what happened when innovative teachers were mentored by more traditional and controlling supervisors who assumed they always knew best. In circumstances like these, we argued, 'mentors may seem more like tormentors'. At Oxford, I had encounters with both.

David Hargreaves turned out to be a terrific mentor and colleague, even if I didn't always fully appreciate what he was doing at the time. David had the office next door to mine – three of us down the end of one corridor: Hargreaves, Hargreaves, and Backhouse! In 1982, he published a brilliant book, *The Challenge for the Comprehensive School*.[12] Unusually, it transcended radical and conservative academic and ideological positions to try, in the early days of Margaret Thatcher's government, to build a consensus around the idea of young people's dignity and the school as a community. Rigorously argued and supported, its prose was also attractive and understandable to everyday educators. It was the work of a true public intellectual.

Cultures of Teaching

When David did a launch event to academic colleagues and leaders from local schools in the department's library at 15 Norham Gardens, I had another Anthony Giddens moment. Here was someone who didn't just weave together different theories. He could do it in an intellectually engaging way that also made people in schools feel professionally inspired and valued. Like Giddens, he stood and talked for precisely his allotted time. But he also supplemented his academic eloquence with everyday examples and captivating charm. For the second time in my career, I thought, 'That's what I want to do!'

Following his lead, I started to teach myself how to write and talk with greater accessibility and fluency – still maintaining depth, but in a way that increased engagement with and got responsiveness from my audiences. I was, in my own way, embarking on the very early stages of becoming a public intellectual too. You couldn't do it all at once then by writing a blog, posting on TikTok or YouTube, going viral, then getting an invite from TED Talks. You had to build it up steadily, piece by piece, over many years.

Hargreaves also team-taught the master's degree classes with me to more teachers and leaders seconded by Tim Brighouse. We planned the material and the pedagogy together, walking round and round the university parks, discussing and arguing intensely about the best curriculum. We engaged the students, sat with different small groups, and debated our positions in the light of each other's contributions and reactions right in front of them. We debriefed in real time (during the quaint Oxford ritual of breaks for morning tea and biscuits) and then at length after each class. I would go on to write a lot about collegiality in the years to come, but rarely would I experience it with greater quality, sincerity, and pedagogical intensity than this.

Through the team teaching and other discussions, as the two Hargreaves, we developed our joint interest in culture and in the symbolic interactionist tradition that we shared, particularly in

The Making of an Educator

relation to the culture of teaching. Both of us had been inspired and influenced by three key American texts: Willard Waller's incisive and also curmudgeonly discussion of what teaching as an occupation does to teachers in his 1932 classic, *The Sociology of Teaching*;[13] Dan Lortie's 1975 book about how teachers in and around Boston and Florida existed in a world of 'presentism', 'conservatism', and 'individualism', which he said were the three defining features of the culture of teaching;[14] and Philip Jackson's *Life in Classrooms*, with its depiction of the overwhelming 'immediacy' (Lortie's presentism) of teachers' working lives and decisions.[15] These three canonical books about the culture of teaching and schooling that started our sociology of education class in Oxford would commence every class I taught on educational change in Britain, the United States, and Canada over the next 30 years.

My relationship with a second potential mentor didn't work out nearly so well. The literature on mentoring is consistent on one point – it is far better to choose your mentor, if you can, rather than have a mentor thrust upon you. David Hargreaves and I had not only our surnames in common but also common traditions and enthusiasms, which included the content of symbolic interactionism, school culture, and community, as well as a kind of collegiality that was genuinely collaborative even and especially when it was vigorously disputatious.

My second potential mentor was assigned by Harry Judge, the head of department. His invitation, which I couldn't really refuse, was to co-teach the master's class in sociology of education with the very distinguished A. H. (Chelly) Halsey. Professor Halsey was one of the world's leading social scientists. He had been educational advisor to the preceding Labour government, and he was currently a Fellow of Nuffield College. More than 25 years my senior, Halsey struck an imposing figure as a doppelganger of the British actor, Frank Finlay.

Our first and only planning meeting, which took place at Nuffield College, was one-sided, to say the least. Halsey and I came from

Cultures of Teaching

different generations and traditions. He co-founded a field known as political arithmetic which detailed the statistics of inequitable access to secondary education and higher education, and the consequences for subsequent social class differences in educational performance and opportunity.[16] It was rigorous, painstaking, and worthy, but to my generation of sociologists in education, who came of age in the countercultural 1960s and early 1970s, it was also decidedly dull. More than that, it seemed to miss the point. Surely, the nature, the content, and the experience of the education to which people did or did not get access was what drew them into achievement or pushed them away. In research terms, so my young cohort of fellow academics believed, this experience within the school and its impact could only be accessed by emerging qualitative methodologies rather than through traditional, 'scientific', quantitative ones.

The classes took place on Halsey's territory, at Nuffield College. Apart from one small concession to my own interests and expertise, it was very much centred around his own orientations. There was no spirited back-and-forth banter of intellectual equals like there was with David Hargreaves. Instead, Halsey and I delivered lectures to the whole class – he one week, me another – followed by class questions and discussion. I still vividly recall standing up to lecture on topics where I was clearly second best, with him sitting in the middle of the front row, staring at me, waiting, or so I felt, for my eventual faux pas. It was intimidating. Sheer torment, in fact.

On the surface, everything was courteous and polite. But the students sensed there was more to it than this. Our lectures were like very high-level versions of *The Simpsons* or of modern animated movies where the messages, and especially the jokes, work at two levels. Superficially, there is one set of messages being communicated to the everyday folk, the children, or, in our case, the students. Then there is another level of sophisticated irony and oblique allusion that only those who have been initiated into the deep mysteries of the subject can fully grasp. Our intrigued students realised something very odd was going on between their two teachers, even if they couldn't figure out the exact details, although it did provoke some fascinating conversations when we all walked back to the department together.

Hargreaves and Halsey were like chalk and cheese. Both were extremely clever and highly accomplished. But there the similarities ended. One was collegial, respectful, engaging, open to argument, and had a mischievous twinkle in the eye, sometimes. The other was hierarchical, pompous, pedagogically conservative, and generationally overprotective of his own paradigm and knowledge base. From both these academics together, from the mentor and the tormentor, I have learned how to be a guardian of long traditions and of classical canons of knowledge, yet also to be open to new paradigms, even when their bearers are critical and confrontational. Senior scholars must show generational generosity by valuing the cultures of the old and the new and not hang on to old intellectual allegiances at any cost.

Meeting in the Middle

Through teaching my courses and being a school governor, my time at Oxford was drawing my research and thinking back towards the culture of schools. For almost a decade, I had wrestled with Grand Theory, then the dizzy heights of educational policy, trying to apply what I was learning to teachers' strategies in different kinds of classrooms. What was missing in my study of middle schools, ironically, was what was happening in the middle. Micro and macro, Left and Right, theory and evidence, why couldn't I be like the singers Zedd, Maren Morris, and Grey, who get frustrated about all the squabbles, fights, and differences with a lover, and ask, 'Why don't we meet in the middle?'[17]

Cultures of Teaching

In 1949, the American sociologist Robert Merton set out a case for what he called 'theories of the middle range'. He complained that sociological theorists had tried, unsuccessfully, to create vast, totalising systems that could explain the whole nature of society, copying the ambitions of physics. These 'overly zealous and defensive' efforts advanced by 'each charismatic sociologist [who] tries to develop his own general system of theory' were 'typically held to be mutually exclusive and largely at odds'.[18] The alternative, Merton argued, was to have 'middle-range theory' that would 'guide empirical inquiry' on subjects that were researchable and (dis)provable. General theories were 'too remote' from these 'delimited' classes of behaviour and organisation 'to account for what is observed'.[19] 'Middle-range theory involves abstractions, of course,' but it is 'close enough to observed data to be incorporated in propositions that permit empirical testing'.[20]

In the sociology of education, macro theory had, true to form, been far removed from classroom practice. Micro theory, meanwhile, was very much concentrated within the classroom. What was missing was something in between, something in that middle range. A big contribution here was the work of Ivor Goodson and Stephen Ball, two young scholars at Sussex University. They looked at groups of teachers in secondary school subject communities such as geography and English departments. These subject subcultures, they found, mediated what teachers thought, how teachers taught, and how they identified with their subject and even with sub-communities within that subject. Goodson and Ball, and a group of other researchers at the time, also linked these subject cultures to evidence on the historical evolution, identity, and status of subjects like geography, English, and mathematics.[21]

Papers on this emerging work were presented at annual St Hilda's Conference gatherings, and Hammersley and I published a collection that included them in 1983.[22] The work showed how subject disciplines were not fixed entities, but changed over time in terms of

The Making of an Educator

what they emphasised or how abstract they became, as they competed for status and recognition against other subjects in the secondary school curriculum. Subjects recruited new members in the upper echelons of secondary school and at university, and those who went into teaching became attached to their subject communities, regarded them as a fundamental part of their teaching identity, and followed career paths with them up to head of department and beyond.

This was the middle range that my work had been lacking. Lortie said there was a culture of individualism in teaching, but he was really focusing only on the primary school years. All this research in secondary schools was adding something else – about how teachers gathered in like-minded sub-groups that shared the same ideals and problems, developed the same strategies, and believed the same things. Was this also true of middle schools, I wondered. The receipt of an unexpected invitation pushed me into and through this final phase of thinking in my PhD that might join up the micro and the macro in a credible way.

The invitation came from Canada. In 1983, at 32 years old, I was invited to deliver the Duncan McArthur Visiting Speaker Series at Queen's University, in Kingston, Ontario, by a Canadian professor who had got to know me and my work when he spent his leave in our department at Oxford. The purpose of the series, I discovered, was to legitimise the faculty of education, located on the geographical periphery of its university, by presenting three lectures to the faculty and a fourth to another department – in this case, sociology – to demonstrate that education scholars were as credible, intellectually, in the wider university space as those from any other discipline. They would pay my airfare, they said, along with an honorarium. I thought they had added a zero in error.

I was accommodated in the university's lavish vice-presidential suite. The pressure of expectation was immense. In mid-air, over the Atlantic, I broke out in a hideous rash that covered all my body

Cultures of Teaching

except my face and hands. I was detained at immigration due to an irregularity with my work permit and was petrified they might strip-search me, discover the apparently contagious rash, and send me straight back home. As if this was not enough, I also threw up in the toilet before two of my lectures. But the series was a great success.

This was the first time I had visited Canada professionally. Pauline and I had been just once before, when I was a graduate student, to visit my brother and his family, and to hike into and camp out in the wilderness among the prowling bears and howling wolves of Algonquin Park. But this time, during a steepening downturn in the fortunes of faculties of education in England during the Margaret Thatcher era, I discovered Canadian colleagues who were smart, thoughtful, collegial, and enthusiastic about being engaged with big ideas, including mine.

For the first time, I glimpsed the possibility that I might want a future career in Canada. But it was also crystal-clear that, unlike England at that time, I would not be considered for any position without a completed PhD. So, I returned to Oxford with a sense of urgency about finally getting my thesis done. My long and twisted relationship with the intellectual albatross around my neck was about to end. I had found the middle range that would save me. I cancelled all my commitments to conferences, I ignored warnings from colleagues that people would forget about me, and I approached completing the thesis with a laser-like hyperfocus that only others who also have ADHD can fully appreciate. I had a mountain of unanalysed interviews and other organisational data to draw on – it was like writing a second thesis altogether.

To begin with, I needed to show, in as convincing and 'objective' a way as possible, that there were indeed two cultures within the middle schools I had studied and within middle schools in general. Two indicators provided especially striking evidence.[23]

1. Year Groups

Staff in both schools were assigned to year groups where they carried out most of their teaching. There weren't enough teachers to have communities of subject specialists. Teachers would congregate and identify on another axis instead – the year group. The bottom and top halves of the schools, I found, were sharply segregated. They were located at different ends of the building. In staff meetings, teachers mainly sat next to colleagues from their own year. Most teachers spent 90% of their time in one year group. By this measure alone, the cultures of primary and secondary schooling persisted and prevailed despite middle school aspirations to achieve smooth transition and unity.

2. Ability Grouping

A common practice in 11–18 comprehensive schools during this period was to organise pupils into ability groups in certain subjects (a practice known as setting), particularly English, maths, and French. In the two middle schools, no more than 15% of the timetable was organised by setting in the lower years. But in the upper years, 50% of the classes in one school and 80% in the other were set by ability, in up to 10 subjects, even including swimming. Some subjects, like French, were set on principle, according to belief that they were inherently difficult to teach in a mixed-ability environment. Subjects like mathematics were set because many teachers didn't have specialist qualifications and weren't confident teaching mixed-ability groups. Last, logistically, the small size of the schools and shortage of specialist teachers meant that when subjects like French and mathematics were set for one class, the other class had to be taught another subject, such as swimming, which was then also set by default. The irony of all this was that middle schools ended up segregating pupils by ability at ages 11–13 far more than conventional secondary schools did.

Cultures of Teaching

The Break in the Middle

The movement from the lower to the upper reaches of the middle school was less like a gradual shift and more like a sudden break. There were some logistical reasons for this that arose from the shortage of specialists and the size of the schools, which restricted the options for setting. But when I looked at my interview transcripts, I found that the main reason was teachers' biographies and identities and the subcultures to which they belonged. Three cultures stood out.

1. Academic-Elementary Teachers

At the top end of the middle schools were two sub-groups of teachers. One of them consisted of teachers with long careers of 20 years or more. They had worked in some combination of secondary schools and upper primary schools, but their formative years were in the 1950s, so they held on to traditional perspectives on teaching and learning. They were guardians of tradition, resentful of young upstarts, and gratefully heading towards retirement. They preferred working with academically successful children, and they stood by subject specialism, grouping by ability, traditional teaching methods, and firm discipline. A younger subset of colleagues, mostly with less than 10 years of experience, shared similar perspectives on traditional teaching, formal relationships with the children, specialist subject teaching, and ability grouping. These teachers were attracted to the upper years of middle schools because they had felt stuck in their careers in lower status secondary modern (vocational) schools and wanted to escape from 'dirty work' with non-academic youths.

2. Developmental Teachers

Three teachers I interviewed, all women, worked in the lower years of the middle school. They had a developmental view of children and their learning, which echoed the principles of the Plowden Report and of open education in general.[24] These teachers were generalists, not specialists, were interested in relationships rather than traditional discipline, and enjoyed being with the children as much as teaching them.

3. Middle Years Teachers

A third group of eight teachers, with less than five years of experience in all but two cases, had been specifically trained for the middle years. They had learned the philosophy of middle schools, but perhaps because of its vagueness or their own lack of seniority, they tended to get absorbed into the other two cultures at the upper or lower ends of the school where they worked. Their culture was not strong enough and their experience not deep enough, it seemed, to withstand or transform the powerful forces of the two cultures that the middle school had inherited. Culture had beaten out policy.

Culture and Change

Any attempt to bring about reform in curriculum, assessment, teaching, or learning ignores culture at its peril. School amalgamations, curriculum integration, and special education inclusion are just three examples of strategies that attempt to merge categories and therefore cultures that have hitherto been kept apart. Teacher cultures are usually an oversight or an afterthought in change efforts. They sabotage reform initiatives, feed resistance, and make a mockery of policy implementation. Romane Viennet and Beatriz Pont at the Organisation for Economic Co-operation and Development (OECD) point out that over 80% of education policies never get implemented properly.[25] One reason is that the policy stakeholders, such as teachers, are treated as the objects of policy, who are informed about it or trained to deliver it, rather than as active and engaged subjects who should be co-creating the policies with governments and system leaders. In this way, culture could become part of the policy and change process rather than viewed as a threat to its realisation.

Culture connects history to destiny, theory to practice, and policy to action. It is one of our greatest leverage points for bringing about positive change in education. At Oxford, I had experienced awkward encounters with high culture. But by working in a department that built partnerships with schools, I started connecting with school culture. Teaching the foundations of symbolic interactionism and its understanding of the generic culture of teaching drew my theoretical interests in the same direction now – towards the middle range of teaching as an occupation and of schools as organisations. It brought me down from the clouds. And the emerging body of work on subject subcultures gave me something to pin my own research work on – an understanding of different cultures within schools and teaching.

The solutions to understanding and changing our schools are to be found neither down in the dirt nor up among the spires. Without ever losing sight of the big picture or of blue-sky thinking completely, they are mainly to be found and formed in the middle, close to where the action is, in the cultures that shape who we are and what we might become. In the end, the closer teachers and researchers can get to the practice and to each other, the more they will be able accomplish together.

With time running out on my contract at Oxford, and with the alluring prospect of a life and career in a country that was not weighed down with the politics and policies of Thatcherism, I developed the long overdue sense of urgency that would see me get my thesis done and start my transition out of early career into a more mature phase. There was just one more step to take to close out this process.

CHAPTER 7

The Great Education Shift

Sent to Coventry

In January 1985, the UK number 1 record was Band Aid's 'Do They Know It's Christmas?'[1] In one hastily penned lyric, Bob Geldof, George Michael, Phil Collins, Bananarama, and an all-star line-up, mourned how 'there won't be snow in Africa this Christmas time'. With the hindsight of greater clarity and cultural sensitivity, we now realise that up to 40% of the population of Africa is Muslim and that the Atlas Mountains and the summit of Kilimanjaro are no strangers to snow. At the start of 1985, though, snow and ice were familiar features of the English landscape, as the nation shivered in the icy grip of a bitterly cold spell that was one of the worst of the century.

This was the year I fell off our Honda on black ice on my way to work. One of my new students, a local head teacher, took pity on me and loaned me her family's old VW Beetle. It had no heating or floor coverings, and I drove it through the winter bundled up in a woolly hat, scarf, and gloves, as Pauline needed our own car for the longer drive to her new school. But I now had the stability of four wheels, and, for my new student's peace of mind, my safety was assured.

The Making of an Educator

I was in another job now at the University of Warwick. Situated on the edge of a housing estate in the city of Coventry, the more bucolic sounding Warwick University avoided being called the University of Coventry in deference to the donors of its land and as a shrewd piece of branding. It was and is a highly rated university, and it gave me the security and status of my first and only tenured university position in England.

But when I *went* to Coventry, it was almost like being *sent* to Coventry. During the English Civil War, Royalist prisoners were sent to Coventry where they would be shunned. In more recent times, trade unions would sometimes send members to Coventry, metaphorically, for crossing picket lines or otherwise breaking ranks. I wasn't ignored in my new job but, for reasons I will explain shortly, for the first and only time in an academic career that has stretched across seven institutions in three countries, as well as several visiting professorships elsewhere, I felt intellectually and professionally alone, devoid of any true colleagues with whom I could collaborate.

I was fortunate to have a job at all, I suppose. As I neared the end of my contract at Oxford, the positions in my discipline, sociology of education, were disappearing everywhere. All the doors were slamming shut. This was a direct consequence of the educational policies of the Thatcher government and the beginning of what I call the Great Education Shift. Although the full force of the national curriculum did not occur until three years later, in 1988, and despite continuing efforts to make secondary education more motivating for less academic students, central government was already imposing its agenda of ideological control in education. It began by setting its sights on the supposedly liberal educational establishment of teacher training.

Teaching Quality

By the time I was due to leave Oxford, it was almost impossible for universities to hire specialists in sociology of education and other generalist disciplines such as philosophy of education, comparative education, and, for a short while, even educational psychology. This was the result of a political pincer movement between a move to narrow the certification required to be a teacher educator and the imposition of government inspections on faculties of education to ensure compliance.

First, education faculties were made to employ teacher educators whose expertise and qualifications were restricted to the conventional subjects of the secondary school curriculum, like history, mathematics, or science. This was meant to erase liberal and socialist ideologies from faculties of education. The government also gained the reluctant consent of universities to open their teacher education programmes to scrutiny by inspectors if they wanted to retain their funding. This would ensure compliance with the new regulations.

No one would know it then, but these reforms would become ground zero of a Great Shift or global transformation in teacher preparation, along with a parallel decline in the status and quality of the teaching profession. Training was to concentrate on core skills in subject teaching, including in primary schools. Considerations of gender equity, anti-racism, economic inequality, and so on were almost completely excised from the teacher education curriculum.[2] Students were required to spend less time on campus and more time in schools. Practice didn't make perfect. Practice just made practice.[3]

Today, only about 20% of the teacher preparation process in England takes place outside schools, and many schools, rather than universities, have become registered providers of teacher education.

The Making of an Educator

There are bestselling texts on reflective practice, but the heavy emphasis on practical training means that there is little opportunity to engage in serious and sustained reflection on the contextual factors in families and society that impact on teacher quality and pupil performance. In the United States, almost 70% of all new teachers in Texas qualify through certification programmes that take place away from institutions of higher education, but elsewhere, after peaking at around 16% of all preparation around 2015, alternative programmes have undergone a decline, suggesting that shortfalls in quality may be coming home to roost.[4]

Around the year 2000, I tried to warn people that this deprofessionalisation of teaching was coming to North America.[5] I had already seen the road map in England. The paper remains one of the top five most cited in the journal that published it. But US experts find it hard to accept that ideas that are introduced there, even bad ones, are not always homegrown and can originate elsewhere. So, the warnings fell on deaf ears.

The state of teacher education in England and Wales was far from perfect, however. One of the consequences of teaching becoming an all-graduate profession in the 1970s was that it led to a surge in recruitment to university education faculties of academics whose strengths were in research and whose interests were more in educational theory than in being experts in and role models for excellent teaching practice. Many classes either tended to take a critical perspective on how teaching perpetuated inequalities or they focused on insights from individual psychology that didn't seem realistic in whole-class circumstances.

Teacher candidates had to spend a lot of time engaging with what was wrong with teaching, and therefore with what might be wrong with themselves, which was dispiriting, to say the least. There weren't clear answers yet on how to develop practical responses to issues like racism through culturally responsive teaching practices, for example.

The Great Education Shift

The practical aspects of on-site teaching were mainly dealt with by teachers who took positions with the university to drive around multiple schools to observe individual students for a lesson or so on each visit. Within the schools themselves, the task of supervising student teachers was often an extra, middle leadership responsibility, which came with little or no additional reward. In a 2013 OECD review of school improvement in Wales, in which I participated, we found these trends were persisting (which led to sweeping reforms after our report was published).[6] Similar problems have been identified in other OECD countries too.[7]

By the 1980s, a two-tier structure was emerging in faculties of education. In the upper echelons are the star researchers who attract big grants, teach graduate students, and find the funding to present at conferences all over the world. Down in the basement of these faculties are the Cinderellas of their subject, almost all women, who do what US sociologist Dan Liston once called the 'domestic labour' of teacher education.[8] They keep everything organised, maintain communication with the schools, troubleshoot when there are problems, and provide logistical and emotional support to their students. These teacher educators get few research opportunities, have limited access to resources, may be able to publish articles only in professional magazines or in lower ranked journals that will accept their small case studies, and are often excluded from key aspects of faculty meetings. They often rightly complain that their star colleagues, including ones whose expertise is teacher education, treat them with condescension.

One former colleague in North America whose case study narratives were composed by and collected from her students, boasted that she had not set foot in a school in 20 years. And don't even get my wife started on all the dinners we have been to where academic colleagues in education will gleefully talk about themselves and their intellectual interests but show no curiosity about

The Making of an Educator

her extensive experiences and expertise on the ground as a teacher and school leader.

One attempt to circumvent the development of these divisive cultures within faculties of education, and to create an effective and functioning bridge between theory and practice, was to create partnerships between education faculties and clusters of schools. Here, student teachers went in groups, along with a supervising faculty member, provided support for each other during their classroom practice, and participated in the culture and professional development of the whole school. These partnerships had various titles, but most became known as school–university partnerships in the United States.[9]

I found myself on the ground floor of this movement when Warwick University set up several partnerships with the city's local education authority. Every Wednesday, I spent all day with a dozen students in a Coventry primary school. The approved curriculum within the university may only have permitted a single class session on race issues in education, but in this school, where many of the children were from Sikh families, race and diversity were an everyday fact of life.

I particularly recall debriefing a mathematics lesson where a store had been set up so the children could buy goods with toy currency as a way of learning about the arithmetic of money values. I asked the group if they noticed anything unusual about what was for sale. One of them sensed where this discussion was headed and interjected, 'How am I supposed to know what these people eat?' 'Well,' I replied, 'could we just ask them? Better still, we could invite them to bring in their own empty packages.' The point of multiculturalism, I explained, was not to teach in a traditional way – from the front – and decide everything for the children, including researching their eating preferences, but to engage with the children as active participants in their own culture. They might bring in packets of curry and sauces but also boxes of cereal, for example.

The Great Education Shift

Who knew until we asked them? Introducing critical perspectives into the practice can enrich the practice, but only if there is still a solid body of knowledge of racism, diversity, and what we would now call inclusion to draw on.

High-performing countries like Finland respect and combine both the knowledge and the practice, and they have managed to sustain high status for the teaching profession as a result.[10] Nations like England and the United States, however, have discarded much of the professional knowledge that informs good practice, they have turned teachers into technicians, and they now find themselves suffering a monumental crisis of teacher recruitment and retention.

The second part of the pincer movement on teacher education was the imposition of external inspections. Back on campus, my own contribution to the teacher preparation programme was a class that addressed what Americans call issues of social context in education, like poverty, family, racial diversity, and so on. It was during the one permitted class on gender that the government-appointed inspectors decided to make their call. My students conspired magnificently to put on the best show ever. Like hyperactive pre-teens, these young 20-somethings flung their hands into the air to answer questions and make informed contributions that were spectacular displays of curiosity, knowledge, and insight.

My students enjoyed their classes, and they were eager to support me in a way that I was not prepared for but warmed my heart. Even though I was in my mid-30s now, I was still almost one of them. But when I queued up at the supermarket checkout one Friday night, holding a fine French burgundy under my arm, and I spied a bottle of Woodpecker cider in a trolley belonging to one of my students, I had to accept that my illusions of eternal youth had finally deserted me. My students were generationally too distant now to be even facsimiles of friends. My early career stage was coming to an end.

Alone Together

If there were no positions in my field, how was it that I even got a job at Warwick? They had two slots to fill – one in special education and the other in psychology, which had made it back on to the list of approved qualifications for teacher educators by that point. They found one person who fitted both sets of criteria, so they treated the remaining position as an open one and duly appointed me.

The search committee was a small group of senior faculty members. The selection process included no opportunity to meet with other faculty, still less with any students. I spent my first few months having to introduce myself to colleagues I had not yet met. The one question I recall was posed by the mercurial professor of arts education, David Jenkins. 'What's the question you would least like us to ask you?' he said. 'That one,' I answered.

Warwick University creatively circumvented the early constraints that Thatcherism had imposed on teacher education appointments so they could hire me, but at the same time, those very policies took away the community and collegiality that, to different degrees, I had been able to find in my previous jobs. There were just no like-minded souls to bond with. People were pleasant enough. There was congeniality, to be sure. But, for me, there was little or no collegiality embedded in the in-depth work of teaching, writing, or research undertaken with others. In one way or another, by taking the social sciences out of teacher education, Thatcherism had successfully destroyed that.

Research efforts and opportunities yielded disappointing results. I worked on an application to the Economic and Social Research Council for a grant to study assessment reform, in partnership with a University of Bristol lecturer, Patricia Broadfoot (who would later become a university vice-chancellor), but the council's research budget and funding opportunities had been deliberately decimated

The Great Education Shift

by the Thatcher government, and, as younger scholars with small track records, we became too discouraged to complete it and send it in. There were funded research evaluations being undertaken within my department of government initiatives in technical and vocational education. But Warwick University had been suitably dubbed 'Warwick University Limited' by the historian E. P. Thompson for a reason, and when one colleague disclosed that the trick was to give the funders the results they wanted to secure further grants, I quickly lost interest.[11]

Side Bets

I was stuck in an institution, without true colleagues, with few prospects of research funding, and with a teacher education agenda that was not aligned with my values.

With my thesis now behind me and my first sole-authored book that it gave rise to going to press, I was ready to move to another level. I had so many ideas and so much energy, but nowhere to put them, professionally. My work felt scattered – a collection of disorganised fragments of odds and ends involving teacher candidates, a few one-term diploma students, and a bit of work with local schools. There seemed to be no coherent narrative or direction for me, or for anyone, under this government. What was I to do?

In 1970, a Jewish German scholar, Otto Hirschman, who had resettled in the United States and become a professor at Harvard, wrote a book of lasting impact called *Exit, Voice, and Loyalty*.[12] When an organisation, movement, or nation you have believed in goes into decline, he asked, what should you do? Hirschman knew what he was talking about. During the Second World War, he had worked with the resistance movement in occupied France to help prominent artists and intellectuals, like the philosopher Hannah Arendt, to escape to freedom across the Pyrenees.

The Making of an Educator

The first option, Hirschman said, is to continue to show *loyalty*, to dig in, stay quiet, and continue working within the organisation. At Warwick, I watched those who took the loyalty route secure their funding streams for government evaluations. They knew which side their bread was buttered on. But that was not for me.

The second option is *exit*, to leave for other opportunities that seem more aligned with one's own beliefs and aspirations and where one's own contributions will be more valued and have more impact. But I was almost in mid-career now, and if I were to take the exit option it would come with considerable risks to other parts of our lives that were going well. My doctoral albatross no longer hung from my neck. I had a secure tenured position at last, and now our children were older, and Pauline and I were both working full-time, we had financial security too. We were living in a large Victorian terraced home in the heart of what has become one of England's most attractive places to live, Leamington Spa. I had traded the Honda for the car my student loaned me, and then for another car we bought second hand, with our own money, from a neighbour. Our vehicles were no longer in need of constant repair, and if I did take up practical tasks, like renovating an antique hall stand, which remains one of my most cherished possessions to this day, it was for the inherent pleasure of it. The kids' school, which they enjoyed, was just down the street. I took them there every morning before heading into work. They made friends with the neighbours, and so did we. We were settled. I was happy and secure at home but profoundly unsatisfied at work. I would take the exit route eventually, but only when all other options had been exhausted.

The third way to go for Hirschman was *voice*. I was still too junior to exercise any credible voice in my own institution against the turning tide of Thatcherism. My critiques of Westminster government policy were embryonic and needed research evidence behind them to have credibility. I did try to stay consistent, though, not to go under and change course, however hard that might have been. This effort, it turned out, had not gone unnoticed.

Twenty years or so down the track, when I was walking along the South West Coast Path with my adult daughter, Lucy, a bike came past us in the woods and skidded to a halt. 'I'd recognise that voice anywhere,' the rider called out upon hearing my loud Northern vowels. He had been a student in one of my master's classes in Oxford and was a deputy head teacher now, approaching retirement. After we reminisced for a bit, he cycled off with a parting remark that took me aback. 'You were the only one who didn't change!' he called out. 'All the others, they adjusted, and they adapted.' Then, as he was about to set off again, he added, 'No, I tell a lie. Not just you. You and Tim Brighouse.' This was high praise indeed.

Oddly, Brighouse features in an additional strategy that Hirschman never considered – developing side hustles, or side bets as the American sociologist Howard Becker once called them.[13] This was made possible through my evolving relationships with schools. My major side bet at Warwick was a small consulting contract with a county education authority to help its leaders develop an alternative system of secondary school assessments known as Records of Achievement – an initiative that had begun with Brighouse while I had been at Oxford.

Assessment and Achievement

Oxfordshire's director of education, Tim Brighouse, was the mastermind of an innovation called the Oxford Certificate of Educational Achievement (OCEA).[14] Before the creation of the national curriculum in 1988, the secretary for education, Sir Keith Joseph, set out to transform secondary education to motivate young people in vocational studies who had become disaffected with a traditional curriculum. Joseph's energy and initiative brought together people from across the ideological spectrum to try and transform secondary schools.

Never one to miss an opportunity to improve learning, especially for the most underserved and marginalised, Brighouse formed a partnership with three large local authorities and Oxford University's Department of Educational Studies to create OCEA.

OCEA used a diverse assessment process to recognise the breadth of young people's accomplishments. It consisted of three components. The 'E' component collated conventional examination results, the 'G' component curated other out-of-school certificates, and the 'P' component might include part-time jobs, acting as a carer for a family member, taking on leadership positions in school, and so on. This record was to be discussed periodically with a tutor who knew the young person well and could use the ongoing record to support their development. Together, these components made up a portfolio – a record of achievement – that could be presented to potential employers or people in further and higher education.

By the autumn of 1984, the Department of Education and Science and the Welsh Office published *Records of Achievement: A Statement of Policy*.[15] It set out four purposes of Records of Achievement:

- To recognise, acknowledge and give credit for what pupils have achieved and experienced, not just in terms of results in public examinations but in other ways as well.
- To contribute to pupils' personal development and progress by improving their motivation, providing encouragement and increasing their awareness of strengths, weaknesses and opportunities.
- To help schools identify the all round potential of their pupils and to consider how well their curriculum, teaching and organisation enable pupils to develop the general, practical and social skills which are to be recorded.

The Great Education Shift

- To provide young people leaving school or college with a short, summary document of record which is recognised and valued by employers and institutions of further and higher education.[16]

When I had been at Oxford, I had been appointed as the university's representative on the 'P' component committee. It wasn't research, but I learned a lot about the potential and design of the component itself, and about underlying issues that had to be addressed concerning certification, credibility, time, privacy, workload, and changing power relationships between pupils and their teachers. I also gained insights into the politics of innovation as different systems worked together to bring about a change that they believed in and in a way they could agree on. It was my first real experience of system change.

For a brief period, before the national curriculum killed it off, the Records of Achievement initiative generated great energy. This is what often happens during a Great Shift. There is a brief period of innovation and opportunity for those who can seize the moment. A range of local authority pilot projects was launched.[17] Warwickshire was one of them. It asked me to work with it on developing the 'P' component of its own record of achievement. For a time, this set me up with a meaningful side bet. It also established an interest and policy concern that I would return to repeatedly over my career – an interest where pupil voice and choice run up against educational selection and inequality.

I signed a contract for a book on assessment with a young educator (even younger than me) to whom I had been introduced. His name was Steve Munby. Steve and I eventually became great friends, and we have been close collaborators for over a decade in leading an international network of government ministers and teacher union leaders to advance humanitarian goals in education.[18] Steve went on to have a stellar career running England's National

The Making of an Educator

College for School Leadership, among other things. In the end, circumstances conspired against us writing this book together – a serious car crash and other life events in Steve's case and movement to another country that led to a set of new priorities in my own. But with a bit of support from one of my graduate students, Steve eventually finished the book himself.[19]

    I met on several occasions with a group of Warwickshire head teachers under the guidance of a local authority advisor. Drawing on my experience of helping to develop OCEA, I drew up a prompt sheet of questions for them to consider when they were making their design decisions. Who would the records be for? What would be recorded? How would the recording be done? When and how often would it happen? Where would all the records – all the files of pupil achievement – be stored, and who would they belong to? And why was all this going to be worthwhile in the first place?

    Records of Achievement and alternative assessments in general were a place in secondary schools where my own and others' paradoxes and tensions about progressivism and pupil autonomy in primary and middle schools played out. How far could pupils be given a voice in their own learning before it backfired and schools reasserted control? At what point would recognition of these new accomplishments for less academic pupils become so popular that they began to affect traditional assessments, examination results, and opportunities among more 'academic' pupils and their more privileged families? When would assessing a broad range of young people's skills, feelings, and accomplishments be liberating, and at what point might it become controlling or intrusive? Would the negotiation of young people's accomplishments that they wanted to record be authentic, or would it become a sham that still rested in the teacher's powerful hands? And when these conversations about achievement, personal accomplishments, and goal setting turned into an institutional norm rather than a temporary project, might it not all become just one more tedious routine that was too overwhelming for teachers to handle?

Records of Achievement also turned into something of a battleground where formative assessment ran up against the hard-edged purpose of educational selection that conventional examinations performed and therefore against their role in perpetuating inequality.

Combining my theoretical foundational knowledge of questioning and critique with my growing practical awareness of school-level issues, my Warwickshire colleagues and I identified and confronted all the possible risks and threats to the policy so that we could address them. I called these record breakers![20]

What are the deal breakers for Records of Achievement and for alternative forms of assessment, right up to this day and age?

Motivation

First, I turned to the German theorist Jürgen Habermas. Habermas argued that capitalist societies had been experiencing and responding to three different crises in their efforts to secure consent and support from their citizens. The third and last of these was what he called a 'motivation crisis'.[21] When unemployment was rampant and opportunities for working-class people to advance and live well were limited, Habermas argued, it was hard to motivate people to participate in and support the social order. In 1984, the unemployment rate in the UK had reached almost 12% – the highest level for over a decade. The spectre of youth unemployment stalked the secondary education system.

Sir Keith Joseph understood the motivation problem and firmly grasped the nettle with the innovations he encouraged in secondary education for non-academic pupils. At the end of 1983, he pledged to introduce pilot projects to support the development of Records of Achievement 'to give an opportunity for a child's successes to be shown' in ways that would 'be particularly encouraging to those who leave school with apparently few achievements to their credit because there is no way of recording such achievements as they have'.[22] One of the four purposes listed by the Department of Education and Science for Records of Achievement, it is worth remembering, was improving pupils' motivation.[23]

Also in 1984, David Hargreaves addressed these motivational issues in an influential review he chaired for the Inner London Education Authority on the future of secondary education.[24] He described four different aspects of achievement. The first two were familiar enough – academic or intellectual-cognitive achievement and practical or applied achievement. Together, these dominated existing secondary school life. Two other areas of achievement were considerably neglected, though.

Personal and social achievement comprised what is now called social and emotional learning, including resilience, communication, and other social skills. Last, and most radical, was motivation. Pupil motivation, Hargreaves said, is not something we should presume or merely hope for. It is the school's responsibility to create it. Motivation is an achievement, an outcome. It includes things like perseverance, self-confidence, the capacity to overcome difficulties, and the ability to deal constructively with failure. Think of it in C. Wright Mills' sociological terms: when one pupil is unmotivated, it is probably a problem with the pupil. When large numbers of pupils are unmotivated, it is a problem with the school, the curriculum, the teaching, or the society.

The downside of this position is that after using every motivational trick in the book, such as projects, different assessments, tutoring, or real-life learning, if jobs have gone and opportunities have shrunk drastically, it is hard to convince young people why they should bother with their schoolwork, even when it is interesting. What is the point? When there is a crisis of motivation, it cannot be left to schools to do all the heavy lifting. Society must motivate our young people too.

The Great Education Shift

Surveillance

One of the most insightful accounts of the threats of continuous record-keeping has been by the French philosopher Michel Foucault in his book *Discipline and Punish*.[25] The book opens with gruesome and graphic descriptions of public spectacles of torture and executions in France before the Republic, which were meant to serve not only as acts of retribution but also as forms of deterrence to would-be criminals who might be watching. Foucault argued that modern discipline is more sophisticated. It has turned into a perpetual, invasive, and pervasive system of surveillance and control. Consider the ubiquitous surveillance cameras on our streets or the algorithms that track our keystrokes online, for example.

For Foucault, the quintessential form of this discipline is the examination. The examination combines the 'techniques of an observing hierarchy' with what he called 'normalizing judgment' – judgement by those in the hierarchy of what is and is not 'normal'. This system makes it possible 'to classify and to punish' people.[26]

Intriguingly, when Foucault referred to the examination, he didn't mean the traditional sit-down examination that is now a familiar feature of secondary schools. He meant continuous assessment. Detailed case records and endless assessments became a 'document for future use'.[27] Individuals were turned into cases who, in the future, could be trained, corrected, classified, and so on. People were subject to constant surveillance. Everything they did was recorded and assessed to manage their selection or exclusion, for example, or to create evidence that could be used against them in the future. This kind of all-seeing, endless continuous assessment would become 'an indefinite discipline, an interrogation without end' in 'a file that was never closed'.[28]

This may sound far-fetched to teachers who just want to have a fairer, fuller, and less final picture of their pupils when they create or pass judgements upon them. But in the 1990s, after I had gone to Canada, I built on the insights I had developed at Oxford and

The Making of an Educator

Warwick to conduct development and research work for the government of Ontario, which introduced alternative forms of assessment in the middle years. There, while our team witnessed the humanistic potential of formative, continuous assessments, we also saw what was lurking on the darker side of the street in terms of surveillance and control.

On the bright side, some teachers took great efforts to involve students in their assessment. They shared their assessment criteria openly. 'How they are going to be evaluated, they get upfront,' one of them said. This enabled students to see 'it's not just a good job, but why it's a good job'. Other teachers went further and 'made up the evaluation criteria together' with their students.[29]

There was more emphasis on student self-assessment, more sharing of assessment targets with students, and more joint reviews of progress between students, teachers, and parents too. They taught their students self-evaluation and peer evaluation. 'I thought they would all give themselves glowing marks,' one teacher commented, 'but they were pretty close to my own.'[30] Teachers collaborated with their students and with each other to develop and apply assessments. It took the mystery out of grading and the arbitrariness out of judgement. On some occasions, they also invited assessments of themselves. Rethinking assessment on these lines could improve relationships between teachers and students and shift the power dynamics between them.

The surveillance side of an all-encompassing and never-ending assessment process also reared its head in these Ontario schools and classrooms, though. Many teachers used checklists to assess affective or emotional attributes, for example, with regard to things like body language, the amount of work produced, making comments to group partners, paying attention, having positive attitudes towards the subject, completing homework, and being willing to ask for help. Many of these affective or emotional attributes seemed to be synonyms for compliance with the norms of schooling, not with behaviour that involved questioning, risk-taking, assertiveness, initiative, or creativity, for example. Teachers occasionally pointed out that it was important not to assess everything, including within a child's portfolio – for instance, when a child who had disabilities or who was simply quiet or shy might stack up poorly on communication skills compared to other children.

Bureaucracy

One of the basic questions about Records of Achievement was how much time would they take? Who would do the work? Where would the time come from? Which bits of the curriculum would have to make room for them? A national evaluation commissioned by the Department of Education and Science recognised that 'finding time to carry out all the new processes associated with recording was the most frequently cited obstacle to the success' of the Records of Achievement initiative.[31] These issues were still prominent when we pursued our work in Ontario, and in other systems long after that.

In Ontario, teachers often had difficulty knowing how to measure outcomes. They wanted to know what indicators like 'exceeds outcome' meant. Meeting outcomes was hard enough; measuring them was harder still. One Ontario teacher put it like this: 'At Grade 9, you are talking about three-, four-, and five-dimensional matrices to really be able to understand it. There are too many twists and turns.'[32] In Scotland, where I have been a government advisor since 2016, curriculum reviews have shown that when multiple outcomes in a curriculum unit are cross-referenced with types of experiences children are going to have, the sheer quantity of assessments can overwhelm everybody.[33]

All this complicated measurement takes time. So do other aspects of the continuous assessment process. Some Ontario teachers felt guilty about discussing assessments with individual children when others in the class might be left to work without those teachers' supervision. Another teacher I worked with in a US project to explore teachers' concepts and experiences of time described himself as being in 'portfolio prison'. He felt as if he 'had to give up many things, including an enormous amount of time both in school and out of school, to work on the portfolios'.[34] He even had to miss a school trip to stay behind with a dozen students who had not completed their portfolios. The image of being in portfolio prison once more conjures up Max Weber's famed iron cage of bureaucracy. Expand what is assessed but leave traditional exams and grades untouched, and everyone will soon feel swamped by the extra work and time demands.

Selection

Assessment in schools fulfils different purposes. Alternative assessments – like continuous and formative assessments, self and peer assessments, and portfolios – capture a more complete picture of people's efforts and accomplishments. They provide more feedback and a clearer sense of progress. And they encourage people to take more responsibility for their own efforts and accomplishments rather than outsourcing all the judgement and responsibility to their teacher or some distant examiner.

But people also want assessment to serve other functions. Sometimes we need reliable assessments that certify people's ability to do a job properly. Driving tests ensure that uncertified drivers don't create mayhem on our roads. We need to know that architects and engineers have been properly trained and qualified before they start building bridges. Teachers should also be thoroughly qualified before they get to work on children's minds. And most people want to be sure that children have mastered one level of learning before they move on to another or proceed to university. At some point, therefore, clear, valid, and transparent criteria must come into play when we certify people and their competencies. Cumbersome records and quirky self-assessments are not sufficient for this purpose.

The Great Education Shift

Selection occurs when certification meets scarcity. The selection function of education is most obvious and most urgent when young people approach the end of their schooling and face the prospect of being accepted for higher education or not, or of getting into a higher rather than a lower status institution. This is why public examinations at the end of secondary school generate immense anxiety among young people. These teenagers' entire futures depend on the grades they get. This selection function is now seeping into children's lives earlier and earlier as competitiveness among families gets more intense.

Across the world, many societies like the UK and United States are experiencing a disturbing trend where young people from working-class families and poorer backgrounds are less and less likely to go to university or to improve their financial status in life compared to their parents. This is known as a decline in *upward* social mobility.[35]

Alongside this trend are two others that Britain's professor of social mobility, Lee Elliot Major, and his co-author, Emily Briant, exposed in their book on equity in education.[36] First, Britain's middle classes are experiencing rapidly rising rates of *downward* as well as upward mobility, they point out. In their 30s and 40s, middle-class adults are less well off than their parents were at that point, less prosperous, and less able to buy their own homes. Second, at the very top, the super elite of the top 1% or 2% is becoming more insulated and isolated from everyone else as it accumulates ever more wealth, finds ways to avoid paying fair taxation, and uses its great riches to buy influence so the system works in its favour.

All this puts extraordinary pressure on the assessment system and on the curriculum that is associated with it. In this respect, the problem with Sir Keith Joseph's inspiring reforms was not that they weren't working but that they were. The surge in motivation instigated by Records of Achievement, alongside the expanding popularity of innovative courses and related assessments in technical and vocational education, began to threaten the opportunities of England's and Wales' traditional elites. And so, the Conservative government pushed back by introducing a subject-based and traditionally assessed national curriculum in 1988, which in many ways was modelled on the curriculum of private and preparatory schools in which most government cabinet ministers had been successful.

Basil Bernstein's insights and ideas were right back in play. As soon as educators mess with the traditional categories of curriculum and assessment that favour elites, then innovative efforts come to an end and the old order is reasserted. Goodbye alternative assessments, curriculum innovations, and progressive pedagogies. Equity and autonomy are eviscerated together in a single battle.

These patterns and problems exist even today. In 2022, I served as one of two experts on an OECD team of four charged with reviewing aspects of the examination system in Ireland and how it had fared during the COVID-19 pandemic.[37] During that time, teachers had to come up with alternative ways of certifying their students' achievements when those students had not been able to go into school and sit traditional examinations.

Ireland has a highly unusual school Leaving Certificate. One hundred percent of young people's future depends on the results they get in a set of final, sit-down exams. This places immense pressure on young people and their families. A vast industry of what are grimly known as private 'grind schools' has grown up where students (with parents who can afford it) go after school to be coached in revision and exam-passing strategies.

Drawing on data that national school student leaders had collected from 20,000 members, students used the COVID-19 crisis and the review to point to the immense threat to young people's well-being that this system created. Many parents and families shared these concerns. As the results of our review evolved, the minister of education announced that in future no more than 60% of a student's final grade would depend on the sit-down exam and that the rest would be collected by teachers through a process of continuous assessment.

Elite parents wanted to retain the examination, however, so they placed pressure on the government to preserve it. The most surprising response was from teachers' unions, though. They could foresee a mushrooming workload for their members. They also argued that it was the examiners' job to assess their pupils, not the teachers'. If it became the teachers' job, they said, the highly competitive, high-stakes nature of the Leaving Certificate would place their members under unreasonable pressure from parents to alter children's grades in the small communities where many teachers worked. Although the Irish minister at the time slowed down the implementation process for a few months, in November 2024, she insisted that the students could not wait and that the reforms would be accelerated.[38]

A similar situation has been occurring in Scotland. COVID-19 raised huge questions about young people's mental health and the negative impact that is exerted on it by traditional examinations. A review led by University of Glasgow Professor Louise Hayward, who had cut her teeth developing her own expertise on assessment during the days of Records of Achievement, advocated for moves away from the dominance of the traditional exam.[39] But as it faces the prospects of uncertainty in a future election, Scotland's government seems uncertain about how to proceed with many of Hayward's recommendations. Inequality and elitism are in constant tension with efforts to achieve greater inclusion and equity, especially where the future of political control hangs in the balance.

Time and Tide

Before I went to Warwick, early career for me had been mainly a pursuit of intellectual growth amid a struggle for institutional

The Making of an Educator

survival. I had moved from one temporary job to the next in a country where Thatcherism's economic austerity and ideological determination were making the opportunities disappear. Miraculously, almost, we arrived at Warwick to take on jobs that gave us financial security at last. My PhD was finally completed. We lived in a lovely spa town. Intellectually, I was ready to move from surviving to thriving. But when I planted my feet on the professional sands of my new job, the tide had gone out.

Research funds were disappearing. Teacher secondments were coming to an end. Teacher education was turning the reflective practice of a profession into basic training for a standardised job. For the first time, I also felt that I didn't have any real colleagues with whom I could work on research, writing, course planning, or team teaching. I had been hired under the radar, almost in secret, to circumvent the teacher training regulations. But this meant that it took months to introduce myself to other faculty members and to try and allay any suspicions about my appointment.

I still learned some things, of course. Being in on the ground floor of school-university partnerships helped to frame my understanding of them in the years ahead. And my involvement with Records of Achievement laid the groundwork for an approach to assessment reform that I could take to governments in the future too. I retained my passion for a humanistic assessment system that gave pupils more autonomy and extended their opportunities for achievement and success. But I was now also armed with the knowledge that I had gained from peering inside the closets where the skeletons of assessment reform were hidden.

The landscape of education and of educational studies in Britain was changing rapidly, though. Even the flickering flames of hope that existed in secondary school curriculum reform for less academic students and in assessment reform initiatives would soon be snuffed out by a very conservative and exclusionary national curriculum.

The Great Education Shift

Although I was finally feeling financially comfortable and very much at home with my family and in my neighbourhood, I was nonetheless profoundly unhappy at work. I felt alone in a university and adrift in a country where I was trying to hang on to bits and pieces of professional flotsam and jetsam that had no coherence, cohesion, or direction. I had laid down some side bets and tried some workarounds, but it wasn't enough. It was time to take up Hirschman's last strategy: exit. It was time for a shift of my own.

CHAPTER 8

A Shot in The Dark

Exeunt

Pauline walked into our library with its view through the French windows into the garden. She leaned over my shoulder and placed a copy of the *Times Education Supplement* under my nose on the desk. It was opened at the jobs pages. 'I've found the perfect job for you,' she said. It was in Canada.

She knew I was unhappy. But when I had scanned the country's universities in my mind's eye, scoping out better alternatives, there was nowhere I wanted to go. The problem was not the institution, I realised. It was the country.

We had endured years of political turmoil and despair. Margaret Thatcher waged war on the unions, the Irish, the Argentinians, the unemployed, the Black population, demonstrators against apartheid, and, later, even the families of bereaved Liverpool football supporters. But none of this prompted us to leave. Even with all this going on around us, our home life was inexplicably happy. Looking back on these years, we often wonder how so many of us managed to eke out any pleasure at all. Yet, somehow, we did.

The immediate and pressing problem was that Margaret Thatcher also waged war on teachers and on social scientists in the

The Making of an Educator

universities, as the Trump Republican government is now doing in the United States. Professional fulfilment no longer seemed possible where I was. My institution and increasingly my whole profession in the UK was becoming the evil twin of everything I would come to write about and advocate for in the coming years. It felt like there was no true collaboration, no culture of collegiality, no sense of community. On our cassette player, Bruce Hornsby was singing about unemployment, poverty, and racism. 'That's just the way it is,' he sang. 'Some things will never change.'[1]

We had visited Canada for personal and professional reasons. We had been impressed. Both my brothers and their families were already there – economic migrants who had left England's working class to take up engineering opportunities across the ocean. So, I sent off my application to work in a university field centre in partnership with local schools – a chance to take the professional legacy that Tim Brighouse had left me and develop it at scale with whole groups of schools.

Over the summer, as my application was sitting in someone's in-tray, Pauline and I sat with our children in a field in France – our first European holiday, under canvas in ready-erected tents. On a hot summer evening, we drank some local wine and speculated about what might happen to the application. And then I said something that in hindsight still seems extraordinary.

If the job didn't come through in Canada, I said, I would keep the security of my position, and we would stay in the community we were growing to love as a family. But I would disengage from my work. I would show up to meetings and teach my classes conscientiously, but I would not bang my head against a brick wall in a futile effort to gain research funds, write journal articles, or develop new collaborations. I would shift the balance of my efforts and satisfactions towards home, take up new interests, and just relax a little more. Disinvestment was my backup strategy. It never crossed Hirschman's mind, but it is one that many disillusioned idealists eventually adopt.[2]

A Shot in The Dark

I sometimes have an untoward sympathy for mid-career teachers who resist educational change. This is probably where it comes from. I still remember what it was like to have energy and imagination yet feel frustrated and blocked. I still recall how easy it was to entertain professional disinvestment as a serious option. As I said in Chapter 1, the reason many people leave teaching or other professional work physically, or lessen their investments professionally, is because of the adults in the organisation or the society and the self-serving agendas they are pursuing. They pull back and turn inward, not in the absence of idealism but because of it.

In August 1986, a call finally came through from Canada. It was not what I was expecting. The head of department of educational administration at the Ontario Institute for Studies in Education (OISE) in Toronto was inviting me to fly over for a job interview in September.

'But I haven't applied for a job in educational administration,' I said.

'No, we know you haven't,' he replied.

'But I don't know anything about educational administration,' I went on.

'No, we know you don't,' he continued.

Bemused as I was, but with a chance to see my brothers in Canada, I was being offered an all-expenses paid flight to Toronto, with three nights in a swanky hotel thrown in. What did I have to lose?

Later, after I had been appointed, I learned there had been more to it. I had indeed applied for a job at OISE to work with schools in one of its field centres. Someone on that search committee was also on the committee for the educational administration position, so I was, in a way, poached for that second post. Apparently, the department had undergone a recent review, and one recommendation was that it should appoint an international scholar from another discipline than educational administration whose work and interests were compatible with the field.

The Making of an Educator

After a few more weeks had gone by and they had interviewed three other international candidates, including my one-time colleague Roger Dale, one of the members of the department showed up at a European conference where I was presenting a paper. On the cobbled streets of Bruges in Belgium, he removed a crumpled sheet of paper from his jacket pocket. It showed how each member of the department had ranked the four candidates. I was rated first by every professor, except one, who ranked me second.

Compared to Warwick, where I had been interviewed by a small search committee and had met no other faculty members or any students, here was a whole community that would be behind my appointment and that would want to make it a success. It was hugely motivating. Terms were discussed and eventually a formal offer was made. But when the call came in with the news, Pauline burst into tears.

Suddenly, it was all too real. The prospects were exciting. A new job, a new country, a new life. But we were 37, not 27. We would be leaving behind a community that we loved; schools and friends that our growing children loved too; a country which, for all its faults, was still ours; widowed mothers who were heading towards their 70s; good friends; treasured memories; and a familiar culture with its country walks, football matches, newspapers, and TV. Not to mention Pauline's own job and career. The internet, email, Skype, and even fax machines either didn't exist or were not yet in everyday use, so the only real-time communication was by analogue telephone. We would be taking a one-way ticket into a new world. There was a lot to give up.

So, we sat down and talked. 'That's OK then,' I said. 'We just won't go.' I meant it. 'We have a lovely home and secure jobs. We'll be no worse off than we already are.'

'But we have to go,' Pauline said. 'You've told them that you're leaving. Everybody knows.'

A Shot in The Dark

'That's true,' I said. 'But I haven't signed my resignation letter. They can't make me leave. I'll suffer some temporary embarrassment for a year or two, and other people may regard me as an unreliable hiring decision for a bit. But I can live with that. It won't be so bad.'

So, then and there, we decided we weren't going. Next day, I walked around town on my own. I am not especially religious, but I went into a church, sat down, and reflected quietly, seeking inspiration and guidance in myself as much as anything. I went back home and tried to call Pauline at work. She was trying to call me. Our messages were the same. 'Alright then,' we both blurted out. 'Let's go'.

We had stared into the abyss of exile and loss. We had considered the feeling that emigration would be almost like inexorable self-deportation. But now we knew we could choose. We had autonomy. So, taking back control of things, we redoubled our resolve to go, and, in truth, we never looked back.

As William Shakespeare (whose birthplace was just a few miles away) wrote whenever all his characters left the stage at once: *Exeunt.*

The Knowledge

In 1865, a test was introduced to certify London taxi drivers. It is called 'The Knowledge'. To pass and to be certified to drive, candidates must take up to four years, spending many hours every week, to memorise thousands of routes, landmarks, hotels, and other venues within a six-mile radius of Charing Cross. To drive a taxi in London, and earn the lucrative income that comes with it, in an expert and effortless way, requires thousands of hours of memorisation and practice.[3]

Malcolm Gladwell popularised this idea when he reported a classic psychological study of elite violinists which claimed that most of their performance success came from thousands of hours of practice – around 10,000, to be precise.[4] Replications of this study have complicated this initial finding where effort and time seemed to triumph over talent. Talent and motivation, it turns out, actually explain a huge amount in the pursuit of excellence. But practice still accounts for about 20–25% of the variance between elite and non-elite performers.[5]

Finding your talent, then exploring and developing it with lots of practice, is what early career is all about. You will never be a virtuoso straight away. After we moved to Canada, my career took off in terms of prize-winning books, highly cited papers, funded research projects, keynote speech invitations, and opportunities to work with governments, for example. But it did not come down to one magic moment of moving countries and cultures. The knowledge and skills I started displaying in Canada and the United States had been under construction, piece by tiny piece, in the UK for many years before. Canada could fairly claim to have launched me, but it was England that really built me.

We would take a modest amount of physical baggage to our new country: half a containerful of the possessions we were just starting to accumulate – an apartment-sized load, as the removal people derisively called it when they delivered our goods in Canada.

The intellectual and professional baggage was considerable, though. Without truly understanding it at the time, I had been packing those bags for more than a decade. What was in them would stay with me for the rest of my life and career. In all the years ahead, at different times, on different projects, in different countries, I would keep coming back to the same professional questions, the same items of professional knowledge, that had occupied me in early career.

A Shot in The Dark

- How can young people and teachers have autonomy to pursue their interests and passions yet still meet high standards?
- How far can we break down boundaries and push for equity and autonomy in a system's curriculum and assessments before the system starts to push back?
- How can we connect what schools do in their everyday practice to deep and broad understandings of the changing world around them?
- How can we meet people where they are and understand why they do what they do before trying to get them to change and do something better?
- How can we bring together cultures, identities, systems, and perspectives that other people try to set apart?
- How do we develop and advance our own intellectual passions and commitments while protecting and actively supporting the ability and dignity of others, including our opponents, to have the intellectual freedom to express theirs?
- How can academics and educators in schools and school systems work together in relationships of mutual understanding and respect?

A Particular Set of Skills

In the 2008 movie *Taken*, the protagonist, played by Liam Neeson, delivers one of the most quoted movie lines of all time as he sets out to rescue his captured daughter. He has, he warns her captors, 'a very particular set of skills. Skills I have acquired over a very long career. Skills that make me a nightmare for people like you.'[6]

Other consummate professionals – doctors, teachers, writers, and speakers – also have particular sets of skills. They may not carry the

The Making of an Educator

same element of menace, but they also take many years to develop over long careers. They begin early. And they don't come ready-made. Being an academic or intellectual in early career extends beyond the content knowledge that people read, write, and speak about. It also involves developing all kinds of other skills and dispositions. Here are 10 of them to bear in mind for anyone embarking on an academic career in education and for those who support them:

1. *Do something badly, if you must, before you do it well,* whether it is speaking, writing, teaching, or advising. There is a moment just before we can do something when we can't. We never truly know when that last moment will be.
2. *Regard writing, speaking, and teaching as skills to keep developing*, not just as gifts that you may be lucky to have or not. Treat them as crafts that you must constantly try to improve, every time, without exception. I still do, including in this book.
3. *Be a mentor, not a tormentor.* Choose your words carefully. Most great mentoring is incidental. It is the right word offered at just the right time, and, if possible, backed by action. Leave the right kind of mark on those who come behind you.
4. *Seize exciting new opportunities*, even if they make you throw up and break out in a rash. You will get over it, and you will learn a lot. Don't overthink the pros and cons and the calculations of work–life balance. Go with your gut sometimes. What you learn may not be immediately obvious or part of a pre-prepared plan. But the insights and new skills it gives you may well last a lifetime.
5. *Instigate feedback.* Respond fully, frankly, but also generously to other people's work. Make it a normal and expected part of your workplace culture. And invite it from others about your own work too, no matter how senior or

accomplished you may become. None of us are perfect. All of us need help to improve.

6 *Find colleagues. Build collaboration.* You will learn something from everyone you collaborate with, and most of the time you will accomplish more together. Bad collaborations – and you will have some – should not deter you from building better collaborations in the future.

7 *Learn to communicate accessibly and attractively.* Connect what you have learned from your research and development to the people it is most supposed to affect – students, teachers, leaders, families, and the public, for example. Communicate it not just so that it is clear but also so that it is engaging and inspiring. Jettison the jargon. Craft your speeches and writing meticulously. Make music from your sentences.

8 *Consider the complicated and sometimes difficult lives that younger scholars have.* They are not just tenure track applications. They may be struggling with money, anxiety, insecurity, raising a young family, or caring for parents back in their country of origin. Their cultural or social class origins might make them uncomfortable with certain aspects of academic life. Don't judge them all in the same way. Consider their differences from each other and from you.

9 *Reach out across the generations.* If you are a younger scholar, try to consider the possibility that those who are more senior and seem to have more status, power, and privileges didn't always get it handed to them on a plate. Especially if they came from a low-income family, a racial or ethnic minority, or, back in the 1980s and 1990s, were women, they will have spent many years struggling to put together their career and a body of work, just as you might sometimes feel you have to do now. Your responsibility is to be a custodian of what built your field (which may also

include criticisms of it) and a champion of how to move that field forward.

10 *Make history deliberately.* In early career, it can sometimes feel like you are staggering from one thing to the next. But you are living in a particular time. You are part of history, and in your own small way, making history. Try to have some self-awareness of what is going on around you and how you are part of it. Later in your career, if you are lucky, your work will leave a larger footprint. You will be making history in a bigger way and, either consciously or subconsciously, you will be drawing on your own generational formation when you were making history before. In some form or other, sometimes when you least expect it, you will keep returning to the things you learned and did early on for the rest of your life.

Better Coping Strategies

Most of the work I conducted in early career was about teachers and teaching. Much of it still is.[7] What might teachers and school leaders pick up from these insights into teaching in the 1970s and 1980s and their implications for today? Here, to close, are 10 lessons for teachers and school leaders that come directly from my work on teachers' coping strategies, cultures and careers of teaching, the interrelationship between experience and research, and the nature and effects of educational and social change.

1. Revisit Your Coping Strategies
Much of the reason why teachers do what they do has to do with the constraints they have to cope with. More and more, school leaders are complaining to me that teachers are changing. They are becoming more transactional. Younger teachers, they say, who

are working in systems that are increasingly bureaucratic, prescriptive, and risk-averse, are doing a competent job but also counting the hours, watching the clock, and sticking to the contract to protect their sanity. Who can blame them? When I was finding things discouraging and overwhelming, I almost took that path myself. But if all you do is knuckle down, eventually you will buckle under. We spend a lot of our lives working. There must be more to it than meeting the minimum requirement – and the same goes for your kids. So, look up and look around. There are better coping strategies out there than being transactional. What might they be?

2. Strengthen Your Core

When the system depresses us, it is essential to take out our moral compass and ensure we stay true to our North Star or Southern Cross. To use another metaphor, it is important to strengthen our core. In a world gone mad, it is the first and most important thing we can do. Remember why you came into teaching. Not to do the minimum, but to change children's lives. Don't just play Hirschman's loyalty card and keep your head down in a system that has gone awry. And don't keep playing that card as a habit once the system picks up again – as it will one day. If you take the exit door, exit your school for a better one (they are out there) or for another job in education rather than leaving the education profession altogether and becoming another statistic in the teacher retention crisis. Speak up. Use your voice when you can. But mostly, especially when you find yourself in a Great Shift, look for the windows of opportunity, the creative alternatives, for where, somewhere in your work, you can put a bit of extra time into things that will bring joy and fulfilment back into the lives of you and your kids. I have seen this in a project I have been leading to develop innovations in 40 schools.[8] Even in unsympathetic systems, teachers have found ways to create joyful and engaging learning for part of the curriculum or for half a day a week, at least. So can you.

3. Get Protection

If you do something different that rattles people's cages, at some point an envious colleague or an angry administrator who feels like they are losing control will come after you. Be ready. If your arteries of professional autonomy and innovation are getting blocked, perform a bypass operation. In case a head of department or other middle manager should make life difficult for you, build a positive relationship with the head teacher or a system administrator, and use your work to draw positive attention to the school rather than to yourself as an eccentric outlier within it. Do this proactively, not reactively. Get parents on your side through the excellent and reassuring continuous feedback you provide about their children's accomplishments. They will help to make you fireproof. And if all else fails, if you are being bullied, harassed, or deliberately sidelined by your superiors, simply for trying to do the right thing for your kids, turn to your union, as I did. That is what it is there for.

4. Find a Friend

The research on early adolescents in secondary schools shows that having just one adult who knows them and cares about them can make a huge difference to their achievement and well-being.[9] The same applies to adults. Finding good friends and colleagues within and outside your workplace can make a massive difference to how your work feels and how effective you are. I have always been able to find at least one close friend or colleague in every place I have worked, except one. The deputy head in the school where I started out was an indispensable ally and support for me. Almost 40 years my senior, she was a silver-haired inspiration. Over 80% of my 38 books have been written or edited with other people. These people have been a big part of what I have become. In early career, it must be said, almost all my close colleagues and collaborators were men – reflecting the gender composition of British universities at the time. In later career, though, they went on to include outstanding women such as Ann Lieberman, Lorna Earl, Alma Harris, Beatriz Pont, and Jess Whitley.

There are always cultures of teaching. Even individualism is a culture. These cultures help to define what we will become. Toxic cultures can make us lonely or bitter. Positive, collaborative cultures make us more effective, more uplifted, and more positively inclined towards transformative change. Find at least one close colleague or friend. Seek out positive cultures. And if they don't already exist, create them yourself.

5. Don't Attract Envy and Invite Enemies
Do something different, strive for the right thing and the greater good, and you will make enemies, whether you want them or not. In a poem that Margaret Thatcher loved to quote, the Scottish writer Charles MacKay asked, 'You have no enemies, you say?' 'Alas!' he continues, 'You've never turned the wrong to right, / You've been a coward in the fight.'[10] You cannot teach or lead from a position of fear. But learn a lesson from my younger self – don't cultivate envy and opposition just for the sake of it or because it enlarges your own ego.

In her landmark work on teachers' emotions, the psychotherapist and Holocaust survivor Isca Salzberger-Wittenberg, who passed away at 100 years of age in 2023, warned teachers who were outrageously innovative or who were especially loved by their pupils against the egotistical urge to attract envy from their peers.[11] Whatever their intellectual merits, my mischievously titled attacks on my Marxist rivals in the early 1980s were also perversely designed to draw attention to me! So, if you are going out on a limb to do the right thing, don't go attracting enemies out of your own need to be adored by your followers and envied by your rivals. Try not to enjoy the limelight too obviously and too much. Show an interest in what your other, less extrovert colleagues are doing. Value your differences. Celebrate their accomplishments as well as your own.

You will have enemies enough. There is no need to go looking for them.

6. Rethink Your Relationship with Research
The time has long gone when teachers could just rely on practical experience without any reference to evidence or research. If teachers are going to have the professional status of doctors, nurses, architects, or engineers, they must take evidence seriously. But this shouldn't mean forcing them to adopt procedures that outside experts decide are best for them and for the young people they teach.

Some years ago, when I went to tell my doctor that I thought I had contracted African tick bite fever, he likely saved my life because he took several kinds of knowledge seriously: my knowledge of my body and the unusual blackened wound that was on it, my knowledge of where I had just been (South Africa), our shared knowledge of the internet (which gave me a one in two million chance of having the disease even after having been bitten), his expert, practical knowledge of what dangerously necrotising flesh looks like, and the specialised knowledge of the colleague he phoned in tropical medicine. This physician expertly combined the knowledge of formal research, of me as a human being, of his specialist colleague, and of practical familiarity with necrotising flesh. And I was a partner in all this with him.

This is the relationship that teachers need to have with research – knowing where to find the right evidence, treating it seriously, discussing and evaluating it with colleagues, and applying it all to the people they know best, possibly with a bit of school-based enquiry and definitely with a lot of experiential knowledge thrown in. Don't ignore research, but don't be oppressed by it either. And engage with many kinds of research and professional knowledge – qualitative as well as quantitative – in a respectful yet assertive and critically reflective way.

A Shot in The Dark

7. Play the Long Game

Hopefully, if you have reached the very end of this book, you are a person who has been in education a long time or who plans to be. The game is a long one. It has countless moves – many that we are not even aware we are making at the time. But if you are driven and guided by a compelling purpose, equipped with a bit of boldness and resilience, and surrounded by at least a few supportive and stimulating colleagues, every move you make will matter in the long run. You may only affect a few children now, but you have many more coming your way in the future – and that is a big impact in sheer numbers alone. Your work and your ideas that affect these children in this moment will, in time, also affect your school, or your system, and even the world beyond that.

If you get frustrated that you only seem able to move the pawns, remember that the rooks, queen, and bishops are right behind them, waiting to come out in the future. And the pawns matter too. Don't underestimate them. Everything I have been able to accomplish in the past 30 years, sometimes on the big stage, would never have been possible without all the unglamorous work that took place out of the limelight in the first 15 years. Trust me, your early years are valuable in their own right. They are also, possibly, leading to something on an even bigger scale as a teacher leader, a head teacher, a policymaker, a teacher educator, or a writer of books later. The frustration as well as the fascination is that you may not know what any of that is just yet. Enjoy the moment. But also remember that you are in it for the long game – just like your pupils!

8. Be a Sleeper

In the world of espionage, there are people called sleepers. They learn the skills of spying, then live for a long time as ordinary members of a foreign community, until their handlers activate them. In education, sleepers learn their knowledge and skills when windows for change and transformation open, especially when there are Great Shifts. When a new order comes into being, everything tightens up, and the windows close again, sleepers take what they learned about innovation and transformation earlier on and just keep it close to their chests for a while, perhaps for decades, until the windows open again. By then, they will have moved on and up in their careers and become leaders in the system. It is then time for the ideas they learned earlier to reappear big time in a slightly altered form – whether it is alternative assessments, project-based learning, pupil voice, or something else.

One of the inalienable aspects of change is that it lives on in people's memories, ready to come back to life whenever favourable conditions return. So, if the project you have committed to or the innovation you have embraced is terminated, if funds get withdrawn, if priorities shift, or if leaders leave, remember what you have learned. Your time will come again. Be a sleeper. Activate what you have been quietly yearning to do for years when your big moments finally arrive.

9. Embrace Opponents

My idea of balance and integration of opposing views in early career was to criticise both sides. I still seek balance and integration, but I try to embrace opposites more now, instead of just attacking them. Teach your pupils in school and your students in higher education to look for merit in their opponents' views wherever they can and to reach across the ideological divide to include and incorporate them. Effective literacy benefits from attention to phonics *and* to reading in context. Leftists like collective responsibility and conservatives like personal responsibility – but responsibility matters for both groups. I learned to engage with both Marxist and pluralist perspectives and to find a middle-range bridge between the micro and the macro. Calling people in rather than calling them out, wherever you can, will increase the impact of your efforts and the originality of your own thinking.

A Shot in The Dark

10. Be Yourself

In all of this, don't lose sight of yourself. Having a sense of belonging is not the same as just fitting in. I stood by my right to use a spoon rather than a fork as an assertion of my class identity. In presentations to mixed groups of school people and academics, I have been known to break into popular song sometimes, which typically delights the school practitioners, even though it can make more stuffy scholars cringe with embarrassment. But it expresses who I am, and it gets engagement from teachers and school leaders who understand well enough that performance and surprise are big parts of teaching. Don't let any imposed 'scientific' method of anything in teaching reduce you to a robot. And don't let any fashionable progressive or edtech bro persuade you that you are not a teacher any more but just a facilitator now either. Nobody should have to be less than they can be, or should have to hide who they are, just to fit in. A big part of teaching at any and every level is who the teacher is. What the teacher does for the teaching is as important as what the teaching does for the teacher.

We perched on our suitcases at the kerb-side, dressed in our best outfits, waiting for the coach to come and take us to Heathrow Airport.

The Making of an Educator

Leaving Home

On 6 August 1987, when our possessions had been shipped away and we had moved out of the home we loved to sleep over in a neighbour's house, we took a taxi to a bus stop on the edge of Stratford-upon-Avon. We perched on our suitcases at the kerb-side, dressed in our best outfits, waiting for the coach to come and take us to Heathrow Airport. Pauline and I were leaving the first half of our lives behind for the second half that awaited us over 3,000 miles away. Across the Atlantic, U2 were at number 1 singing, 'I still haven't found what I'm looking for'.[12]

We had gone through a great educational and political shift. Now was the time to embark on a major geographical and cultural one. Apart from my job, we had no precise targets to aim at. We were taking a shot at a new life. It would turn out well in the end. But in truth, it was pretty much a shot in the dark.

Endnotes

Preface

1 D. H. Hargreaves, *Schooling Re-imagined: Educating for a More Ethical Society* (Bloomsbury, 2024).
2 A. Hargreaves, *Moving: A Memoir of Education and Social Mobility* (Solution Tree Press, 2020).

Introduction: The Great Shift

1 K. Mannheim, 'The Problem of Generations', in *Essays on the Sociology of Knowledge*, ed. P. Kecskemeti (Routledge, 1952; original work published 1927), pp. 276–322 at p. 310.
2 For my own take on the transgender–gender-critical feminism debate, see A. Hargreaves, 'There is a Way Out of Cancel Culture, But It's Not Free Speech', *Times Higher Education* (15 February 2024). https://www.andyhargreaves.com/a-way-out-of-cancel-culture.html. For a more extended discussion of identity issues and identity politics in education and society, see D. Shirley and A. Hargreaves, *The Age of Identity: Who Do Our Kids Think They Are ... and How We Can Help Them Belong* (Corwin Press, 2024). Two other thoughtful books on this topic are Y. Mounk, *The Identity Trap: A Story of Ideas and Power in Our Time* (Penguin, 2023) and J. Ahluwalia, *Both, Not Half: A Radical New Approach to Mixed Heritage Identity* (Mango Publishing, 2024).
3 A. Woo, M. K. Diliberti, and E. D. Steiner, *Policies Restricting Teaching About Race and Gender Spill Over into Other States and Localities: Findings from the 2023 State of the American Teacher Survey* (RAND, 2024). https://www.rand.org/pubs/research_reports/RRA1108-10.html
4 R. Luscombe, 'Florida Schoolkids May Have to Study "Threat of Communism

The Making of an Educator

in the US"', *The Guardian* (4 February 2024). https://www.theguardian.com/us-news/2024/feb/09/florida-schools-communism-history-bills-desantis

5. Trump is quoted in R. Leingang, 'Republican President-Elect Says He Wants to Dismantle the US Education Department and Fire "Radical Left Accreditors"', *The Guardian* (18 November 2024). https://www.theguardian.com/us-news/2024/nov/18/trump-education-policies

6. J. Fitzgerald, F. Yousif, and K. Epstein, 'Trump Puts All US Government Staff on Paid Leave "Immediately"', *BBC News* (23 January 2025). https://www.bbc.com/news/articles/cgj288ywj23o

7. A. Hargreaves, *Moving: A Memoir of Education and Social Mobility* (Solution Tree Press, 2020).

8. A. Hargreaves, English Middle Schools: An Historical and Ethnographic Study [unpublished PhD thesis, University of Leeds, 1985].

9. A. Giddens, *Beyond Left and Right: The Future of Radical Politics* (Polity Press, 1994); A. Giddens, *The Third Way: The Renewal of Social Democracy* (Polity Press, 1999). My own effort in more recent times to establish a position that extends beyond the Third Way can be read in A. Hargreaves and D. Shirley, *The Fourth Way: The Inspiring Future for Educational Change* (Corwin Press, 2009).

10. One of the most notable examples is former assistant secretary of education for President George H. Bush, Diane Ravitch, who self-converted from being an official advocate of traditional standards and testing to becoming the United States' most virulent and public critic of standardised testing. See D. Ravitch, *The Death and Life of the Great American School System: How Testing and Choice Are Undermining Education* (Basic Books, 2011). Harvard University Professor Richard Elmore didn't only reverse his position on the value of top-down instructional reform but also edited a collection on how other educators had changed their minds on important issues too. See R. Elmore, *I Used to Think … and Now I Think* (Harvard Education Press, 2011).

11. See, for example, D. Ravitch, 'Why I Object to the Term "Science of Reading"', [blog] (25 November 2020). https://dianeravitch.net/2020/11/25/why-i-object-to-the-term-science-of-reading; D. C. Berliner, 'Comment: Educational Research: The Hardest Science of All', *Educational Researcher*, 31(8) (2002), 18–20. https://doi.org/10.3102/0013189X031008018; and D. Wiliam, *Leadership for Teacher Learning* (Solution Tree Press, 2016).

12. See, for example, the definition and uses of evidence-based practices by the ResearchED organisation: https://researched.org.uk and by the Education Endowment Foundation: https://educationendowmentfoundation.org.uk/education-evidence. For an early yet thorough critique, see G. Biesta, 'Why "What Works" Won't Work: Evidence-Based Practice and the Democratic Deficit in Educational Research', *Educational Theory*, 57 (2007), 1–22. https://doi.org/10.1111/j.1741-5446.2006.00241.x

13. On the criticisms of weight loss drugs and their side effects, see N. Triggle, 'Why Weight Loss Drugs May Be No Obesity Silver Bullet', *BBC News* (15 October 2024). https://www.bbc.com/news/articles/czxgqp1nd1jo

Endnotes

14 For an analysis of the interests invested in highly processed foods and their addictive effects, see C. van Tulleken, *Ultra-Processed People: Why We Can't Stop Eating Food That Isn't Food* (Vintage Books, 2024).
15 Osler's quote is cited in O. Sacks, *An Anthropologist on Mars: Seven Paradoxical Tales* (Vintage Books, 1996), p. 3.
16 See M. Weber, *Economy and Society: An Outline of Interpretive Sociology*, tr. G. Roth and C. Wittich (University of California Press, 1978; original work published 1925).
17 K. Marx, 'Theses on Feuerbach', in K. Marx and F. Engels, *Collected Works. Vol. 5: 1845–1847* (Lawrence & Wishart, 1976), no. 11, p. 5.
18 Children's author Philip Pullman first introduces the concept of dæmons in *Northern Lights* (Scholastic Books, 1995), the first of the 'His Dark Materials' trilogy, which is now mass marketed and a highly popular movie, *The Golden Compass*.

Chapter 1: A Shot at Teaching

1 Cat Stevens, 'Father and Son', on *Tea for the Tillerman* (Island Records, 1970).
2 D. Lortie, *Schoolteacher: A Sociological Study* (University of Chicago Press, 1975), p. 101.
3 B. Plowden, *Children and Their Primary Schools: A Report of the Central Advisory Council for Education (England). Vol. 1: Report* [Plowden Report] (HMSO, 1967), p. 187. I cited it in A. Hargreaves, 'Progressivism and Pupil Autonomy', *Sociological Review*, 25(3) (1977), 585–621.
4 M. E. Brown and N. Precious, *The Integrated Day in the Primary School* (Ward Lock Education, 1967).
5 P. Freire, *Pedagogy of the Oppressed* (Continuum, 1970).
6 I. Illich, *Deschooling Society* (HarperCollins, 1972).
7 A. S. Neill, *Summerhill: A Radical Approach to Child-Rearing* (Penguin, 1967).
8 R. Skidelsky, *English Progressive Schools* (Penguin, 1969).
9 B. Schwartz, *The Paradox of Choice: Why More is Less* (HarperCollins, 2004).
10 E. Blishen (ed.), *The School That I'd Like* (Penguin, 1969).
11 S. E. Anderson, 'Moving Change: Evolutionary Perspectives on Educational Change', in A. Hargreaves, M. Fullan, A. Lieberman, and A. Datnow (eds), *The Second International Handbook of Educational Change* (Springer, 2010), pp. 65–84.
12 A. Lawlor, 'For Mathematician and Teacher, Zoltan Dienes, Play was the Thing', *Globe and Mail* (Canada) (4 February 2014). https://www.theglobeandmail.com/news/national/education/for-mathematician-and-teacher-zoltan-dienes-the-play-was-the-thing/article16701934
13 Lawlor, 'For Mathematician and Teacher, Zoltan Dienes, Play was the Thing'.
14 Simon and Garfunkel, 'Cecilia', on *Bridge Over Troubled Water* (Columbia Records, 1970).
15 N. Bennett, *Teaching Styles and Pupil Progress* (Open Books, 1976).

16 The quoted author is J. Taylor, *Organising and Integrating the Infant Day* (George Allen and Unwin, 1971), quoted in Bennett, *Teaching Styles and Pupil Progress*, p. 161.

Chapter 2: The Paradox of Pupil Autonomy

1. A. Hargreaves, *Moving: A Memoir of Education and Social Mobility* (Solution Tree Press, 2020).
2. See N. Gross, J. B. Giacquinta, and M. Bernstein, *Implementing Organizational Innovations: Sociological Analysis of Planned Educational Change* (Basic Books, 1971); and L. M. Smith and P. Keith, *Anatomy of Educational Innovation* (Wiley, 1971).
3. N. Bennett, *Teaching Styles and Pupil Progress* (Open Books, 1976).
4. D. Fink, The Attrition of Change (unpublished doctoral dissertation, Open University, 1997), p. 353.
5. C. B. Cox and R. Boyson (eds), *Black Paper 1975: The Fight for Education* (Vol. 4) (Dent, 1975), p. 1.
6. B. Bernstein, *Class, Codes, and Control. Vol. 3: Towards a Theory of Educational Transmissions* (Routledge, 1975), p. 96.
7. Bernstein, *Class, Codes, and Control*, p. 96.
8. This is discussed in H. Entwistle, *Antonio Gramsci: Conservative Schooling for Radical Politics* (Routledge & Kegan Paul, 1979).
9. Q. Hoare and G. Nowell-Smith, *Antonio Gramsci: Selections from the Prison Notebooks* (Lawrence & Wishart, 1971), p. 32, n. 7.
10. P. Thompson, 'Why Michael Gove's Invocation of Gramsci Misses the Point of His Work', *The Guardian* (6 February 2013). https://www.theguardian.com/commentisfree/2013/feb/06/michael-gove-gramsci-misses-point
11. R. Sharp and A. Green, *Education and Social Control: A Study in Progressive Primary Education* (Routledge & Kegan Paul, 1975), p. 224.
12. Sharp and Green, *Education and Social Control*, p. 51.
13. Sharp and Green, *Education and Social Control*, p. 52.
14. Sharp and Green, *Education and Social Control*, pp. 121–124.
15. D. H. Hargreaves, 'Whatever Happened to Symbolic Interactionism?' in L. Barton and R. Meighan (eds), *Sociological Interpretations of Schooling and Classrooms: A Reappraisal* (Nafferton Books, 1978), pp. 7–22 at p. 7.
16. I raise these sorts of leadership paradoxes and dilemmas in my book, A. Hargreaves, *Leadership from the Middle: The Beating Heart of Educational Transformation* (Routledge, 2023). For a discussion of leadership paradoxes in organisations, see L. S. Luscher, *Managing Leadership Paradoxes* (Routledge, 2018).
17. A. Berlak and H. Berlak, *Dilemmas of Schooling: Teaching and Social Change* (Routledge, 1981).
18. A. Berlak and H. Berlak, 'The Dilemmas of Schooling: An Application and Interpretation of G. H. Mead's Social Behaviorism'. Paper presented to the

Endnotes

American Educational Research Association, Washington, DC, April 1975. https://citeseerx.ist.psu.edu/document?repid=rep1&type=pdf&doi=f764a3aa67f2afe95c44ba7bcd3132aae2389952

19 B. Bernstein, 'Elaborated and Restricted Codes: Their Social Origins and Some Consequences', *American Anthropologist*, 66(6) (1964), 55–69. http://www.jstor.org/stable/668161

20 W. Labov, 'The Logic of Nonstandard English', *Georgetown Monographs on Language and Linguistics*, 22 (1969), 1–31.

21 B. Bernstein, 'Class and Pedagogies: Visible and Invisible', in *Class, Codes, and Control. Vol. 3: Towards a Theory of Educational Transmissions* (Routledge & Kegan Paul, 1975), pp. 107–129 at p. 121 [my emphasis].

22 A. Hargreaves, 'Progressivism and Pupil Autonomy', *Sociological Review*, 25(3) (1977), 585–621 at 607.

23 A. Hargreaves, 'The Significance of Classroom Coping Strategies', in L. Barton and R. Meighan (eds), *Sociological Interpretations of Schooling and Classrooms: A Reappraisal* (Nafferton Books, 1978), pp. 73–100.

24 A. Hargreaves, *Changing Teachers, Changing Times: Teachers' Work and Culture in the Postmodern Age* (Bloomsbury; Teachers College Press, 1994), p. 95.

25 The following school-based description is drawn and adapted from its original publication in Hargreaves, 'The Significance of Classroom Coping Strategies'.

26 L. Cohen, 'Everybody Knows', on *I'm Your Man* (Columbia Records; Leonard Cohen Stranger Music, 1988).

27 See D. Shirley and A. Hargreaves, 'Engagement with Learning: Being Fully Present Rather Than Chronically Absent', *Practical Literacy*, 29(3) (2024), 4–7; P. Mervosh and F. Paris, 'Why School Absences Have "Exploded" Almost Everywhere', *New York Times* (29 March 2024). https://www.nytimes.com/interactive/2024/03/29/us/chronic-absences.html

28 T. Hollweck, M. Cotnam-Kappel, A. Hargreaves, and A. Boultif, 'Playing Our Way Out of the Pandemic', *EdCan Network* (26 April 2023). https://www.edcan.ca/articles/playing-out-of-the-pandemic

29 See A. Hargreaves, G. Ayson, and S. Karunaweera, 'The Power of Play', *Educational Leadership*, 82(4) (1 December 2024). http://www.ascd.org/el/articles/the-power-of-play

Chapter 3: Classroom Coping Strategies

1 A. Hargreaves, 'The Significance of Classroom Coping Strategies', in L. Barton and R. Meighan (eds), *Sociological Interpretations of Schooling and Classrooms: A Reappraisal* (Nafferton Books, 1978), pp. 73–100.

2 L. Dwyer-Hemmings, '"A Wicked Operation"? Tonsillectomy in Twentieth-Century Britain', *Medical History*, 62(2) (2018), 217–241. https://doi.org/10.1017/mdh.2018.5

The Making of an Educator

3 The following school-based description is drawn and adapted from its original publication in A. Hargreaves, 'Experience Counts, Theory Doesn't: How Teachers Talk About Their Work', *Sociology of Education*, 57 (1984), 244–254.

4 A. Hargreaves and T. Dawe, 'Paths of Professional Development: Contrived Collegiality, Collaborative Culture and the Case of Peer Coaching', *Teaching and Teacher Education*, 6(3) (1990), 227–241. https://doi.org/10.1016/0742-051X(90)90015-W

5 P. Woods, 'Teaching for Survival', in P. Woods and M. Hammersley, *School Experience: Explorations in the Sociology of Education* (Croom Helm, 1977). Reprinted in A. Hargreaves and P. Woods, *Classrooms and Staffrooms: The Sociology of Teachers and Teaching* (Open University Press, 1984), pp. 48–63.

6 I. Westbury, 'Conventional Classrooms, Open Classrooms and the Technology of Teaching', *Journal of Curriculum Studies*, 5(2) (1973), 99–121.

7 D. Tyack and W. Tobin, 'The Grammar of Schooling: Why Has It Been So Hard to Change?' *American Educational Research Journal*, 31(3) (1994), 453–480.

8 Woods, 'Teaching for Survival', p. 51.

9 Hargreaves, 'The Significance of Classroom Coping Strategies', p. 77.

10 E. C. Hughes, 'Good People and Dirty Work', *Social Problems*, 10(1) (1962), 3–11. https://doi.org/10.2307/799402

11 P. G. Cressey, *The Taxi-Dance Hall: A Sociological Study in Commercialized Recreation and City Life* (AMS Press, 1972; originally published 1932).

12 B. Stenross and S. Kleinman, 'The Highs and Lows of Emotional Labor: Detectives' Encounters with Criminals and Victims', *Journal of Contemporary Ethnography*, 17(4) (1989), 435–452.

13 P. Sahlberg, *Finnish Lessons 3.0: What Can the World Learn from Educational Change in Finland?* (Teachers College Press, 2021).

14 Crosby, Pevar, and Raymond, 'Time is the Final Currency', on *CPR* (Sampson Music, 1998).

15 This example is described more fully in A. Hargreaves and M. T. O'Connor, *Collaborative Professionalism: When Teaching Together Means Learning for All* (Corwin, 2018).

16 S. Hargreaves, 'Words Are Flowing Out Like Endless Rain into a Paper Cup: ChatGPT and Law School Assessments', *Legal Education Review*, 33(1) (2023), 69. https://doi.org/10.53300/001c.83297

17 S. E. Steimler, Y. Lindvig, T. Skandsen, J. I. Wærness, and M. Faannessen, *Leading Educational Change in the Era of AI* (Learnlab, 2024).

18 Details about the Ottawa Catholic Board's use of AI can be found on the staff website at https://sites.google.com/ocsb.ca/aiattheocsb/home and on the parents' website at https://www.ocsb.ca/why-ocsb/humane-use-of-technology/artificial-intelligence-at-the-ocsb.

19 D. Day and Q. Gu, *The New Lives of Teachers* (Routledge, 2010).

Endnotes

Chapter 4: How to Build a Theory

1. Z. Bauman, *Identity: Conversations with Benedetto Vecchi* (Polity Press, 2004), p. 25.
2. R. Miliband, *The State in Capitalist Society* (Basic Books, 1969).
3. L. Taylor and S. Cohen, *Psychological Survival: The Experience of Long-Term Imprisonment* (Penguin, 1972).
4. A. Giddens, *The Constitution of Society: Outline of the Theory of Structuration* (Polity Press, 1984).
5. A. Giddens, *The Third Way: The Renewal of Social Democracy* (Polity Press, 1999).
6. A. Hargreaves and D. Shirley, *The Fourth Way: The Inspiring Future for Educational Change* (Corwin Press, 2009).
7. Mike + the Mechanics, 'The Living Years', on *Living Years* (Atlantic Records; WEA, 1988).
8. My first effort from the conference was published as A. Hargreaves, 'Synthesis and the Study of Strategies: A Project for the Sociological Imagination', in P. Woods (ed.), *Pupil Strategies* (Croom Helm, 1980), pp. 162–197. My thinking on this issue was later developed as A. Hargreaves, 'The Micro–Macro Problem in Educational Research', in R. Burgess (ed.), *Issues in Educational Research: Qualitative Methods* (Falmer Press, 1985), pp. 21–47.
9. C. W. Mills, *The Sociological Imagination* (Oxford University Press, 1959).
10. S. Bowles and H. Gintis, *Schooling in Capitalist America: Educational Reform and the Contradictions of Economic Life* (Basic Books, 1976).
11. P. Woods, 'Teaching for Survival', in P. Woods and M. Hammersley, *School Experience: Explorations in the Sociology of Education* (Croom Helm, 1977). Reprinted in A. Hargreaves and P. Woods, *Classrooms and Staffrooms: The Sociology of Teachers and Teaching* (Open University Press, 1984), pp. 48–63; P. Woods, 'Relating to Schoolwork: Some Pupil Perceptions', *Educational Review*, 30(2) (1978), 167–175; P. Woods, *The Divided School* (Routledge, 1979).
12. A. Hargreaves, 'Synthesis and the Study of Strategies', p. 192.
13. Coldplay, 'feelslikeimfallinginlove', on *Moon Music* (Parlophone Records; Atlantic Records, 2024).
14. B. Cosin, I. Dale, G. Esland, D. Mackinnon, and D. Swift (eds), *School and Society: A Sociological Reader* (2nd edn) (Routledge & Kegan Paul, 1977).
15. M. Hammersley and P. Woods (eds), *The Process of Schooling* (Routledge & Kegan Paul, 1976); R. Dale, G. Esland, and M. MacDonald (eds), *Schooling and Capitalism* (Routledge & Kegan Paul, 1977).
16. A. Hargreaves, 'Teaching and Control' [course unit for E200: Contemporary Issues in Education] (Open University, 1981).
17. This video is still available in the Open University digital archive at https://www.open.ac.uk/library/digital-archive/program/video:FOUE031S, although with access to university staff only.
18. K. Lewin, 'Psychology and the Process of Group Living', *Journal of Social Psychology*, 17(1) (1943), 113–131 at 118.

19 M. Fullan, *The Six Secrets of Change: What the Best Leaders Do to Help Their Organizations Survive and Thrive* (Jossey-Bass, 2011).
20 The value of both building theory inductively and of testing existing or new theory with the evidence was first outlined in B. Glaser and A. Strauss, *The Discovery of Grounded Theory: Strategies for Qualitative Research* (Sociology Press, 1967).
21 A. Hargreaves and M. Fullan, *Professional Capital: Transforming Teaching in Every School* (Teachers College Press, 2012).
22 S. Brinkmann, 'Doing Without Data', *Qualitative Inquiry*, 20(6) (2014), 720–725.
23 A. Hargreaves, 'The Emotional Geographies of Teaching', *Teachers' College Record*, 103(6) (2001), 1056–1080.
24 A. Hargreaves and D. Fink, *Sustainable Leadership* (Wiley, 2006).

Chapter 5: Bias and Integrity

1 J. Gould, 'Scholarship or Propaganda?' *Times Educational Supplement* (4 February 1977). See also, for example, B. Crick, 'Red Sails on the Campus: "Marxist Bias" Report', *The Observer* (25 September 1977), p. 10.
2 M. Hammersley, 'Accusations of Marxist Bias in the Sociology of Education During the 1970s: Academic Freedom Under Threat?' (2015), p. 41. https://martynhammersley.wordpress.com/wp-content/uploads/2013/03/hammersley-marxist-bias-and-academic-freedom.pdf. A more condensed and accessible version of this paper is M. Hammersley, 'An Ideological Dispute: Accusations of Marxist Bias in the Sociology of Education During the 1970s', *Contemporary British History*, 30(2) (2016), 242–259. https://doi.org/10.1080/13619462.2015.1112275
3 Hammersley, 'Accusations of Marxist Bias'.
4 R. Dale, G. Esland, and M. MacDonald (eds), *Schooling and Capitalism: A Sociological Reader* (Routledge & Kegan Paul, 1977), p. 1.
5 M. Hammersley and P. Woods (eds), *The Process of Schooling* (Routledge & Kegan Paul, 1976).
6 See, for example, L. E. Major and E. Briant, *Equity in Education: Levelling the Playing Field of Learning* (John Catt Educational, 2023); M. J. Sandel, *The Tyranny of Merit: What's Become of the Common Good?* (Farrar, Straus & Giroux, 2020); M. Stewart, 'The 9.9 Percent is the New American Aristocracy', *The Atlantic* (June 2018). www.theatlantic.com/magazine/archive/2018/06/the-birth-of-a-new-american-aristocracy/559130; and the classic M. Young, *The Rise of the Meritocracy 1870–2033* (Penguin, 1961).
7 M. Weber, *The Protestant Ethic and the Spirit of Capitalism* (Scribner, 1958), p. 182; see also D. H. Hargreaves, *Beyond Schooling: An Anarchist Challenge* (Routledge, 2019).
8 M. Mazzucato, *The Value of Everything: Making and Taking in the Global Economy* (Public Affairs, 2018); K. Raworth, *Doughnut Economics: Seven Ways to Think Like a 21st Century Economist* (Chelsea Green, 2017).

Endnotes

9. Hammersley, 'Accusations of Marxist Bias', p. 29.
10. The most influential exposition of the relative autonomy argument in the 20th century was by Nicol Poulantzas who had a spirited debate with Ralph Miliband about whether relative autonomy was a theoretical or empirical question. See N. Poulantzas, 'The Problem of the Capitalist State', *New Left Review*, 78 (November–December 1969), 67–78.
11. L. Althusser, *For Marx* (New Left Books, 1969). The iconic phrase 'the last instance' occurs 15 times in the main text, beginning on p. 105. In relation to its 'lonely hour', the last instance appears on p. 113.
12. A. Hargreaves, 'The Ideology of the Middle School', in A. Hargreaves and L. Tickle (eds), *Middle Schools: Origins, Ideology and Practice* (Harper & Row, 1980), pp. 82–105.
13. A. Hargreaves, 'The Politics of Administrative Convenience: The Case of Middle Schools', in B. Cosin and M. Hales (eds), *Education, Policy and Society: Theoretical Perspectives* (Routledge & Kegan Paul, 1983), pp. 199–225.
14. R. Collins, 'Some Comparative Principles of Educational Stratification', *Harvard Educational Review*, 47(1) (1977), 1–27.
15. A. Hargreaves, 'The Politics of Administrative Convenience', in J. Ahier and M. Flude (eds), *Contemporary Education Policy* (Croom Helm, 1983), pp. 23–57 at p. 41.
16. E. O. Wright, *Class, Crisis and the State* (New Left Books, 1979), pp. 15–16.
17. Hargreaves, 'The Politics of Administrative Convenience', p. 49.
18. A. Hargreaves, 'Apple Crumbles? Review Essay on the Work of Michael Apple', *Journal of Curriculum Studies*, 16(2) (1984), 206–210.
19. A. Hargreaves and M. Hammersley, 'CCCS Gas! Politics and Science in the Work of the Centre for Contemporary Cultural Studies', *Oxford Review of Education*, 8(2) (1982), 139–144.
20. A. Hargreaves, 'Resistance and Relative Autonomy Theories: Problems of Distortion and Incoherence in Recent Marxist Analyses of Education', *British Journal of Sociology of Education*, 3(2) (1982), 108–126.
21. The examples to which I pointed were the highly cited works of P. Willis, *Learning to Labour* (Saxon House, 1977) and J. Anyon, 'Social Class and School Knowledge', *Curriculum Inquiry*, 11(1) (1981), 3–42.
22. Hargreaves, 'Resistance and Relative Autonomy Theories', 113.
23. Hargreaves, 'Resistance and Relative Autonomy Theories', 120.
24. Hargreaves and Hammersley, 'CCCS Gas!' 143.
25. G. Greene, *Monsignor Quixote* (Penguin, 1982), p. 41.
26. L. Elliot, 'World's 26 Richest People Own As Much As Poorest 50%, Says Oxfam', *The Guardian* (21 January 2019). https://www.theguardian.com/business/2019/jan/21/world-26-richest-people-own-as-much-as-poorest-50-per-cent-oxfam-report
27. H. Damluji, 'The Contribution of Wealth: How Tax Justice Can Deliver Global Public Goods', *Carnegie Endowment for International Peace* (8 August 2024). https://carnegieendowment.org/research/2024/08/the-contribution-of-wealth-how-tax-justice-can-deliver-global-public-goods?lang=en

28 A. Hargreaves, 'Marxism and Relative Autonomy' [Unit 22: Conflict and Change in Education] (Open University, 1984).

Chapter 6: Cultures of Teaching

1 E. C. Hughes, 'Good People and Dirty Work', *Social Problems*, 10(1) (1962), 3–11. https://doi.org/10.2307/799402
2 For a fictionalised biopic of this unlikely underdog hero, see *Eddie the Eagle* (20th Century Studios, 2016).
3 F. J. Roethlisberger and W. J. Dickson, *Management and the Worker* (Harvard University Press, 1939).
4 A. Hargreaves, Friendship and Output in the Work Situation (unpublished undergraduate dissertation, University of Sheffield, 1972).
5 J. D. Vance, *Hillbilly Elegy: A Memoir of a Family and Culture in Crisis* (HarperCollins, 2016); T. Westover, *Educated: A Memoir* (Random House, 2018).
6 This came out of an extended personal communication between us.
7 Garth Brooks, 'Friends in Low Places', on *No Fences* (Capitol Records Nashville, 1990).
8 I have written about this more fully in A. Hargreaves, 'Towards a Social Geography of Teacher Education', in I. Z. Holowinsky and N. K. Shimahara (eds), *Teacher Education in Industrialized Nations* (Routledge, 1995), pp. 3–40.
9 This description of Brighouse's work draws directly on my tribute to Sir Tim and his legacy in A. Hargreaves, 'Tim Brighouse: Sustainability Maker', in D. Cameron, S. Munby, and M. Waters (eds), *Unfinished Business: The Life and Legacy of Tim Brighouse* (Crown House Publishing, 2024), pp. 39–42.
10 A. Hargreaves, E. Baglin, P. Henderson, P. Leeson, and T. Tossell, *Personal and Social Education: Choices and Challenges* (Blackwell, 1988).
11 A. Hargreaves and M. Fullan, 'Mentoring in the New Millennium', *Theory Into Practice*, 39(1) (2000), 50–56.
12 D. H. Hargreaves, *The Challenge for the Comprehensive School: Culture, Curriculum and Community* (Routledge, 1982).
13 W. Waller, *The Sociology of Teaching* (Wiley, 1932).
14 D. Lortie, *Schoolteacher: A Sociological Study* (University of Chicago Press, 1975).
15 P. Jackson, *Life in Classrooms* (Holt, Rinehart & Winston, 1968).
16 A. H. Halsey, A. Heath, and J. M. Ridge, *Origins and Destinations: Family, Class and Education in Modern Britain* (Clarendon Press, 1980).
17 Zedd, Maren Morris, and Grey, 'The Middle' (Interscope Records, 2018).
18 R. K. Merton, 'On Sociological Theories of the Middle Range', in *Social Theory and Social Structure* (Simon & Schuster; Free Press, 1949), pp. 39–53 at p. 49.
19 Merton, 'On Sociological Theories of the Middle Range', p. 39.
20 Merton, 'On Sociological Theories of the Middle Range', p. 39.
21 I. F. Goodson, 'Subjects for Study: Aspects of a Social History of Curriculum', *Journal of Curriculum Studies*, 15(4) (1983), 391–408; I. F. Goodson and S. J.

Endnotes

Ball (eds), *Defining the Curriculum: Histories and Ethnographies* (Falmer Press, 1985).

22 See M. Hammersley and A. Hargreaves (eds), *Curriculum Practice: Some Sociological Case Studies* (Falmer Press, 1983). An analytical history of the St Hilda's ethnography conferences has been written by G. Walford, 'The Oxford Ethnography Conference: A Place in History?' *Ethnography and Education*, 6(2) (2011), 133–145. https://doi.org/10.1080/17457823.2011.587354

23 The following findings form a significant part of the book from my PhD thesis. It was also my first solely authored book: A. Hargreaves, *Two Cultures of Schooling: The Case of Middle Schools* (Falmer Press, 1986).

24 B. Plowden, *Children and Their Primary Schools: A Report of the Central Advisory Council for Education (England). Vol. 1: Report* [Plowden Report] (HMSO, 1967).

25 R. Viennet and B. Pont, 'Education Policy Implementation: A Literature Review and Proposed Framework', *OECD Education Working Papers*, No. 162 (OECD Publishing, 2017). https://doi.org/10.1787/fc467a64-e

Chapter 7: The Great Education Shift

1 Band Aid, 'Do They Know It's Christmas?' (Phonogram, 1984). The song was rewritten and re-released on multiple occasions in connection with other fundraising efforts, such as those related to the Ebola epidemic and homelessness, but the song continues to be the subject of withering criticism for its colonialist and West-centric depiction of the entire African continent. See, for example, W. Easterly, 'Celebrity Musicians Can't Feed the World: The Trouble with Live Aid, Live 8, and Pop Star Condescension', *Slate Magazine* (29 April 2014). https://slate.com/technology/2014/04/live-aid-band-aid-usa-for-africa-did-pop-stars-and-hit-songs-help-ethiopia-famine-victims.html

2 I analysed the changing policy approach to what was officially called teaching quality in a paper that was published soon after I left England. See A. Hargreaves, 'Teaching Quality: A Sociological Analysis', *Journal of Curriculum Studies*, 20(3) (1988), 211–231.

3 This is a turn of phrase brilliantly coined by Deborah Britzman in her book, *Practice Makes Practice: A Critical Study of Learning to Teach* (SUNY Press, 1991).

4 J. King and J. Yin, *The Alternative Teacher Certification Sector Outside Higher Education* (Center for American Progress; American Association of Colleges for Teacher Education, 2022).

5 A. Hargreaves, 'Four Ages of Professionalism and Professional Learning', *Teachers and Teaching: Theory and Practice*, 6(2) (2000), 151–182.

6 A. Hargreaves, 'Building the Professional Capital for Schools to Deliver Successful Change', in B. Pont, A. Hargreaves, H. Timperley, and M. Kools, *Improving Schools in Wales* (OECD Publishing, 2014), pp. 64–90.

7. OECD, *Improving Lower Secondary Schools in Norway 2011*. Reviews of National Policies for Education (OECD Publishing, 2011). http://dx.doi.org/10.1787/9789264114579-en; P. Sahlberg, P. Broadfoot, J. Coolahan, J. Furlong, and G. Kirk, *Aspiring to Excellence: Final Report of the International Review Panel on the Structure of Initial Teacher Education in Northern Ireland* (Department for Employment and Learning, 2014).
8. D. Liston, 'Work in Teacher Education: A Current Assessment of US Teacher Education', in I. Z. Holowinsky and N. K. Shimahara (eds), *Teacher Education in Industrialized Nations: Issues in Changing Social Contexts* (Routledge, 1995), pp. 87–124 at p. 104.
9. W. A. Firestone and J. L. Fisler, 'Politics, Community, and Leadership in a School–University Partnership', *Educational Administration Quarterly*, 38(4) (2002), 449–493. https://doi.org/10.1177/001316102237669
10. P. Sahlberg, *Finnish Lessons 3.0: What Can the World Learn from Educational Change in Finland?* (Teachers College Press, 2021).
11. E. P. Thompson, *Warwick University Limited: Industry, Management and the Universities* (Penguin, 1970).
12. A. O. Hirschman, *Exit, Voice, and Loyalty: Responses to Decline in Firms, Organizations, and States* (Harvard University Press, 1972).
13. H. Becker, 'Notes on the Concept of Commitment', *American Journal of Sociology*, 66 (1960), 32–40.
14. This description of Brighouse's work draws directly on my tribute to Sir Tim and his legacy in A. Hargreaves, 'Tim Brighouse: Sustainability Maker', in D. Cameron, S. Munby, and M. Waters (eds), *Unfinished Business: The Life and Legacy of Tim Brighouse* (Crown House Publishing, 2024), pp. 39–42.
15. Department of Education and Science/Welsh Office, *Records of Achievement: A Statement of Policy* (HMSO, 1984).
16. The four purposes appear in P. Broadfoot, M. James, S. McMeeking, D. Nuttall, and B. Stierer, *Records of Achievement: Report of the National Evaluation of Pilot Schemes* (HMSO, 1988), pp. v–vi. https://www.researchgate.net/publication/323280776_Records_of_achievement_-_Report_of_the_national_evaluation_of_pilot_schemes
17. Broadfoot et al., *Records of Achievement*.
18. Information about the ARC Education Collaboratory can be located at www.atrico.org.
19. S. Munby and P. Phillips, *Assessing and Recording Achievement* (Prentice-Hall, 1989).
20. A. Hargreaves, 'Record Breakers? Issues in Pupil Records of Achievement', in P. Broadfoot (ed.), *Profiles and Records of Achievement: Issues and Problems* (Holt, Rinehart & Winston, 1986), pp. 203–227. My analysis of records of achievement and of assessment strategies in general is explored in detail in Part 2 of A. Hargreaves, *Curriculum and Assessment Reform* (Open University Press, 1989).
21. J. Habermas, *Legitimation Crisis* (Heinemann, 1976).
22. K. Joseph, Statement to the House of Commons. *Hansard* HC Deb. vol. 49

Endnotes

cols 149–150 (22 November 1983). https://api.parliament.uk/historic-hansard/commons/1983/nov/22/records-of-achievement

23 Broadfoot et al., *Records of Achievement*, p. v.
24 D. H. Hargreaves, *Improving Secondary Schools: Report of the Committee on the Curriculum and Organisation of Secondary Schools* (Inner London Education Authority, 1984).
25 M. Foucault, *Discipline and Punish: The Birth of the Prison* (Penguin, 1977).
26 Foucault, *Discipline and Punish*, p. 184.
27 Foucault, *Discipline and Punish*, p. 135.
28 Foucault, *Discipline and Punish*, p. 137.
29 A. Hargreaves, L. Earl, S. Moore, and S. Manning, *Learning to Change: Teaching Beyond Subjects and Standards* (Jossey-Bass, 2001), p. 74.
30 Hargreaves et al., *Learning to Change*, p. 63.
31 Broadfoot et al., *Records of Achievement*, p. 104.
32 Hargreaves et al., *Learning to Change*, p. 61.
33 I was involved in the first of these reviews of Scotland's Curriculum for Excellence in 2015. See OECD, *Improving Schools in Scotland: An OECD Perspective* (OECD Publishing, 2015).
34 N. E. Adelman, K. P. Walking-Eagle, and A. Hargreaves, *Racing with the Clock: Making Time for Teaching and Learning in School Reform* (Teachers College Press, 1997), p. 19.
35 For an account of the nature and origins of the concept of social mobility and its presence in contemporary society, including its effects on my own family background, see my memoir of a working-class upbringing in the North of England: A. Hargreaves, *Moving: A Memoir of Education and Social Mobility* (Solution Tree Press, 2020).
36 L. E. Major and E. Briant, *Social Mobility Equity in Education* (John Catt Education, 2023).
37 OECD, 'Implementation of Ireland's Leaving Certificate 2020–2021: Lessons from the COVID-19 Pandemic', *OECD Education Policy Perspectives*, No. 73 (OECD Publishing, 2023). https://doi.org/10.1787/e36a10b8-en
38 C. O'Brien, 'Students "Cannot Afford to Wait" for Leaving Certificate Reform – Norma Foley', *Irish Times* (19 November 2024). https://www.irishtimes.com/ireland/education/2024/11/19/teachers-protest-in-bid-to-delay-leaving-cert-reform
39 Scottish Government, *It's Our Future: Report of the Independent Review of Qualifications and Assessment* (2023). https://www.gov.scot/publications/future-report-independent-review-qualifications-assessment/documents

Chapter 8: A Shot in the Dark

1 Bruce Hornsby and the Range, 'The Way It Is', on *The Way It Is* (RCA Records, 1986).
2 J. W. Little, 'The Emotional Contours and Career Trajectories of (Disappointed) Reform Enthusiasts', *Cambridge Journal of Education*, 26(3) (1996), 345–359.

https://doi.org/10.1080/0305764960260304
3 J. Rosen, 'The Knowledge, London's Legendary Taxi-Driver Test, Puts Up a Fight in the Age of GPS', *New York Times* (10 November 2014). https://www.nytimes.com/2014/11/10/t-magazine/london-taxi-test-knowledge.html
4 M. Gladwell, *Outliers: The Story of Success* (Little, Brown, 2008).
5 B. N. MacNamara and M. Maitra, 'The Role of Deliberate Practice in Expert Performance: Revisiting Ericsson, Krampe & Tesch-Römer (1993)', *Royal Society Open Science,* 6(6) (2019), 190327. https://doi.org/10.1098/rsos.190327; and, outside musicians' expertise, see B. N. Macnamara, D. Moreau, and D. Z. Hambrick, 'The Relationship Between Deliberate Practice and Performance in Sports: A Meta-Analysis', *Perspectives on Psychological Science,* 11(3) (2016), 333–350. https://doi.org/10.1177/1745691616635591
6 P. Morel (dir.), *Taken* (EuropaCorp; M6 Films; Grive Productions; Canal+; TPS Star, 2008).
7 The most recent of these works is A. Hargreaves (in process), *Changing Teachers for Challenging Times* (Bloomsbury; Teachers College Press).
8 See, for example, A. Hargreaves, G. Ayson, and S. Karunaweera, 'The Power of Play', *Educational Leadership,* 82(4) (1 December 2024). http://www.ascd.org/el/articles/the-power-of-play
9 One of the earliest pieces of research that came up with this finding was E. Karp, *The Dropout Phenomenon in Ontario Secondary Schools* (Queen's Printer for Ontario, 1988).
10 C. Mackay, 'No Enemies', in *Selected Poems and Songs* (BiblioBazaar, 2009).
11 I. Salzberger-Wittenberg, G. Henry, and E. Osborne, *The Emotional Experience of Learning and Teaching* (Routledge & Kegan Paul, 1983).
12 U2, 'I Still Haven't Found What I'm Looking For', on *The Joshua Tree* (Island Records, 1987).

References

Adelman, N. E., Walking-Eagle, K. P., and Hargreaves, A. (1997). *Racing with the Clock: Making Time for Teaching and Learning in School Reform* (Teachers College Press).

Ahluwalia, J. (2024). *Both, Not Half: A Radical New Approach to Mixed Heritage Identity* (Mango Publishing).

Anderson, S. E. (2010). 'Moving Change: Evolutionary Perspectives on Educational Change', in A. Hargreaves, M. Fullan, A. Lieberman, and A. Datnow (eds), *The Second International Handbook of Educational Change* (Springer), pp. 65–84.

Anyon, J. (1981). 'Social Class and School Knowledge', *Curriculum Inquiry*, 11(1), 3–42.

Bauman, Z. (2004). *Identity: Conversations with Benedetto Vecchi* (Polity Press).

Becker, H. (1960). 'Notes on the Concept of Commitment', *American Journal of Sociology*, 66, 32–40.

Bennett, N. (1976). *Teaching Styles and Pupil Progress* (Open Books).

Berlak, A. and Berlak, H. (1975). 'The Dilemmas of Schooling: An Application and Interpretation of G. H. Mead's Social Behaviorism'. Paper presented to the American Educational Research Association, Washington, DC, April. https://citeseerx.ist.psu.edu/document?repid=rep1&type=pdf&doi=f764a3aa67f2afe95c44ba7bcd3132aae2389952

Berlak, A. and Berlak, H. (1981). *Dilemmas of Schooling: Teaching and Social Change* (Routledge).

Berliner, D. C. (2002). 'Comment: Educational Research: The Hardest Science of All', *Educational Researcher*, 31(8), 18–20. https://doi.org/10.3102/0013189X031008018

Bernstein, B. (1964). 'Elaborated and Restricted Codes: Their Social Origins and Some Consequences', *American Anthropologist*, 66(6), 55–69. http://www.jstor.org/stable/668161

Bernstein, B. (1975a). 'Class and Pedagogies: Visible and Invisible', in *Class, Codes, and Control. Vol. 3: Towards a Theory of Educational Transmissions* (Routledge & Kegan Paul), pp. 107–129.

Bernstein, B. (1975b). *Class, Codes, and Control. Vol. 3. Towards a Theory of Educational transmissions* (Routledge).

Biesta, G. (2007). 'Why "What Works" Won't Work: Evidence-based Practice and the Democratic Deficit in Educational Research', *Educational Theory*, 57, 1–22. https://doi.org/10.1111/j.1741-5446.2006.00241.x

Blishen, E. (ed.) (1969). *The School That I'd Like* (Penguin).

Bowles, S. and Gintis, H. (1976). *Schooling in Capitalist America: Educational Reform and the Contradictions of Economic Life* (Basic Books).

Brinkmann, S. (2014). 'Doing Without Data', *Qualitative Inquiry*, 20(6), 720–725.

Britzman, D. (1991). *Practice Makes Practice: A Critical Study of Learning to Teach* (SUNY Press).

Broadfoot, P., James, M., McMeeking, S., Nuttall, D., and Stierer, B. (1988). *Records of Achievement: Report of the National Evaluation of Pilot Schemes* (HMSO). https://www.researchgate.net/publication/323280776_Records_of_achievement_-_Report_of_the_national_evaluation_of_pilot_schemes

Cameron, D., Munby, S., and Waters, M. (eds) (2024). *Unfinished Business: The Life and Legacy of Tim Brighouse* (Crown House Publishing).

Collins, R. (1977). 'Some Comparative Principles of Educational Stratification', *Harvard Educational Review*, 47(1), 1–27.

Cosin, B., Dale, I., Esland, G., Mackinnon, D., and Swift, D. (eds) (1977). *School and Society: A Sociological Reader* (2nd edn) (Routledge & Kegan Paul).

Cox, C. B. and Boyson, R. (eds) (1975). *Black Paper 1975: The Fight for Education* (Vol. 4) (Dent).

Cressey, P. G. (1972 [1932]). *The Taxi-Dance Hall: A Sociological Study in Commercialized Recreation and City Life* (AMS Press).

Crick, B. (1977). 'Red Sails on the Campus: "Marxist Bias" Report', *The Observer* (25 September).

Dale, R., Esland, G., and MacDonald, M. (eds) (1977). *Schooling and Capitalism* (Routledge & Kegan Paul).

Damluji, H. (2024). 'The Contribution of Wealth: How Tax Justice Can Deliver Global Public Goods', *Carnegie Endowment for International Peace* (8 August). https://carnegieendowment.org/research/2024/08/the-contribution-of-wealth-how-tax-justice-can-deliver-global-public-goods?lang=en

Day, D. and Gu, Q. (2010). *The New Lives of Teachers* (Routledge).

Department of Education and Science/Welsh Office (1984). *Records of Achievement: A Statement of Policy* (HMSO).

Dwyer-Hemmings, L. (2018). 'A "Wicked Operation"? Tonsillectomy in Twentieth-Century Britain', *Medical History*, 62(2), 217–241. https://doi.org/10.1017/mdh.2018.5

Easterly, W. (2014). 'Celebrity Musicians Can't Feed the World: The Trouble with Live Aid, Live 8, and Pop Star Condescension', *Slate Magazine* (29 April). https://slate.com/technology/2014/04/live-aid-band-aid-usa-for-africa-did-pop-stars-and-hit-songs-help-ethiopia-famine-victims.html

Elliot, L. (2019). 'World's 26 Richest People Own As Much As Poorest 50%, Says Oxfam', *The Guardian* (21 January). https://www.theguardian.com/business/2019/jan/21/world-26-richest-people-own-as-much-as-poorest-50-per-cent-oxfam-report

Elmore, R. (2011). *I Used to Think … and Now I Think* (Harvard Education Press).

References

Entwistle, H. (1979). *Antonio Gramsci: Conservative Schooling for Radical Politics* (Routledge & Kegan Paul).

Fink, D. (1997). The Attrition of Change [unpublished doctoral dissertation, Open University).

Firestone, W. A. and Fisler, J. L. (2002). 'Politics, Community, and Leadership in a School-University Partnership', *Educational Administration Quarterly*, 38(4), 449–493. https://doi.org/10.1177/001316102237669

Fitzgerald, J., Yousif, F., and Epstein, K. (2025). 'Trump Puts All US Government Staff on Paid Leave "Immediately"', *BBC News* (23 January). https://www.bbc.com/news/articles/cgj288ywj23o

Foucault, M. (1977). *Discipline and Punish: The Birth of the Prison* (Penguin).

Freire, P. (1970). *Pedagogy of the Oppressed* (Continuum).

Fullan, M. (2011). *The Six Secrets of Change: What the Best Leaders Do to Help Their Organizations Survive and Thrive* (Jossey-Bass).

Giddens, A. (1984). *The Constitution of Society: Outline of the Theory of Structuration* (Polity Press).

Giddens, A. (1994). *Beyond Left and Right: The Future of Radical Politics* (Polity Press).

Giddens, A. (1999). *The Third Way: The Renewal of Social Democracy* (Polity Press).

Gladwell, M. (2008). *Outliers: The Story of Success* (Little, Brown).

Glaser, B. and Strauss, A. (1967). *The Discovery of Grounded Theory: Strategies for Qualitative Research* (Sociology Press).

Goodson, I. F. (1983). 'Subjects for Study: Aspects of a Social History of Curriculum', *Journal of Curriculum Studies*, 15(4), 391–408.

Goodson, I. F. and Ball, S. J. (eds) (1985). *Defining the Curriculum: Histories and Ethnographies* (Falmer Press).

Gould, J. (1977). 'Scholarship or Propaganda?' *Times Educational Supplement* (4 February).

Greene, G. (1982). *Monsignor Quixote* (Penguin).

Gross, N., Giacquinta, J. B., and Bernstein, M. (1971). *Implementing Organizational Innovations: Sociological Analysis of Planned Educational Change* (Basic Books).

Habermas, J. (1976). *Legitimation Crisis* (Heinemann).

Halsey, A. H., Heath, A., and Ridge, J. M. (1980). *Origins and Destinations: Family, Class and Education in Modern Britain* (Clarendon Press).

Hammersley, M. (2015). 'Accusations of Marxist Bias in the Sociology of Education During the 1970s: Academic Freedom Under Threat?'. https://martynhammersley.wordpress.com/wp-content/uploads/2013/03/hammersley-marxist-bias-and-academic-freedom.pdf

Hammersley, M. (2016). 'An Ideological Dispute: Accusations of Marxist Bias in the Sociology of Education During the 1970s', *Contemporary British History*, 30(2), 242–259. https://doi.org/10.1080/13619462.2015.1112275

Hammersley, M. and Hargreaves, A. (eds) (1983). *Curriculum Practice: Some Sociological Case Studies* (Falmer Press).

Hammersley, M. and Woods, P. (eds) (1976). *The Process of Schooling* (Routledge & Kegan Paul).

Hargreaves, A. (1972). Friendship and Output in the Work Situation (unpublished undergraduate dissertation, University of Sheffield).

Hargreaves, A. (1977). 'Progressivism and Pupil Autonomy', *Sociological Review*, 25(3), 585–621.
Hargreaves, A. (1978). 'The Significance of Classroom Coping Strategies', in L. Barton and R. Meighan (eds), *Sociological Interpretations of Schooling and Classrooms: A Reappraisal* (Nafferton Books), pp. 73–100.
Hargreaves, A. (1980a). 'The Ideology of the Middle School', in A. Hargreaves and L. Tickle (eds), *Middle Schools: Origins, Ideology and Practice* (Harper & Row), pp. 82–105.
Hargreaves, A. (1980b). 'Synthesis and the Study of Strategies: A Project for the Sociological Imagination', in P. Woods (ed.), *Pupil Strategies* (Croom Helm), pp. 162–197.
Hargreaves, A. (1981). 'Teaching and Control' [course unit for E200 Contemporary Issues in Education] (Open University).
Hargreaves, A. (1982). 'Resistance and Relative Autonomy Theories: Problems of Distortion and Incoherence in Recent Marxist Analyses of Education', *British Journal of Sociology of Education*, 3(2), 108–126.
Hargreaves, A. (1983a). 'The Politics of Administrative Convenience', in J. Ahier, and M. Flude (eds), *Contemporary Education Policy* (Croom Helm), pp. 23–57.
Hargreaves, A. (1983b). 'The Politics of Administrative Convenience: The Case of Middle Schools', in B. Cosin and M. Hales (eds), *Education, Policy and Society: Theoretical Perspectives* (Routledge & Kegan Paul), pp. 199–225.
Hargreaves, A. (1984a). 'Apple Crumbles? Review Essay on the Work of Michael Apple', *Journal of Curriculum Studies*, 16(2), 206–210.
Hargreaves, A. (1984b). 'Experience Counts, Theory Doesn't: How Teachers Talk About Their Work', *Sociology of Education*, 57, 244–254.
Hargreaves, A. (1985a). English Middle Schools: An Historical and Ethnographic Study [unpublished PhD thesis, University of Leeds].
Hargreaves, A. (1985b). 'The Micro-Macro Problem in Educational Research', in R. Burgess (ed.), *Issues in Educational Research: Qualitative Methods* (Falmer Press), pp. 21–47.
Hargreaves, A. (1986a). 'Record Breakers? Issues in Pupil Records of Achievement', in P. Broadfoot (ed.), *Profiles and Records of Achievement: Issues and Problems* (Holt, Rinehart & Winston), pp. 203–227.
Hargreaves, A. (1986b). *Two Cultures of Schooling: The Case of Middle Schools* (Falmer Press).
Hargreaves, A. (1988). 'Teaching Quality: A Sociological Analysis', *Journal of Curriculum Studies*, 20(3), 211–231.
Hargreaves, A. (1989). *Curriculum and Assessment Reform* (Open University Press).
Hargreaves, A. (1994). *Changing Teachers, Changing Times: Teachers' Work and Culture in the Postmodern Age* (Bloomsbury; Teachers College Press).
Hargreaves, A. (2000). 'Four Ages of Professionalism and Professional Learning', *Teachers and Teaching: Theory and Practice*, 6(2), 151–182.
Hargreaves, A. (2001). 'The Emotional Geographies of Teaching', *Teachers' College Record*, 103(6), 1056–1080.
Hargreaves, A. (2014). 'Building the Professional Capital for Schools to Deliver Successful Change', in B. Pont, A. Hargreaves, H. Timperley, and M. Kools, *Improving Schools in Wales* (OECD Publishing), pp. 64–90.

References

Hargreaves, A. (2020). *Moving: A Memoir of Education and Social Mobility* (Solution Tree Press).

Hargreaves, A. (2023). *Leadership from the Middle: The Beating Heart of Educational Transformation* (Routledge).

Hargreaves, A. (2024a). 'There is a Way Out of Cancel Culture, But It's Not Free Speech', *Times Higher Education* (15 February). https://www.andyhargreaves.com/a-way-out-of-cancel-culture.html

Hargreaves, A. (2024b). 'Tim Brighouse: Sustainability Maker', in D. Cameron, S. Munby, and M. Waters (eds), *Unfinished Business: The Life and Legacy of Tim Brighouse* (Crown House Publishing), pp. 39–42.

Hargreaves, A. (in process), *Changing Teachers for Challenging Times* (Bloomsbury; Teachers College Press).

Hargreaves, A., Ayson, G., and Karunaweera, S. (2024). 'The Power of Play', *Educational Leadership*, 82(4) (1 December). http://www.ascd.org/el/articles/the-power-of-play

Hargreaves, A., Baglin, E., Henderson, P., Leeson, P., and Tossell, T. (1988). *Personal and Social Education: Choices and Challenges* (Blackwell).

Hargreaves, A. and Dawe, T. (1990). 'Paths of Professional Development: Contrived Collegiality, Collaborative Culture and the Case of Peer Coaching', *Teaching and Teacher Education*, 6(3), 227–241. https://doi.org/10.1016/0742-051X(90)90015-W

Hargreaves, A., Earl, L., Moore, S., and Manning, S. (2001). *Learning to Change: Teaching Beyond Subjects and Standards* (Jossey-Bass).

Hargreaves, A. and Fink, D. (2006). *Sustainable Leadership* (Wiley).

Hargreaves, A. and Fullan, M. (2000). 'Mentoring in the New Millennium', *Theory Into Practice*, 39(1), 50–56.

Hargreaves, A. and Fullan, M. (2012). *Professional Capital: Transforming Teaching in Every School* (Teachers College Press).

Hargreaves, A. and Hammersley, M. (1982). 'CCCS Gas! Politics and Science in the Work of the Centre for Contemporary Cultural Studies', *Oxford Review of Education*, 8(2), 139–144.

Hargreaves, A. and O'Connor, M. T. (2018). *Collaborative Professionalism: When Teaching Together Means Learning for All* (Corwin).

Hargreaves, A. and Shirley, D. (2009). *The Fourth Way: The Inspiring Future for Educational Change* (Corwin Press).

Hargreaves, A. and Tickle, L. (eds) (1980). *Middle Schools: Origins, Ideology and Practice* (Harper & Row).

Hargreaves, D. H. (1978). 'Whatever Happened to Symbolic Interactionism?' in L. Barton and R. Meighan (eds), *Sociological Interpretations of Schooling and Classrooms: A Reappraisal* (Nafferton Books), pp. 7–22.

Hargreaves, D. H. (1982). *The Challenge for the Comprehensive School: Culture, Curriculum and Community* (Routledge).

Hargreaves, D. H. (1984). *Improving Secondary Schools: Report of the Committee on the Curriculum and Organisation of Secondary Schools* (Inner London Education Authority).

Hargreaves, D. H. (2019). *Beyond Schooling: An Anarchist Challenge* (Routledge).

Hargreaves, D. H. (2024). *Schooling Re-imagined: Educating for a More Ethical Society* (Bloomsbury).

Hargreaves, S. (2023). 'Words Are Flowing Out Like Endless Rain into a Paper Cup: ChatGPT and Law School Assessments', *Legal Education Review*, 33(1). https://doi.org/10.53300/001c.83297

Hegel, G. W. F. (1820). *Grundlinien der Philosophie des Rechts: Naturrecht und Staatswissenschaft im Grundrisse* (Nicolai'sche Buchhandlung).

Hegel, G. W. F. (2001 [1820]). *Philosophy of Right* (Batoche Books).

Hirschman, A. O. (1972). *Exit, Voice, and Loyalty: Responses to Decline in Firms, Organizations, and States* (Harvard University Press).

Hoare, Q. and Nowell-Smith, G. (1971). *Antonio Gramsci: Selections from the Prison Notebooks* (Lawrence & Wishart).

Hollweck, T., Cotnam-Kappel, M., Hargreaves, A., and Boultif, A. (2023). 'Playing Our Way Out of the Pandemic', *EdCan Network* (26 April). https://www.edcan.ca/articles/playing-out-of-the-pandemic

Hughes, E. C. (1962). 'Good People and Dirty Work', *Social Problems*, 10(1), 3–11 https://doi.org/10.2307/799402

Illich, I. (1972). *Deschooling Society* (HarperCollins).

Jackson, P. (1968). *Life in Classrooms* (Holt, Rinehart & Winston).

Joseph, K. (1983). Statement to the House of Commons. *Hansard* HC Deb. vol. 49 cols 149–150 (22 November). https://api.parliament.uk/historic-hansard/commons/1983/nov/22/records-of-achievement

Karp, E. (1988). *The Dropout Phenomenon in Ontario Secondary Schools* (Queen's Printer for Ontario).

King, J. and Yin, J. (2022). *The Alternative Teacher Certification Sector Outside Higher Education* (Center for American Progress; American Association of Colleges for Teacher Education).

Labov, W. (1969). 'The Logic of Nonstandard English', *Georgetown Monographs on Language and Linguistics*, 22, 1–31.

Lawlor, A. (2014). 'For Mathematician and Teacher, Zoltan Dienes, Play was the Thing', *Globe and Mail* (Canada) (4 February). https://www.theglobeandmail.com/news/national/education/for-mathematician-and-teacher-zoltan-dienes-the-play-was-the-thing/article16701934

Leingang, R. (2024). 'Republican President-Elect Says He Wants to Dismantle the US Education Department and Fire "Radical Left Accreditors"', *The Guardian* (18 November). https://www.theguardian.com/us-news/2024/nov/18/trump-education-policies

Lewin, K. (1943). 'Psychology and the Process of Group Living', *Journal of Social Psychology*, 17(1), 113–131.

Liston, D. (1995). 'Work in Teacher Education: A Current Assessment of US Teacher Education', in I. Z. Holowinsky and N. K. Shimahara (eds), *Teacher Education in Industrialized Nations: Issues in Changing Social Contexts* (Routledge), pp. 87–124.

Little, J. W. (1996). 'The Emotional Contours and Career Trajectories of (Disappointed) Reform Enthusiasts', *Cambridge Journal of Education*, 26(3), 345–359. https://doi.org/10.1080/0305764960260304

Lortie, D. (1975). *Schoolteacher: A Sociological Study* (University of Chicago Press).

Luscher, L. S. (2018). *Managing Leadership Paradoxes* (Routledge).

Luscombe, R. (2024). 'Florida Schoolkids May Have to Study "Threat of Communism in the US"', *The Guardian* (4 February). https://www.theguardian.

References

com/us-news/2024/feb/09/florida-schools-communism-history-bills-desantis

Mackay, C. (2009). 'No Enemies', in *Selected Poems and Songs* (BiblioBazaar).

MacNamara, B. N. and Maitra, M. (2019). 'The Role of Deliberate Practice in Expert Performance: Revisiting Ericsson, Krampe & Tesch-Römer (1993)', *Royal Society Open Science*, 6(6), 190327. https://doi.org/10.1098/rsos.190327

Macnamara, B. N., Moreau, D., and Hambrick, D. Z. (2016). 'The Relationship Between Deliberate Practice and Performance in Sports: A Meta-Analysis', *Perspectives on Psychological Science*, 11(3), 333–350. https://doi.org/10.1177/1745691616635591

Major, L. E. and Briant, E. (2023). *Equity in Education: Levelling the Playing Field of Learning* (John Catt Educational).

Mannheim, K. (1952 [1927]). 'The Problem of Generations', in *Essays on the Sociology of Knowledge*, ed. P. Kecskemeti (Routledge), pp. 276–322.

Marx, K. (1976). 'Theses on Feuerbach', in K. Marx and F. Engels, *Collected Works. Vol. 5: 1845–1847* (Lawrence & Wishart).

Mazzucato, M. (2018). *The Value of Everything: Making and Taking in the Global Economy* (Public Affairs).

Merton, R. K. (1949). 'On Sociological Theories of the Middle Range', in *Social Theory and Social Structure* (Simon & Schuster; Free Press), pp. 39–53.

Mervosh, P. and Paris, F. (2024). 'Why School Absences Have "Exploded" Almost Everywhere', *New York Times* (29 March). https://www.nytimes.com/interactive/2024/03/29/us/chronic-absences.html

Miliband, R. (1969). *The State in Capitalist Society* (Basic Books).

Mills, C. W. (1959). *The Sociological Imagination* (Oxford University Press).

Mounk, Y. (2023). *The Identity Trap: A Story of Ideas and Power in Our Time* (Penguin).

Neill, A. S. (1967). *Summerhill: A Radical Approach to Child-Rearing* (Penguin).

O'Brien, C. (2024). 'Students "Cannot Afford to Wait" for Leaving Certificate Reform – Norma Foley', *Irish Times* (19 November). https://www.irishtimes.com/ireland/education/2024/11/19/teachers-protest-in-bid-to-delay-leaving-cert-reform

OECD (2011). *Improving Lower Secondary Schools in Norway 2011. Reviews of National Policies for Education* (OECD Publishing). http://dx.doi.org/10.1787/9789264114579-en

OECD (2015). *Improving Schools in Scotland: An OECD Perspective* (OECD Publishing).

OECD (2023). 'Implementation of Ireland's Leaving Certificate 2020–2021: Lessons from the COVID-19 Pandemic', *OECD Education Policy Perspectives*, No. 73 (OECD Publishing). https://doi.org/10.1787/e36a10b8-en

Plowden, B. (1967). *Children and Their Primary Schools: A Report of the Central Advisory Council for Education (England). Vol. 1: Report* [Plowden Report] (HMSO).

Poulantzas, N. (1969). 'The Problem of the Capitalist State', *New Left Review*, 78 (November–December), 67–78.

Pullman, P. (1995). *Northern Lights* (Scholastic Books).

Ravitch, D. (2011). *The Death and Life of the Great American School System: How Testing and Choice Are Undermining Education* (Basic Books).

Ravitch, D. (2020). 'Why I Object to the Term "Science of Reading"' [blog] (25 November). https://dianeravitch.net/2020/11/25/why-i-object-to-the-term-science-of-reading

Raworth, K. (2017). *Doughnut Economics: Seven Ways to Think Like a 21st Century Economist* (Chelsea Green).

Roethlisberger, F. J. and Dickson, W. J. (1939). *Management and the Worker* (Harvard University Press).

Rosen, J. (2014). 'The Knowledge, London's Legendary Taxi-Driver Test, Puts Up a Fight in the Age of GPS', *New York Times* (10 November). https://www.nytimes.com/2014/11/10/t-magazine/london-taxi-test-knowledge.html

Sacks, O. (1996). *An Anthropologist on Mars: Seven Paradoxical Tales* (Vintage Books).

Sahlberg, P. (2021). *Finnish Lessons 3.0: What Can the World Learn from Educational Change in Finland?* (Teachers College Press).

Sahlberg, P., Broadfoot, P., Coolahan, J., Furlong, J., and Kirk, G. (2014). *Aspiring to Excellence: Final Report of the International Review Panel on the Structure of Initial Teacher Education in Northern Ireland* (Department for Employment and Learning).

Salzberger-Wittenberg, I., Henry, G., and Osborne, E. (1983). *The Emotional Experience of Learning and Teaching* (Routledge & Kegan Paul).

Sandel, M. J. (2020). *The Tyranny of Merit: What's Become of the Common Good?* (Farrar, Straus & Giroux).

Schwartz, B. (2004). *The Paradox of Choice: Why More is Less* (HarperCollins).

Scottish Government (2023). *It's Our Future: Report of the Independent Review of Qualifications and Assessment*. https://www.gov.scot/publications/future-report-independent-review-qualifications-assessment/documents

Sharp, R. and Green, A. (1975). *Education and Social Control: A Study in Progressive Primary Education* (Routledge & Kegan Paul).

Shirley, D. and Hargreaves, A. (2024a). *The Age of Identity: Who Do Our Kids Think They Are ... and How We Can Help Them Belong* (Corwin Press).

Shirley, D. and Hargreaves, A. (2024b). 'Engagement with Learning: Being Fully Present Rather Than Chronically Absent', *Practical Literacy*, 29(3), 4–7.

Skidelsky, R. (1969). *English Progressive Schools* (Penguin).

Smith, L. M. and Keith, P. (1971). *Anatomy of Educational Innovation* (Wiley).

Steimler, S. E., Lindvig, Y., Skandsen, T., Wærness, J. I., and Faannessen, M. (2024). *Leading Educational Change in the Era of AI* (Learnlab).

Stenross, B. and Kleinman, S. (1989). 'The Highs and Lows of Emotional Labor: Detectives' Encounters with Criminals and Victims', *Journal of Contemporary Ethnography*, 17(4), 435–452.

Stewart, M. (2018). 'The 9.9 Percent is the New American Aristocracy', *The Atlantic* (June). www.theatlantic.com/magazine/archive/2018/06/the-birth-of-a-new-american-aristocracy/559130

Taylor, J. (1971). *Organising and Integrating the Infant Day* (George Allen and Unwin).

Taylor, L. and Cohen, S. (1972). *Psychological Survival: The Experience of Long-Term Imprisonment* (Penguin).

Thompson, E. P. (1970). *Warwick University Limited: Industry, Management and the Universities* (Penguin).

References

Thompson, P. (2013). 'Why Michael Gove's Invocation of Gramsci Misses the Point of His Work', *The Guardian* (6 February). https://www.theguardian.com/commentisfree/2013/feb/06/michael-gove-gramsci-misses-point

Triggle, N. (2024). 'Why Weight Loss Drugs May Be No Obesity Silver Bullet', *BBC News* (15 October). https://www.bbc.com/news/articles/czxgqp1nd1jo

Tyack, D. and Tobin, W. (1994). 'The Grammar of Schooling: Why Has It Been So Hard to Change?' *American Educational Research Journal*, 31(3), 453–480.

van Tulleken, C. (2024). *Ultra-Processed People: Why We Can't Stop Eating Food That Isn't Food* (Vintage Books).

Viennet, R. and Pont, B. (2017). 'Education Policy Implementation: A Literature Review and Proposed Framework', *OECD Education Working Papers*, No. 162 (OECD Publishing). https://doi.org/10.1787/fc467a64-e

Walford, G. (2011). 'The Oxford Ethnography Conference: A Place in History?' *Ethnography and Education*, 6(2), 133–145. https://doi.org/10.1080/17457823.2011.587354

Waller, W. (1932). *The Sociology of Teaching* (Wiley).

Weber, M. (1958). *The Protestant Ethic and the Spirit of Capitalism* (Scribner).

Weber, M. (1978 [1925]). *Economy and Society: An Outline of Interpretive Sociology*, tr. G. Roth and C. Wittich (University of California Press).

Westbury, I. (1973). 'Conventional Classrooms, Open Classrooms and the Technology of Teaching', *Journal of Curriculum Studies*, 5(2), 99–121.

Wiliam, D. (2016). *Leadership for Teacher Learning* (Solution Tree Press).

Willis, P. (1977). *Learning to Labour* (Saxon House).

Woo, A., Diliberti, M. K., and Steiner, E. D. (2024). *Policies Restricting Teaching About Race and Gender Spill Over into Other States and Localities: Findings from the 2023 State of the American Teacher Survey* (RAND). https://www.rand.org/pubs/research_reports/RRA1108-10.html

Woods, P. (1977). 'Teaching for Survival', in P. Woods and M. Hammersley, *School Experience: Explorations in the Sociology of Education* (Croom Helm). Reprinted in A. Hargreaves and P. Woods, *Classrooms and Staffrooms: The Sociology of Teachers and Teaching* (Open University Press, 1984), pp. 48–63.

Woods, P. (1978). 'Relating to Schoolwork: Some Pupil Perceptions', *Educational Review*, 30(2), 167–175.

Woods, P. (1979). *The Divided School* (Routledge).

Wright, E. O. (1979). *Class, Crisis and the State* (New Left Books).

Young, M. (1961). *The Rise of the Meritocracy 1870–2033* (Penguin).